The Decolonization of Portuguese Africa

The Decolonization of Portuguese Africa

Metropolitan Revolution and the Dissolution of Empire

NORRIE MACQUEEN

Longman
London and New York

Addison Wesley Longman Limited
Edinburgh Gate,
Harlow, Essex CM20 2JE,
United Kingdom
and Associated Companies throughout the world

Published in the United States of America
by Addison Wesley Longman Inc., New York

© Addison Wesley Longman Limited 1997

First published 1997

ISBN 0 582 25993 2 PPR
ISBN 0 583 25994 0 CSD

British Library Cataloguing in Publication Data
A catalogue record for this book is available from the British Library

Library of Congress Cataloging-in-Publication Data
Macqueen, Norrie, 1950–
The decolonization of Portuguese Africa : metropolitan revolution and the
dissolution of empire / Norrie Macqueen.
p.   cm.
Includes bibliographical references and index.
IBN 0-582-25993-2 (PPR). – ISBN 0-582-25994-0 (CSD)
1. Africa, Portuguese-speaking–Politics and government.
2. Decolonization–Africa, Portuguese-speaking. I. Title.
DT36.5.M33   1997
960'.097569–dc20   96-34685
                                                                            CIP

Set by 7 in 10/12pt Baskerville

Produced by Longman Singapore Publishers (Pte) Ltd.
Printed in Singapore

For Betsy and Triona

Contents

Preface

This book aims to provide an overview of one of the most far-reaching events in post-Second World War history: the end of Portugal's 500-year empire in Africa. The structure of its analysis of the decolonization process is essentially triangular. It explores the three dimensions of African nationalism, European revolution and the politics of the international system both individually and in their interconnections.

Within this general scheme, however, the book places a stress on the metropolitan environment and in particular on the events surrounding the Lisbon coup of April 1974. This emphasis implies no devaluation of the African and international perspectives. The aim is simply to redress an imbalance in the published work which has been available in English up to the present. Since the 1960s a considerable body of material has emerged on the liberation struggles in Portuguese Africa and, later, on the development of the new states which emerged from decolonization. The focus of these studies has generally been an African one, offering little systematic analysis of the interconnections between revolutionary nationalism in lusophone Africa and the 'revolutionary process' in the metropole.

Similarly, the 1970s was a period of significant change in the management of relations between the superpowers. The decade began with the flowering of *détente* and ended with its collapse. International relations specialists, therefore, have tended to offer interpretations of developments on the African 'periphery' of the central balance at this time in systemic rather than local terms. There have been few attempts to tie these great shifts in superpower relationships to the unfolding of revolutionary politics and the process of decolonization in Lisbon during 1974 and 1975. My intention therefore has been twofold: to point up the metropolitan bases of imperial dissolution and to attempt to integrate these with the other causal factors to be found in Africa and in the broad international system.

Portugal enforces a 'thirty-year rule' on access to foreign affairs and colonial ministry documents (and offers no guarantee that the most important material will be released even after that period). This has not, though, been as great a disability in the preparation of this book as might be expected. The explosion of political expression which followed the collapse of the old regime in Portugal in 1974 created a climate in which considerations of state secrecy hardly constrained public revelation. The publication of instant memoirs and collections of personal papers – often including state documents – became a growth industry in Lisbon in the mid and later 1970s. At the same time, a recently free press was pushing its new liberties to their limit and was unintimidated by official disapproval. More recently, the twentieth anniversary of the revolution brought a second wave of public disclosure and reinterpretation from participants in the revolution. Many of the central actors of 1974 and 1975 have been remarkably frank in published reminiscences and interviews.

In this respect I must express my own gratitude for the time and patience of a number of figures involved in the decolonization process who made themselves available for interview in 1995. I owe a great debt to: Dr António de Almeida Santos who was minister for interterritorial coordination (effectively 'decolonization minister') in the first to fourth provisional governments in Portugal from May 1974 to August 1975; Rear Admiral Vítor Crespo who was high commissioner in Mozambique during the transitional government there in 1974 and 1975, and later Portuguese minister for cooperation (in succession to Almeida Santos) in the fifth and sixth provisional governments in 1975 and 1976; and Brigadier Pedro Pezarat Correia who led the Armed Forces Movement in Angola during the transition and later served on the Portuguese Council of the Revolution. All were extremely accommodating, frank in their expression of views and forbearing in the face of my far from elegant Portuguese.

These meetings took place in the course of a series of visits to Portugal in 1994 and 1995 which was made possible by a research grant from the British Academy and by generous leave from my former institution, the University of Sunderland. Among the many debts incurred in these trips one of the more significant was to Dr Natércia Coimbra, archivist at the 25 April Documentation Centre of the University of Coimbra, who was of enormous help both in Coimbra and in subsequent correspondence. Staff at the Portuguese national library and at the newspaper library of the Lisbon municipality were also unfailingly helpful. Beyond these conventional and formal sources, a multitude of influences have come to bear on the book from conversations and disputations held under a variety of circumstances in Mozambique, Portugal and here in Britain over the past twenty-odd years.

Finally, the book would never have been completed without the (almost) limitless good humour of my wife Betsy and daughter Catriona and their toleration of absences abroad and mounting irrationality of behaviour at home.

Norrie MacQueen
University of Dundee

List of Maps

List of Abbreviations

AC	Civic Association (Associação Cívica) [São Tomé & Príncipe]
ANP	Popular National Action (Acção Nacional Popular) [Portugal and the colonies]
CDS	Social Democratic Centre (Centro Democrático Social) [Portugal]
CND	National Decolonization Commission (Comissão Nacional de Descolonização)
CONCP	Conference of Nationalist Organizations of the Portuguese Colonies (Conferência das Organizações Nacionalistas das Colónias Portuguesas)
Copcon	Continental Operational Command (Comando Operacional do Continente) [Portugal]
Coremo	Revolutionary Committee of Mozambique (Comité Revolucionária de Moçambique)
CUF	Manufacturing Combine Co. (Companhia União Fabril)
DGS	Directorate-General of Security (Direcção-Geral de Segurança)
EFTA	European Free Trade Association
FAPLA	Popular Forces for the Liberation of Angola (Forças Armadas Populares de Libertação de Angola)
FARN	Broad Front of National Resistance (Frente Ampla de Resistência Nacional) [Cabo Verde]
FICO	('I stay') Front for Western Continuity (Frente para a Continuação Ocidental) [Mozambique]
FLEC	Front for the Liberation of the Cabinda Enclave (Frente de Libertação do Enclave de Cabinda)
FLING	Front for the Liberation and Independence of Guiné (Frente de Libertação e Independência da Guiné)
FNLA	Angolan National Liberation Front (Frente Nacional para a Libertação de Angola)
FPL	Free Popular Front (Frente Popular Livre) [São Tomé & Príncipe]

FRA   Angolan Resistance Front (Frente de Resistência Angolana)

FRAIN   African Front for National Independence (Frente Africana de Independência Nacional)

Frecomo   Mozambique Common Front (Frente Comum de Moçambique)

Frelimo   Mozambique Liberation Front (Frente de Libertação de Moçambique)

FUR   Angolan United Front (Frente Unida Angolana)

GE   Special (Operations) Groups (Grupos Especiais)

GEP   Special Paratroop Groups (Grupos Especiais Paraquedistas)

GRAE   Revolutionary Government of Angola in Exile (Governo Revolucionário de Angola no Exílio)

Gumo   Mozambique United Group (Grupo Unido de Moçambique)

JSN   Junta of National Salvation (Junta de Salvação Nacional)

MAC   Anti-Colonialist Movement (Movimento Anti-Colonialista)

Manu   Makonde National Union [Mozambique]

MDG   Guiné Democratic Movement (Movimento Democrático da Guiné)

MFA   Armed Forces Movement (Movimento das Forças Armadas)

MLG   Liberation Movement of Guiné (Movimento de Libertação da Guiné)

MLSTP   Movement for the Liberation of São Tomé & Príncipe (Movimento para a Libertação de São Tomé e Príncipe)

MNR   National Resistance Movement (Movimento Nacional de Resistência) [Mozambique]

MPD   Movement for Democracy (Movimento para Democracia) [Cabo Verde]

MPLA   Popular Movement for the Liberation of Angola (Movimento Popular de Libertação de Angola)

MPP   Movement for Peace (Movimento para a Paz) [Guiné]

MUD   United Democratic Movement (Movimento Unido Democrático) [Portugal]

OAU   Organization of African Unity

PAICV   African Party for the Independence of Cabo Verde (Partido Africano para a Independência de Cabo Verde)

PAIGC   African Party for the Independence of Guiné and Cabo Verde (Partido Africano para a Independência da Guiné e Cabo Verde)

PCA	Angolan Communist Party (Partido Comunista Angolano)
PCD	Democratic Convergence Party (Partido de Convergência Democrática) [São Tomé & Príncipe]
PCDA	Angolan Christian Democratic Party (Partido Cristão Democrático Angolano)
PCN	National Coalition Party (Partido Coligação Nacional) [Mozambique]
PCP	Portuguese Communist Party (Partido Comunista Português)
PIDE	International and State Defence Police (Polícia Internacional e de Defesa do Estado)
PPD	Popular Democratic Party (Partido Popular Democrática) – see PSD [Portugal]
PS	Socialist Party (Partido Socialista) [Portugal]
PSD	Social Democratic Party (Partido Social Democrática) – renamed from PPD [Portugal]
PSP	Public Security Police (Polícia de Segurança Pública)
Renamo	Mozambican National Resistance (Resistência Nacional Moçambicana)
SADF	South African Defence Force
SWAPO	South West Africa Peoples Organization
UDCV	Democratic Union of Cabo Verde (União Democrática de Cabo Verde)
Udenamo	National Democratic Union of Mozambique (União Democrática Nacional de Moçambique)
Unami	National African Union of Independent Mozambique (União Nacional Africana de Moçambique Independente)
Unipomo	Union for Peace among the Peoples of Mozambique (União para a Paz do Povo de Moçambique)
UN	National Union (União Nacional) [Portugal and Colonies]
UNAVEM	United Nations Angola Verification Mission
UNITA	National Union for the Total Independence of Angola (União Nacional para a Independência Total de Angola)
UNOMOZ	United Nations Operation in Mozambique
UPA	Union of the Peoples of Angola (União dos Povos de Angola)
UPICV	People's Union of the Cabo Verde Islands (União do Povo das Ilhas de Cabo Verde)
UPNA	Union of the Peoples of Northern Angola (União dos Povos do Norte de Angola)

CHAPTER ONE

Portuguese Africa, the 'New Imperialism' and the Estado Novo

Portugal and the 'Scramble'

Two related assumptions have frequently been made about the position of Portugal and its African territories from the time of the European imperial 'scramble'. Both are significant in the perspectives they have imposed on the nature of Portugal's collapse in Africa. Both are essentially mistaken. The first is that Portugal's fragmentary presence in Africa was haplessly and helplessly buffeted by the intervention of the major European actors in the 1870s and 1880s and survived, barely, by good luck and the indulgence of others rather than by any political skill on the part of Lisbon. The second is that, having survived the partition of Africa in this way, Portugal maintained its empire as an anachronism, untouched by the broader political and economic objectives and methods pursued by 'modern' imperial powers like Britain, Germany and France. In this view, the wilful disregard of Portugal for the realities of the international system and the way it developed in the twentieth century ended inevitably with bitter and protracted colonial wars. In short, these wars were fought against not only the nationalists of Portuguese Africa but against history itself.[1]

The foundations of Portugal's 'third empire' in the late nineteenth century were certainly weak. Its origins lay in the role of coastal possessions in supporting the previous empires: the 'first' in east Asia in the sixteenth century, and the 'second' based on Brazil in the seventeenth and eighteenth centuries. The original function of the African territories had been as supply points on the sea routes to Asia. This role had been performed by the Atlantic archipelagos of Cabo Verde and São Tomé & Príncipe, by the mainland ports of

Bissau and Luanda and by Ilha de Moçambique, off the northern coast of what was to become the mainland territory of Mozambique. With the decline of Portugal's east Asian empire – which by the nineteenth century consisted only of the enclaves of Goa and Damião in India, part of the island of Timor within the Dutch East Indies archipelago and the port of Macão in southern China – the African mainland and its interior became more significant. Now Portugal's African presence was put to the service of the second empire. West Africa, particularly Angola and the Congo hinterland, provided slaves for the plantations of Brazil while São Tomé & Príncipe and Cabo Verde served as entrepôts in the trade.

With the independence of Brazil in 1822, however, and the increasing international pressure against the slave trade, Portugal's presence in Africa lacked any obvious purpose. Effective administration was maintained only in the Atlantic archipelagos. In Guiné the Portuguese presence was scant in the extreme and in Angola it extended little beyond the ports of Luanda and Lobito. In Mozambique, apart from the virtually autonomous *prazos* (agricultural estates developed from the seventeenth century along the Zambezi basin) Lisbon's authority was exercised only on Ilha de Moçambique, at a few points on the Indian Ocean coastline and in isolated riverine strongholds. In 1877, on the eve of partition, the governor-general of Angola, Almeida e Albuquerque, had acknowledged that 'it is sadly necessary to confess that our empire in the interior is imaginary'.[2] Such administration and commerce as Portugal's limited holdings did enjoy was supervised for the most part not by metropolitan colonialists but by a heterogeneous Creole population which was 'Portuguese' only to the degree that it had emerged from earlier imperial undertakings. In Cabo Verde and São Tomé & Príncipe the population as a whole was Creole. In Angola Creoles developed and maintained the slave trade. In Mozambique the Creole elite was involved in trade with India and eventually succeeded in taking control of the Zambezi *prazos*. Generally speaking, metropolitan merchant-adventurers, even in the mid-nineteenth century, continued to view the remnants of the second, South American, empire rather than Africa as their natural area of operations and accordingly devoted their energies and resources to Brazil. As the European partition began, therefore, the concept of 'Portuguese Africa' was questionable in terms both of territory and population.

Yet this unpromising position at the starting blocks of the 'new imperialism', far from bringing Portuguese Africa to the verge of extinction, contributed to a dramatic reinvigoration of Lisbon's imperial project. The internationalization of African imperialism in the 1880s provided a 'systemic' pull towards Africa which acted in parallel with the push of political and economic developments in the metropole.

The challenges to Portugal's position in Africa *appeared* at times extremely threatening, but their menace tends to weaken on examination. Certainly Lisbon lost its claim to the hinterland of the Zaire-Congo (present-day Zaire) in the 1880s to Belgium, largely as a result of Léopold II's fast diplomatic footwork at the Berlin Conference. But it was worth considering what exactly had been 'lost'. The extent of Portugal's exploitation of the area, let alone its effective occupation of it, were limited indeed. The ending of the slave trade to Brazil in 1836, which had been the primary purpose of Portugal's presence in west-central Africa, stripped Portugal's possession of the Congo basin of much of its *raison d'être*. The very circumstances of Portugal's defeat on the issue – with Lisbon's claim being supported against that of Belgium by Britain – highlighted the complexity of imperial diplomacy at this time. In other situations this complexity could and did operate in Portugal's favour.

Portugal had emerged successfully from a similar challenge in the previous decade when the French president, acting in arbitration, found in its favour against British complaints over its control of Delagoa Bay in east Africa. Britain had been anxious to acquire control of this part of the coast (within which the capital of Mozambique, Lourenço Marques, was located) because it formed a major outlet for the rapidly developing Transvaal. In fact, in both the Congo and the Indian Ocean Portugal constituted a useful piece on the political chessboard upon which the partition of Africa was played out. This role of geographic and diplomatic counter also protected Portugal from periodic Anglo-German aspirations for the division of Angola and Mozambique between them. Mutual mistrust between the two larger imperial powers gave an importance to Portugal's continued presence which it would not have had in a more serene political environment. Yet it would be wrong to consider Portugal's role in these manoeuvres as purely passive. Lisbon's own management of such issues as the Anglo-German relationship was not to be underestimated; considerable acumen was shown in its avoidance of legal and financial traps which might have facilitated the partition of its territories.[3]

Portugal proved adept at exploiting the 'customary' rights under international law that its presence, however notional, afforded it.

The widely observed legalities surrounding colonial expansion in Africa frequently belie the image of a 'scramble'. As if in recognition of the inherent danger of imperial competition spinning off into international anarchy, residual legal forms tended to receive a regard which did not reflect the balance of raw power between the participants. As one participant clearly short of such power, Portugal benefited greatly from this legalism. The implicit respect for prior 'possession' in the process of partition worked more to Portugal's favour than to its disadvantage.

Even Portugal's supposed national humiliation in Africa, the British ultimatum of 1890, was largely a self-inflicted reversal rather than the gratuitous insult to national honour complained of at the time. Certainly it was the assertion of British *force majeure* which ended one of Portugal's more ambitious imperial dreams. Lisbon's plan had been to establish a single colony across the breadth of Africa by connecting Mozambique and Angola and thus create a Portuguese *mapa côr de rosa* (rose-coloured map) from Indian Ocean to Atlantic. Ultimately God, in the form of Protestant interests anxious to preserve Livingstone's missionary advances in Nyassaland, allied with Mammon, personified by Cecil Rhodes and his ambition for a British Cape to Cairo axis, to ensure that London forced Lisbon to desist. Yet the Portuguese project, though extravagant, was not so completely destined to fail as has often been assumed in retrospect.[4] The ultimatum was not an inevitable and automatic response by Britain, and without it there would have been no obvious obstruction to the creation of an inter-oceanic Portuguese empire, however questionable its durability. And, regardless of the feasibility of the ambition, the very fact that Portugal pursued it is itself significant. It was hardly the behaviour of a nation, so to speak, 'more scrambled against than scrambling'. The enduring impact of the *mapa côr de rosa* affair on Portugal's African position was, moreover, not the ultimatum itself, but the Anglo-Portuguese Treaty of the following year which formalized Portugal's imperial frontiers with a helpfully relaxed approach to the criterion of 'effective occupation'.

These largely favourable international conditions represented one side of the 'imperial temptation' for Portugal. There were also considerable domestic forces at work. The drive for a third empire began in response to the particularly difficult economic circumstances in which Portugal found itself in the 1870s after some decades of relative prosperity. Portugal's misfortune at this time was twofold. Firstly, the prices of the primary products typical of Mediterranean Europe were in sharp decline. Secondly, the strategy of retreat into protectionism pursued by the more developed economies of northern Europe was unavailable to Portugal with its small domestic market.[5] When the *haute bourgeoisie* of the Portuguese Monarchy looked to new sources of wealth and investment it found its options restricted. Although still the favoured destination for emigrants, Brazil was gradually withdrawing from Lisbon's political and cultural orbit and its economic opportunities were increasingly open to non-Portuguese competition. Closer Iberian integration was obstructed by political nationalism and fears that nascent Portuguese industry would be suffocated by a more powerful Spain. Domestic imperatives therefore drove Portugal towards Africa, whose promise seemed to be endorsed by the enthusiasm with which it was regarded by the economically more successful states to the north. Both politically and economically the Portuguese imperialist became inseparable from the Portuguese progressive.[6]

By 1914, therefore, international opportunity and domestic imperatives had combined to transform Portugal into a major imperial power. Having confronted from a position of some weakness the accelerating interest in Africa of its European neighbours, Portugal emerged with a dramatically enhanced place in the international pecking order. As D.K. Fieldhouse has observed: 'in place of mythical claims she now had internationally recognized territories . . . Portugal as an African power rubbed shoulders with the great north European industrial giants . . . '.[7]

The remaining decades of Portuguese colonialism in Africa were to see economic policies and administrative doctrines alternate among a variety of models. The principal track of this movement was between the extremes of imperial integration and colonial autonomy. This dichotomy defined the imperial debate in Portugal throughout the twentieth century up to the very point of imperial dissolution.

Consolidating the Empire

The two decades which framed the twentieth century – from the British ultimatum in 1890 to the fall of the Monarchy in Portugal in 1910 – were ones in which Lisbon worked to transform the 'imaginary' empire of the 1870s into a set of overseas possessions comparable in their administration and economic status with those of the other 'new imperialists'. The first priority was to give some reality to the notion of 'effective occupation'. This was a quasi-legal requirement which was increasingly difficult to evade as the frontiers agreed in the 1880s and 1890s took on more and more concrete form throughout Africa. It is difficult to date exactly the completion of the process of 'pacification' in Portuguese Africa. Actions which in one view indicate the continuing strength of pre-colonial political forms and loyalties might in another represent merely a passing disaffection within an established colonial hegemony. It is probably reasonable to date the effective – if always tentative – assertion of European control in Mozambique from 1913. A similar level of control was established in Angola and Guiné respectively in 1914 and 1915. Tellingly, the last areas and peoples to be brought under European control – the Makonde in northern Mozambique, the Bakongo of the Dembos area of northern Angola and the Balanta of southern Guiné – were among the first and fiercest of those to rise against it five decades later.

Beyond the obvious objective of achieving political and military control, the effect of the 'campaign for Africa' was to focus public attention on the new 'colonies' (as they were called under the Republic after 1910) and to create a popular identification with the imperial project. In this way the idea of empire was assimilated into the national political culture. It was in these pre-First World War years that some of the most insidious imperial myths were born, conceived from the African enthusiasm of the 1880s and 1890s and brought to term by the military campaigns of the 1900s. The rhetoric of Portugal's unique, multiracial, pluricontinental destiny may have had its most sententious expression during the dictatorship after 1932 but it long pre-dated the corporatism of the Salazar regime. It was, moreover, a mindset which cross-cut otherwise fundamental divisions of left and right throughout Portugal's imperial history.

Hand in hand with military control went the development of administrative structures and the exploitation of economic resources. Administration varied across Africa. In Mozambique it was entrusted in large part to concession companies which were involved mainly in the sugar and cotton plantation sector. The Companhia de Moçambique was established in 1888 and operated in the central part of the country in the provinces of Sofala and Manica. The Niassa Company came into being in 1891 and covered the then remote northern areas of the colony. The territory of the Zambezi Company (1892) lay between that of the others and was concerned with the exploitation of the Zambezi basin from Quelimane on the coast into Tete province in the west. The advantages of this arrangement were colonial administration on the cheap and the provision of foreign capital (mostly British) for the development of the colony. The disadvantages included an inevitable weakness of metropolitan control and only limited economic benefits from enterprises which were fundamentally under-capitalized and primarily responsible to foreign investors.[8]

As the resources of the Transvaal, Southern Rhodesia and Nyassaland began to be developed, Mozambique's economic potential was increasingly seen as lying in its ports which provided outlets for these land-locked colonies. This role became ever more important with the expansion of the railway system in southern Africa. In 1894 the line between Lourenço Marques and the Transvaal was opened and two years later that between Beira and Umtali. Later, another 'service resource' became a major source of revenue: migrant labour to South Africa's mines. A 1926 treaty between Portugal and South Africa fixed a quota of 100,000 workers who would be reimbursed in part by gold remittances to the Bank of Portugal which then paid the miners on their return to Mozambique in local currency.[9]

The preponderance of foreign investment in the concession companies as well as the provision of Mozambique's infrastructural and labour services to its British-controlled neighbours fostered an image of Portugal's possessions as 'an empire within an empire'. Already heavily dependant on British markets for its exports as well as British direct investment in the metropole, it appeared that Portugal was now extending this peripheral status to the imperial frontier. But whatever the nature of economic relationships underlying colonial development, Lisbon saw in Africa a key economic asset at the turn of the century. The wealth exported from Lourenço Marques and Beira may not have been Portuguese but the port fees and duties were flowing in; the gold mined by Mozambican labour in the Transvaal might not be Portuguese gold but a useful proportion of it found its way into Lisbon's reserves. And, the agricultural and mineral wealth of the Mozambican interior remained to be evaluated and exploited.

As Mozambique's centre of economic gravity moved southward with the development of its ports, so the significance of the Portuguese state in the administration of the territory grew in relation to the authority of the concession companies to the north. The military campaigns of the first years of the century made Lisbon's control much less fragmentary. The Portuguese state was now supplanting the powers both of private companies and of the old Creole elite. These changes created a requirement for formal constitutional models of colonial administration. The preference of the republican regime was for a considerable degree of local autonomy for both Mozambique and Angola. In 1921, in pursuit of the Republic's programme of political development for the African colonies, the former cabinet minister Brito Camacho was appointed high commissioner in Mozambique. The new title, replacing that of 'governor-general', was emblematic of the Republic's push towards administrative devolution, that is devolution to the European settler elite.

The economic development of Angola had not been entrusted to concession companies as in Mozambique. With the decline of the slave trade Angola's economic importance lay in the plantation sector with initially rubber then later coffee and cotton as the main products. Like Mozambique, Angola with its long coast offered ports and railheads to the territories of the interior, in particular Northern Rhodesia and the Belgian Congo which relied on the Benguela railway to transport their copper exports for shipment from the port of Lobito. In 1917 the formation of the diamond prospecting company Diamang with British, French, American and Belgian as well as Portuguese investment was an early indication of future mineral wealth. By the 1930s, however, coffee had become the main source of Angola's wealth. Large plantations were cleared in the northern highlands (on occasion by former Brazilian planters now seeking their labour at source rather than, as previously, *via* the slave trade). It was to be in the coffee plantations of northern Angola that the most violent and most widespread assaults on the apparatus of Portuguese imperialism would take place at the beginning of the armed struggle.

Angola's high commissioner, appointed with Camacho Brito in 1921, was General Norton de Matos who had been minister of war during Portugal's participation in the First World War. Norton de Matos occupies a complex and somewhat contradictory place in Portugal's imperial mythology. 'Liberal' in his advocacy of extensive colonial autonomy from the metropole, he was at the same time a committed colonialist and far from enlightened in his attitude towards the native populations of the Portuguese territories. Employing his proconsular authority to its limit, he drove on the economic development of Angola in the early part of the 1920s through the ruthless exploitation of native labour and extensive speculative borrowing.[10]

The overthrow of the Republic by a rightist military coup in 1926 brought a major change in colonial policies. The reforms of 1926 were initially designed to end a number of abuses which had emerged in the colonies as a result of the devolution of power under the Republic.[11] In particular Portugal had been subjected to considerable international criticism for its maintenance of forced labour practices.[12] The 1926 changes, however, were merely the beginning of a thorough-going process of constitutional definition and consolidation for the empire. What emerged was a political and economic regime in Portuguese Africa which would remain essentially unchanged until its collapse half a century later.

Africa and the Estado Novo

The military dictatorship in power between 1926 and 1933, with due political diffidence, was conscious of its own limited experience and abilities in governance. Accordingly, it drew on the skills of a range of civilians sympathetic to its right-wing Catholic ethos. One of these was a former law lecturer from Coimbra University who had been elected to parliament in 1921, António de Oliveira Salazar. Joining the government as finance minister in 1928 Salazar had become acting colonial minister in 1930. In June of that year what might fairly be described as the key legislative statement of twentieth-century Portuguese imperialism, the Colonial Act (*Acto Colonial*), was published. The Act, which was eventually to be incorporated in Salazar's *Estado Novo* (New State) constitution of 1933, laid down the guiding doctrine of Portuguese colonial policy during the period in which Salazar maintained his dictatorial grip from his appointment as head of government in June 1932 until his incapacitation in September 1968.

The empire, twenty-two times the area of the metropole, was central to Salazar's mission to claim for Portugal the unlikely identity of world power. Africa lay at the heart of the corporatist nationalism of the *Estado Novo*. It was to be both a symbol and a tangible asset around which the nation could be mobilized to face an uncertain future. The essence of this doctrine was mediated by the Colonial Act with its uncompromising emphasis on centralization and administrative integration. In some respects, though, the Act represented continuity as much as change in imperial policy. It gave constitutional expression to many elements of the imperial mythology which emerged from the 'campaign for Africa' in the early 1900s. In the words of James Duffy, the Act 'was a decisive document precisely because it acknowledged a Portuguese tradition in Africa and sought to give it a kind of legislative reality'.[13]

Where the Act *was* unequivocal in marking change was in its absolute rejection of the republican 'heresy' of colonial autonomy. The position of governor-general was reinstated in place of the proconsular office of high commissioner. The expression 'Portuguese Colonial Empire' (*Império Colonial Português*) was introduced to replace the loose terminology of 'colonies' and Portugal's 'historic' civilizing mission was asserted. A powerful strand of economic protectionism was also woven into the Act. The colonies were to be interdependent with each other and with the metropole. Chartered companies would cease to operate (though only after the termination of their existing agreements) and national economic interests were to be specially protected against the incursion of foreign capital. The ground was now prepared for the growth of a handful of large Portuguese monopolies (or 'oligopolies') which, as essential components of the corporate *Estado Novo*, dominated much of the economic activity of Portuguese Africa in the 1950s and 1960s.

In its economic nationalism the Colonial Act represented a response to broader international conditions as the post-1929 slump became global. To this extent Salazar's interest in the empire was analogous to that of the old elite of the Monarchy which responded to the economic crisis of the 1870s by re-directing its attention from depressed Europe to enticing Africa. Even amidst the relative stagnation of the 1930s and 1940s tangible economic benefits accrued to the metropole. Primary products from Africa, in particular sugar, cotton and coffee, permitted significant import substitution and were invaluable to the domestic market during the Second World War. Gold remittances for Mozambican mine labour in South Africa added significantly to Lisbon's reserves while the strict budgetary discipline imposed by the regime on the colonies minimized financial demands on the metropole.

It was, though, in the post-1945 period that Africa seemed to fulfil its economic promise for Portugal. With an imperial economy largely undamaged by the war, Portuguese investment increased in relation to foreign capital. Existing sources of revenue were supplemented by the first significant earnings from mineral extraction (iron in Angola and coal in Mozambique). Less visibly, Africa began in the 1950s to attract a significant proportion of Portugal's flow of emigrants which had hitherto favoured Brazil and other parts of Latin America. Between 1955 and 1968 the white population of Angola tripled from 100,000 to 300,000, while in the period from 1950 to 1968 that of Mozambique quadrupled from 50,000 to 200,000 out of total populations of, respectively, 5½ million and 8¼ million. In contrast to patterns in English-speaking Africa much of this migration was short-term rather than permanent, but of those who did settle the largest proportion were from the impoverished rural areas of central and southern Portugal. With little or nothing to return to in the metropole and with a relatively narrow political world-view, they combined with the ideologues of the regime to resist the reforms which might just have achieved the eventual dissolution of Portuguese Africa without recourse to armed struggle.

On the international level the 1950s brought particular difficulties for Portuguese imperialism. World wars engender postwar institutions to mobilize war-sensitized consciences. Portugal had already been denounced in the League of Nations in the 1920s for its colonial labour practices. Now, in the post-Second World War years, the United Nations turned its attention to the basic question of colonialism. Initially denied membership of the UN along with other wartime neutrals by Soviet obstruction, Portugal sought to improve its prospects by re-packaging its imperialism in a legally sanitized form. This was done by means of a constitutional amendment in 1951 by which the expression 'Colonial Empire' was entirely expunged.[14] Henceforth Portugal's possessions became 'Overseas Provinces' (*Províncias Ultramares*) – and as such integral parts of 'one state single and indivisible' (*um estado une e indivisível*). (The idea was, of course, not especially novel; it followed closely the French formulation applied to Algeria and Indo-China.) Although the immediate motive for the introduction of the Overseas Provinces concept was purely pragmatic, the effect was to give constitutional reality to integration. In the attempt to circumvent United Nations criticism Salazar had, wittingly or unwittingly, underlined his rejection of all notion of colonial decentralization.[15]

The African Perspective

What of the experiences and the reactions of the colonized during this period of imperial assertion and consolidation? The indigenous population of Portuguese Africa (Africans and Creoles) was roughly eight million by 1910, of which about seven million were in Angola and Mozambique. Two factors, largely peculiar to Portuguese imperialism, determined much of their political, economic and social experience. One was the relative backwardness of the imperial power itself. This impacted on the indigenous experience in a variety of ways. Just as Portugal had lagged behind the other powers in abolishing slavery only in 1876, so it was well into the twentieth century before forced labour and compulsory production of cash crops were ended.[16] Even after formal abolition, systematic abuses of the 'contract' labour system continued, particularly in relation to the recruitment of Angolan workers for the cocoa plantations of São Tomé & Príncipe.[17] The limitations of metropolitan resources also affected the provision of basic social services, a responsibility which devolved increasingly after 1930 on Catholic missions. Although empirical comparisons are virtually impossible, it is reasonable to suggest that the indigenous populations of Portuguese Africa, at least up until the 1960s, were the most disadvantaged of the European empires.[18]

Ironically, this in itself does not refute the doctrine of 'one state single and indivisible'. Extreme deprivation, illiteracy and exploit-ation were suffered by a considerable section of the metropolitan population as well throughout the imperial period. Migration to Africa, moreover, did not in itself guarantee a dramatic improvement in the standard of living of the white settler. If the lot of the African in the Portuguese empire compared unfavourably with that of his or her counterpart elsewhere, so did that of the European. White bus and train conductors, even white domestic servants, were common, most so in Angola where in 1960 there were some 7000 white unemployed.[19] The other shared experience between metropole and colony was an absence of effective political participation. The greater part of the history of the third empire was played out under authoritarianism of one form or another. In this sense of *relative* disadvantage between metropole and colony, the lot of 'Portuguese' Africans was probably closer to that of their colonizers than was the case in the other European empires. How much comfort the colonized drew from this shared political and economic privation remains unrecorded.

Although without political power, the native (or *indígena*) did have the opportunity to become 'assimilated' to the status of 'civilized' (*civilizado*) if he or she could demonstrate certain 'skills and qualities'. These included facility with the Portuguese language, financial self-sufficiency and 'appropriate conduct'. It was, however, a perquisite which proved less than irresistible. By 1950 there were only about 30,000 *assimilados* in Angola and 4300 in Mozambique. In the absence of any political rights in the empire there was little obvious benefit to becoming assimilated. The allure of 'civilization' was slight when its one tangible consequence was the privilege of paying extra taxes. The status of *assimilado* ended in 1961 when

Lisbon, once more with an eye to international opinion, undertook some further cosmetic reforms to its administrative regime in Africa. Henceforth all inhabitants of Angola, Mozambique and Guiné-Bissau were, regardless of their own preferences, elevated to the status of Portuguese citizen.

TABLE 1.1   *Approximate population and area of Portuguese Africa at decolonization (1974–75)*

Territory	Population (000s)	Area (000 sq. km)
Angola	5 500	1 247
Mozambique	8 250	802
Guiné-Bissau	550	36
Cabo Verde	280	4
São Tomé & Príncipe	75	1
(Portugal	8 500	92)

For all these fertile grounds of grievance, an anti-colonial movement was slow to emerge and spasmodic in its manifestations when it did. Separated by language from the larger populations of the French and British empires and without their possibilities for even limited political organization, African nationalism in the Portuguese empire grew from the most testing conditions. Little initial support was forthcoming even from the broader pan-African movement. Amílcar Cabral, the leader of the nationalist struggle in Guiné-Bissau and the foremost theorist of anti-colonialism in lusophone Africa, recalled that as late as 1960 a fellow-delegate at the Tunis All-African Peoples' Conference insisted that 'it's different for you . . . you're doing all right with the Portuguese'.[20] Portugal's luso-tropical mythology, it appeared, had made headway even among African nationalists.

Early protest and resistance in the lusophone territories tended to be fragmented. It emerged separately from different sections of colonial society and the strands remained largely uncoordinated into the 1950s. Indeed one effect of the shared experience of repression between the metropole and Africa was that one strand of African resistance, that of the urbanized intellectual, began with more points of contact with the anti-regime forces in Portugal than it did with its peasant and proletarian counterparts in the colonies. Both Portuguese dissident and African nationalist experienced the same disenfranchisement and worked under the shadow of the same secret police. In this at least they were indisputably part of a single political culture, *une e indivisível.*

The first movements which could loosely be described as nationalist in a modern sense emerged among the educated urban Africans and *mestiços* (mixed race) in the 1920s and 1930s in both Angola and Mozambique. These were usually cultural organizations rather than explicitly political ones. As early as 1920 the African League (Liga Africana) had been founded in Lisbon as a social and intellectual focus for Africans studying in metropolitan universities. Among the more significant organizations in the colonies themselves were the National African League (Liga Nacional Africana) and the African Club (Grémio Africano) in Angola and the Centre for Africans of Mozambique (Centro Associativo dos Negros de Moçambique). A number of quasi-political magazines were published in the inter-war years as well, such as *Brado Africano* (*The African Cry*) in Mozambique. Participation in this movement was, however, restricted to a politically aware sub-stratum of an already narrow layer of colonial society. Its impact on either the broader African 'masses' or the colonial state was insignificant. Pan-Africanism was only slowly catching the imagination of the emerging nationalists of the colonial empires and, as we have observed, lusophone nationalists were doubly disadvantaged by language and their uniquely oppressive colonial regime.

A range of technical, social and cultural obstacles (not unique to the Portuguese colonies) prevented the cross-fertilization of urban theorizing and the daily experience of the rural poor. Against this background the colonial state had little difficulty in controlling embryonic nationalism without any extensive recourse to the formidable powers of repression it was developing in the metropole. It was not until 1957, for example, that it was felt necessary to export the metropolitan security police to the colonies. A truly effective nationalist movement only began in lusophone Africa with the recognition that even limited change within the authoritarian centralism of the empire was impossible by purely political means.

The process by which this movement emerged will be explored in the next chapter, as will the parallel agents of imperial dissolution at work outside of Africa. Quite independently at first, but later in tandem with African resistance, the forces of economic modernization in Portugal itself were slowly but irremediably undermining the foundations of the *Estado Novo*. And, just as these African and European elements began to inter-react, the logic of world politics after 1945 was pointing unerringly to the end of the colonial empires. Portugal, which in the 1880s and 1890s had proved quite adept at exploiting global trends to its own benefit, now in the 1950s and 1960s seemed imprisoned by the gains of that earlier age and incapable of acknowledging, let alone responding to, its passing.

Notes

1 The fundamental arguments on either side of the debate about the 'success' of Portuguese imperialism are to be found in R.J. Hammond, *Portugal and Africa 1815–1910: A Study in Uneconomic Imperialism* (Stanford CT: Stanford University Press 1966) and Gervaise Clarence-Smith, *The Third Portuguese Empire 1825–1975: A Study in Economic Imperialism* (Manchester: University Press 1985). The books' subtitles indicate their respective positions.

2 Quoted in José Friere Antunes, *O Factor Africano* (Lisbon: Bertrand 1990), p.27.

3 David M. Abshire, 'From the Scramble for Africa to the "New State" ', David M. Abshire and Michael A. Samuels, eds, *Portuguese Africa: A Handbook* (London: Pall Mall 1969), p.75.

4 See Richard J. Hammond, 'Uneconomic imperialism: Portugal in Africa before 1910', L.H. Gann and Peter Duignan, eds, *Colonialism in Africa 1870–1960*, vol.1: *The History and Politics of Colonialism 1870–1914* (Cambridge: CUP 1969), pp.365–6.

5 Clarence-Smith, *The Third Portuguese Empire*, p.8. The population of Portugal was about 5 million at this time.

6 Friere Antunes, *O Factor Africano*, p.25.

7 D.K. Fieldhouse, *The Colonial Empires: A Comparative Study from the Eighteenth Century* (London: Macmillan 1982), p.351.

8 R.A.H. Robinson, *Contemporary Portugal: A History* (London: George Allen and Unwin 1979), p.114.

9 After six months on full pay 60 per cent of a miner's wage would be remitted to Portugal in gold bars at conversion rates favourable to Lisbon. This gold could then be sold on at market prices. See Mário Azevedo, ' "A sober commitment to liberation?" Mozambique and South Africa 1974–79', *African Affairs* 79(317) October 1980, p.571. The system and its human costs are explored in Ruth First's *Black Gold: The Mozambican Miner, Proletarian and Peasant* (Brighton: Harvester Wheatsheaf 1983).

10 In later life Norton de Matos's hostility to the Salazar regime led him to contest the presidential election of 1949. His antipathy was not driven by any progressive political instincts, however. His opposition to the regime derived from the centralizing thrust of imperial policy under Salazar. As a leading Freemason he was also offended by the religiosity which permeated the rhetoric and practices of Salazarist colonialism.

11 A.H. de Oliveira Marques, *History of Portugal*, vol.2: *From Empire to Corporate State* (New York: Columbia University Press 1972), pp.226–7.

12 On Labour practices before 1921 see Hammond, 'Uneconomic imperialism', pp.373–5.

13 James Duffy, 'Portuguese Africa 1930 to 1960', L.H. Gann and Peter Duignan, eds, *Colonialism in Africa 1870–1960*, vol.2: *The History and Politics of Colonialism 1914–1960* (Cambridge: CUP 1970), p.172.

14 António de Figueiredo, *Portugal: Fifty Years of Dictatorship* (Harmondsworth Middlesex: Penguin 1975), p.206.

15 Portugal entered the UN as part of the 'package deal' of 1955 which

admitted a balanced number of states from each cold war bloc. The verbal sophistries of the 1951 reform had no impact on its application.

16 Following the reforms of 1926 labour in Portuguese Africa could, in theory, only be conscripted for public works beneficial to the labourer (a system similar to that employed in the French territories). Fieldhouse, *The Colonial Empires*, pp.353–54.

17 On the scandals surrounding contract labour at the beginning of the twentieth century see Malyn Newitt, *Portugal in Africa: The Last Hundred Years* (London: Hurst and Co. 1981), pp.207–11.

18 Illiteracy rates in 1960 in the main colonies varied between about 91 per cent (Mozambique) and 99 per cent (Guiné). They improved noticeably as greater resources were devoted to education in the 1960s and early 1970s. By the time of independence Mozambique's rate stood at 75 per cent. Grupo de pesquisa sobre a descolonização portuguesa, *A Descolonização Portuguesa: Aproximação a um Estudo*, vol.2 (Lisbon: Instituto Amaro da Costa 1982), p.127.

19 Franz Ansprenger, *The Dissolution of the Colonial Empires* (London: Routledge 1989), p.269.

20 Foreword by Amílcar Cabral to Basil Davidson, *For the Liberation of Guiné*, (Harmondsworth Middlesex: Penguin 1968), pp.9–10.

CHAPTER TWO

Nationalist Consolidation and the Wars of Liberation

The Emergence of Militant Nationalism in Portuguese Africa

A complex of factors underlay the development of the anti-colonial movement in Portuguese Africa in the 1950s. At the global level there was the rapidly widening contrast between political developments in the British and French empires and their evident absence in that of Portugal. The movement on the part of the more developed imperial powers towards decolonization at this time was interrelated with the growing anti-colonialism of the United Nations and with the cold war positioning of United States policy towards the growing Afro-Asian bloc in world politics. In 1960 alone some twenty new African states emerged from the decolonization process. Yet just at the time when Paris and London, with American urging, were initiating the sequence of political processes and rituals which would lead to imperial dissolution, Lisbon appeared to be tightening its colonial grip. This could be seen formally with the 1951 'reform' which converted the 'Colonial Empire' into integral 'overseas provinces' but it was also evident at the social level with the huge growth in white migration to the colonies which was underway in the mid-1950s.

Portugal's perverseness in the face of the winds of change in Africa was also apparent in its intensifying repression in the colonies which, in a classic cycle of causality, grew with increased agitation for greater political and economic freedoms. In 1953 the violence historically embedded in the labour relations of São Tomé & Príncipe exploded in widespread disorder resulting in about 1000 deaths in a single week. Lisbon's quiet removal of its governor, widely seen as responsible for the bloodbath, was the extent of its response to international criticism. Any expression of protest in the colonies became subject to systematic and savage repression. In 1957 the regime's political police, the PIDE (Polícia Internacional e de Defesa do Estado – International and State Defence Police), established headquarters in all of the African territories and began to build up a formidable network of informers to match that already operating in the metropole. In June 1960 in Mueda in northern Mozambique about 500 protesters died when police and troops opened fire on a demonstration of Makonde cotton labourers. Cotton workers were also the victims in a similar incident in January 1961 in Malanje in central Angola when many hundreds also died. In August 1960 about 50 strikers had been killed in the Pidjiguiti docks in Guiné-Bissau. This catalogue of massacre and violent repression emerged less from the calculated deployment of terror as an instrument of control than from assumptions about the relationship between state and subject common throughout the Portuguese empire, including in the metropole itself. In Africa, however, distance and racial attitudes which were sharply at odds with the official ideology of tolerant integration removed virtually all restraint.

With an ironic appropriateness, the unravelling of the 'one and indivisible' empire had firm trans-imperial roots. The tradition of African and *mestiço* elites undergoing higher education in the metropole may have been designed to develop a unified lusophone culture but by the 1950s it was merely facilitating the coordination of emerging nationalisms. The Centre for African Studies, established in Lisbon in 1951, was later described by Mário Soares as the 'cradle of African leadership'. It provided a focus for the generation of political theorists and guerrilla commanders whose movements would come to power after the collapse of the empire. Dominant figures in the coming armed struggles such as Agostinho Neto and Mário de Andrade of Angola, Amílcar Cabral of Guiné-Bissau and Marcelino dos Santos of Mozambique served their political apprenticeships together in the metropole. The sense of a unified struggle was further enhanced by the fact that many of them were first active in metropolitan-oriented dissident groups like the leftist front, the United Democratic Movement (MUD: Movimento Unido Democrático) and the Portuguese Communist Party (PCP). As Soares later observed, these metropolitan connections were to prove enduring. Common exposure 'to the iron rigour of Salazarist policy' meant that 'the bonds of sympathy with anti-Fascist groups in Portugal were never broken'.[1]

In Angola the sense of a unified, empire-wide struggle against the

Lisbon regime was underlined by the important early role of the Angolan Communist Party (PCA: Partido Comunista Angolano) which had begun in 1948 as a cell of the Portuguese party. The PCA with other less organized groupings would finally coalesce into the Popular Movement for the Liberation of Angola (MPLA: Movimento Popular de Libertação de Angola) in December 1956. Originally led by Viriato da Cruz and Mário de Andrade, the social and geographical bases of MPLA strength reflected its political origins. From its foundation it drew its main support from urbanized Africans and *mestiços* (both da Cruz and Andrade were of mixed race). It was strongest around the Luanda area where it established an ethnic following among the local 1.3 million-strong Mbundu. The MPLA represented in many ways a genuine alliance between intelligentsia and proletariat, social categories more usually associated with Europe than sub-Saharan Africa in the mid-1950s. The numerical limits of this base and the tensions inherent in the management of an ideological movement of the character of the MPLA were to cause grave difficulties within the organization in the later 1960s and early 1970s.

There were other strands in the anti-colonial movement in Angola, as elsewhere in lusophone Africa, whose origins and ideological positions were less cosmopolitan. The most significant of these in the 1950s was the movement which emerged from the internal politics of the Bakongo ethnic group. About 650,000 strong in Angola itself, the importance of the Bakongo ethnic group was enhanced by the fact that its distribution straddled the border with the Belgian Congo (later Zaire). As events within Angola and in the broader region developed in the late 1950s and 1960s, the Bakongo became one of the most significant ethnic elements in the anti-colonial equation. From the first Portuguese expansion into the interior, relations had been established with the traditional Congo monarchy which came to occupy a special position in the colonial regime. Although in the ruthlessly centralized Portuguese system of the mid-twentieth century this fell far short of British practices of 'indirect rule', it nevertheless conferred a significant identity on the Bakongo within Angola.[2] The death of the Bakongo king Dom Pedro VII in 1955 opened up a succession struggle in which the Union of the Peoples of Northern Angola (UNPA: União dos Povos do Norte de Angola) was formed in support of a Protestant heir against Portuguese attempts to impose a Catholic on the throne. The main force behind the movement was the Léopoldville-based Holden Roberto who although Angolan by nationality had spent most of his life in the Belgian Congo. Aside from the Baptist faith which underlay his activism on the succession issue, Roberto was evidently influenced by Patrice Lumumba, the radical prime minister of the Congo after independence.[3] This leftist affinity was not to prove enduring, however. In 1958 the regionalist 'Northern' designation was dropped and the UPNA became the Union of the Peoples of Angola (UPA), a title change which asserted a multi-ethnic national identity that the movement never achieved in reality. It was, though, the UPA which would effectively begin the armed struggle in Portuguese Africa in February 1961. Renamed again in 1962 to become the National Front for the Liberation of Angola (FNLA: Frente Nacional de Libertação de Angola), it became the numerically largest of the anti-Portuguese forces in Angola up until 1974.

The year in which the MPLA came into being in Angola, 1956, was a significant one in Guiné-Bissau as well. In September of that year a small group of predominantly Cabo Verdean activists formed the African Independence Party which later became the African Independence Party for the Independence of Guiné and Cabo Verde (PAIGC: Partido Africano para a Independência da Guiné e Cabo Verde). There was in fact a nationalist grouping in existence already in Portuguese Guiné, the Front for the Liberation and Independence of Guiné (FLING: Frente para a Libertação e Independência da Guiné) which had been formed in 1953 from a number of smaller groups. FLING remained in some sort of existence through to the Portuguese revolution, after which it presented a momentary complication in negotiations over the transfer of power. Its durability was due in no small part to the variable but continuing support of the president of neighbouring Senegal, Léopold Senghor, who kept his political options open by spreading his favour between FLING and the PAIGC.[4] FLING was, however, largely inactive in the 1960s, and concentrated much of its limited energies on criticism of the PAIGC's 'non-African' leadership.[5] Largely clandestine for the first three years of its existence, the PAIGC assumed a high public profile in the aftermath of the Pidjiguiti dock strike in 1959 in which it had been deeply involved. The following year PIDE repression forced the leadership out of Guiné and led it to seek refuge and support for the coming armed struggle in both of its francophone neighbours, Senegal and Guinea-Conakry. In this way the war in Guiné-Bissau was to become something of an issue between the two bordering states and their respective leaders, the 'moderate' Léopold Senghor and the 'radical' Ahmed Sekou Touré.

The dominating figure within the PAIGC was Amílcar Cabral. A *mestiço* Cabo Verdean, though Guinean born, Cabral had trained in Portugal as an agronomist. His profession equipped him with a considerable knowledge of both the conditions of the rural masses and of the political climate throughout the empire. He had, for example, been in Angola during the mid-1950s in the period just prior to the formation of the MPLA.[6] Cabral was the most theoretically profound of the nationalist leaders in Portuguese Africa. For him decolonization was a continuing process rather than a single event and one whose scope transcended the formal transfer of power by the colonial state. To Cabral, therefore, the mere substitution of the colonial state by a 'national' one did not in itself amount to 'decolonization'. This required a continuing struggle which was not merely political or even economic but profoundly psychological as well.[7] This position was one which would create strains within the PAIGC during the armed struggle and which would complicate the always difficult situation in which non-Guineans dominated its leadership.

Mozambique was the last of the colonies to establish a truly national independence movement with the creation of Frelimo (Frente de Libertação de Moçambique) in June 1962. As in Angola, regional and ethnically based movements were already in existence. The Makonde National Union (Manu) drew its support from the Makonde ethnic group of the north while the National Democratic Union of Mozambique (Udenamo: União Democrática Nacional de Moçambique) was southern-based. A third movement, the National African Union of Independent Mozambique (Unami: União Nacional Africana de Moçambique Independente) was based in Tete in the centre of the country. These groups had been formed in exile and were led from abroad. They were therefore distanced from their putative internal power bases.[8] In 1962, under pressure from Julius Nyerere of Tanzania and Kwame Nkrumah of Ghana, the three movements came together in Dar es Salaam to form Frelimo.[9] The new movement was weaker than either the MPLA or the PAIGC in terms of its ideological and structural cohesion. It emerged from external pressure rather than a clear indigenous commitment to a unified national liberation struggle. The choice of leader was indicative of this weakness. Its first president was Eduardo Mondlane, an American-educated United Nations official and perhaps the most distinguished black Mozambican of his generation. Mondlane was clearly an individual of great ability and his nomination as Frelimo leader owed at least as much to his national and international standing as his commitment to nationalist struggle. Almost immediately following the establishment of the new movement he returned to the United States and his post at the UN.[10] These weaknesses in Frelimo's initial construction would only be resolved after a protracted series of internal struggles and schisms fought out in parallel with the war against Portugal.

As well as Nyerere and Nkrumah, a third source of pressure had been brought to bear on the Mozambican movements to unite in 1962. This came from the Conference of Nationalist Organizations of the Portuguese Colonies (CONCP: Conferência das Organizações Nacionalistas das Colónias Portuguesas), a coordinating body which had been established in Algiers by the UPA, MPLA and PAIGC in April 1961. It was in fact the third incarnation of a coordinating structure. In 1957 the Anti-Colonialist Movement (MAC: Movimento Anti-Colonialista) had been formed by Angolan and Guinean nationalists in Paris. This evolved into the African Front for National Independence (FRAIN: Frente Africana de Independência Nacional) in Tunis in 1960. It was clearly of great importance to the CONCP to bring Mozambique into the broader movement and a considerable achievement when it managed to do so, whatever the problems implicit in creating a national liberation movement by external exhortation.

The Wars Begin

By the middle of 1962 each of the major African territories had its national liberation movement in place. The weaknesses of these movements – dependence on foreign sponsorship and refuge, narrowness of social and geographic support, unresolved potential for factionalism – cannot detract from the basic achievement. They had been formed in the face of a colonial state capable of deploying massive repressive resources. They had created in the CONCP the embryo of what would prove to be an extremely effective international coordinating agency. Moreover, the movements exhibited a high degree of ideological cohesion with remarkably similar political and economic programmes (though Frelimo lagged in this during the first years). The pursuit of national independence and the development strategies of the post-colonial states which would emerge from this were to be based on a Marxism pragmatically adapted to African realities. The armed struggles against Portugal and the refinement of 'Afro-Marxism' as a development strategy advanced hand in hand through the 1960s.

Despite these common and unifying factors among the nationalist movements, it would be misleading to suggest that the three African wars began in any kind of coordinated way. Each of the guerrilla campaigns emerged from local circumstances. There were clearly common factors at work. The decolonizing *zeitgeist* in sub-Saharan Africa in the first years of the 1960s has already been mentioned. Within lusophone Africa itself, precedent was clearly a factor. The revolts in Angola at the beginning of 1961 obviously influenced the thinking and timing of the PAIGC's first substantial move in January 1963 which in turn played a part in the initiation of guerrilla activity in Mozambique the following year. But the struggles remained essentially national ones.

Both during and after the period of the armed struggles there was a tendency shared by quite disparate ideological interests to present the nationalist uprisings as a single African 'war'. For the Salazar government this served the image of Portugal in the front-line of the global anti-communist crusade, confronting a single malign force. The regime was also disposed to see the wars through the mystical lens of the indivisible empire with all revolts against the single pluricontinental entity being, in essence, one assault.

On the left, both African and metropolitan, the idea of a unified armed struggle was important in the presentation of events as part of a common anti-imperialist resistance and as a united Euro-African struggle against 'fascism'. Beyond ideological rhetoric and political purpose, however, there is little to support the proposition of a single armed struggle in Portuguese Africa. Between 1961 and 1974 each of the three territories fought out its own war at its own pace, with means and objectives specific to itself. In the case of Angola, indeed, it is unclear whether it is reasonable to speak in terms even of a single *national* struggle. The conflicts *between* the three nationalist movements which were eventually involved in the fighting frequently reached an intensity which suggested civil war rather than mere inter-group rivalry, even before the collapse of the Lisbon regime. For this reason any exploration of 'Portugal's African war' needs to have as its primary focus the development of each armed struggle in its own national context.

In the case of Angola both the MPLA and the UPA claimed to have initiated the liberation war in February–March 1961. The MPLA would point to the calendar and their rivals to impact and consequences. During 1959 and 1960 the MPLA had been subjected to a major campaign of repression by the colonial authorities. A large number of its leading cadres had been arrested and the organization, now with a weakened leadership, opted for a dramatic gesture. At dawn on 4 February 1961 about 200 MPLA members and supporters from Luanda's *muçeques* (African townships) attacked the São Paulo de Luanda prison and other government targets in the city.[11] It was a futile gesture in itself and merely provided the occasion for further PIDE repression and reprisal attacks by white mobs.[12] It would, though, assume a mythic importance in the history of the movement, eventually occupying a corresponding place to Castro's attack on the Moncada barracks in the legend of the Cuban revolution. It was also the first and last significant incident of urban guerrilla activity anywhere in the empire during the course of the wars. The failure of the attack and the evident capacity of the authorities (and settlers) to strike back in the cities persuaded not just the MPLA but the PAIGC and Frelimo as well that, regardless of the rhetoric of proletarian solidarity, the guerrilla struggles had greatest chance of success in the bush. And, ideally, the bush should be contiguous with the frontier of a sympathetic neighbour.

Much more serious for the Portuguese than the Luanda attacks was the outbreak of widespread violence in the coffee-growing areas of northern Angola on 14–15 March. The uprising was influenced by events across the border in the former Belgian Congo where the northern Bakongo were involved in the civil war which followed Belgium's precipitate withdrawal in mid-1960. Orchestrated by Roberto's UPA, the rebellion itself caused the deaths of somewhere between 300 and 500 Europeans and perhaps 1500 Africans. This, though, was insignificant compared to the carnage wrought by white reprisals and, from May 1961, the belated reaction of the Portuguese military. In all between 30,000 and 50,000 Africans died at this time, with several times that number seeking refuge over the border with their fellow Bakongo in the new Congo Republic.[13] From a total strength of about 3000 at the beginning of 1961, Portugal had increased its military presence by the end of the year to 50,000 and the territory settled down to fourteen years of spasmodic guerrilla warfare.

In Guiné-Bissau the military phase of the PAIGC's campaign began on 23 January 1963 with an attack on the Portuguese barracks at Tite in the south of the territory. According to the PAIGC's official history, the decision to pursue the military option was taken at a meeting in September 1959 soon after the Pidjiguiti massacre. Following the initial violence of the dock strike there was a wave of PIDE repression against known political activists. Industrial action and other forms of non-violent pressure, it was agreed, would be futile.[14] In this way an initial faith in the possibilities of political organization among the urban proletariat gave way to a focus on rural guerrilla warfare. This was, as we have observed, a truth forced upon the MPLA in Luanda after the failure of its attacks in February 1961 and was to be recognized throughout Portuguese Africa. A period of intense political activity followed in Guiné which, Amílcar Cabral insisted, was a necessary preparation for the armed struggle. That struggle when it got underway was to be the most intense in the empire, the most unremitting in its violence and proportionately the most extensive in its area of operation.

In contrast to the controlled preparation of the PAIGC in Guiné, Frelimo's armed struggle began precipitately and in some confusion on 26 September 1964. Its first act involved an armed attack on the administrative post at Chai in the northern province of Cabo Delgado, the hinterland of the Makonde who soon came to dominate Frelimo's military cadres. In preparation for the first attacks guerrillas had been infiltrated into the area from bases across the Rovumo river in Tanzania.

The decision to launch the armed struggle at this time had been forced on Frelimo. Sporadic and disorganized violence had already broken out in northern Mozambique and the Portuguese response to this threatened the effectiveness of Frelimo's activities before they had properly begun.[15] Just as events in the neighbouring Congo influenced the UPA uprising in northern Angola in 1961, so the ferment in northern Mozambique in September 1964 was due in part to the independence of neighbouring Malawi a few weeks previously.[16] This abrupt and under-planned first phase of the armed struggle caused considerable early set-backs for Frelimo and in consequence a much more circumspect approach was taken to the war from about 1965.[17] Inevitably, these early difficulties fed factional conflicts which festered unresolved within the organization throughout the latter part of the 1960s.

Metropolitan Politics and the Onset of the Wars

By the end of 1964 Portugal, one of the poorest countries of western Europe, was embroiled in three separate guerrilla wars in another continent. There was, moreover, no sign that it sought any political accommodation and some indication that it might actually be capable of resolving the crisis by force. Paradoxically, the onset of the wars had the effect of consolidating the Salazar regime and muting existing internal criticism of its colonial policies. The obvious need for military protection from the metropole silenced such limited settler separatism as there had been. In Angola in particular the flirtation of sections of the European population with autonomist ideas was quickly abandoned now that the security guarantees implicit in integration with the metropole had suddenly assumed great significance.[18] Additionally, at the end of the fateful year of 1961, India's annexation of Goa and its humiliation of the Portuguese forces there created a groundswell of national indignation in the metropole and in settler communities in Africa. As a result, the regime's centralizing nationalism, far from suffering for its lack of international realism, revived in popularity.[19] Salazar's stratagem of blaming the Goa débâcle on the shortcomings of the garrison – and by extension on the armed forces as an institution – may have sown a wind for the future but it would be his successor who would reap the whirlwind. In the meantime the old dictator had demonstrated his instinct for manipulating competing sections of the national elite to his own advantage.[20]

The crisis of 1961 did not pass without some internal difficulties for the regime, but the challenges themselves were less significant than the relative ease with which Salazar dealt with them. The Lisbon government had been under some pressure since the 1958 presidential elections when reformist elements had fielded General Humberto Delgado, a former air force officer and diplomat who had considerable national prestige. His defeat by the regime's nominee, the impeccably Salazarist Admiral Américo Thomáz, in a crassly rigged poll aggravated rather than reduced political restiveness among the middle as well as working class.[21] A rather more piratical (literally) attack was made on the regime by the actions of the quixotic Captain Henrique Galvão, a former colonial administrator of uncertain politics, who in January 1961 led the hijack of the Portuguese liner the *Santa Maria* in the Caribbean. He then crossed the Atlantic all the while issuing anti-Salazarist statements. Considerable speculation surrounded his intentions and destination. At one point it appeared he might be *en route* to Luanda to establish a Portuguese government in exile and there was speculation that the MPLA attack on the central prison may have been coordinated with Galvão.[22] Whatever its objective, if indeed any had been pre-planned, the *Santa Maria* affair focused world attention on Portugal on the very eve of the Angolan uprising and the beginning of the colonial wars.

In April 1961 dissent emerged at the centre of the regime itself when the defence minister General Júlio Botelho Moniz conspired to remove Salazar. The origins of the *crise Botelho Moniz* remain somewhat obscure but at the core of the affair was the ambiguity of the relationship between the civilian and military components of the regime which had been a characteristic of Portuguese politics since the beginnings of the *Estado Novo*.[23] The *pronunciamento* of 1926 had, after all, been a military coup, and the civilian architects of the *Estado Novo* (most notably Salazar himself) had originally been put in their positions at the grace and favour of the military. In April 1961 the Angolan crisis was a few weeks old and metropolitan control had yet to be reasserted. The army was being subjected to increasing criticism and there was a fear, reasonably founded in the light of events in Goa at the end of the year, that Salazar was setting the military up as scapegoat. In this period of imperial and international confusion such suspicions opened cleavages in the regime which were normally well-sealed by mutual self-interest. Within the ministry of defence and the senior officer corps there was a reformist grouping which saw the Angolan uprising as part of the broader 'winds of change' blowing across Africa. These officers, with the support of the defence minister who was himself by tradition a military man, were evidently anxious to explore political rather than military solutions. Confronted with an intractable civilian leadership, this group laid plans for a coup.[24] The move failed, as did a subsequent, somewhat half-hearted assault by dissident officers on the Beja barracks the following January. Immune from the regime's more savage mechanisms of repression and control, the conspirators were merely transferred to new posts, dismissed, or at worst detained for short periods. Not even Salazar could be confident of unleashing his political police on the military with impunity.

Salazar weathered this particular storm, but its origins in colonial policy were ominous. Like the Goa crisis at the end of the year, the *crise Botelho Moniz* contributed to difficulties for the regime, if not Salazar himself, in the longer term. It exposed, briefly, a seed of military dissent on Africa. Although this was to remain largely dormant for the next decade, it would eventually cross-fertilize with others to bring the dissolution of the empire.[25] For now, though, the regime survived the initial shock of the Angolan uprising and the momentarily greater blow of the loss of Goa. Discord between the military and civilian leaders was soon eased, not least by the enlarged national role – and accompanying resources – that the colonial wars offered the soldiers. Salazar's commitment to maintain the one and indivisible empire remained in all substantial regards, his resolution if anything reinforced by the Botelho Moniz conspiracy.[26]

The affair did, though, necessitate a cabinet re-shuffle which led indirectly to some peripheral reform in African policy. The new colonial minister (or, in the approved language of the regime, the 'overseas' minister: *ministro do ultramar*), Adriano Moreira, was part of an infusion of new blood admitted to the higher levels of the regime in the early 1960s by Salazar as his own physical powers began to wane. Moreira was a former director of the Escola Superior Colonial, the main training centre for colonial administrators, and seemed to promise in his reforms of 1961–62 some erosion of the hardest edges of colonial policy if not its essential character. In September 1961 the Native Statute was repealed, bestowing Portuguese citizenship on all. The following year colonial labour regulations were revised and regulations were introduced to prevent the alienation of native land and end compulsory cultivation.[27] Moreira's own relatively liberal outlook apart, a principal purpose of these reforms was to provide the regime with some protection, however thin, from the international criticism which was mounting in response to developments in Angola. Their actual impact in Africa was extremely limited, and local abuses over labour continued regardless of the new statutes from Lisbon. Nor was Moreira's ministry an enduring one; it lasted only until the end of 1962. From then until Salazar's retirement in 1968 there was no movement in the regime's position sufficient to change the terms of the conflicts in Africa.

The War in Angola

The momentum of revolt in Angola in 1961 was not sustained. The violence of the reaction, both official and unofficial, on the part of the colonial state and its supporters imposed a sullen calm on the northern areas of the country among those Africans who had not sought refuge across the border in the Congo or in other parts of Angola. For the next two years elements of the UPA and those MPLA cadres who had escaped Luanda and the repression after the events of February 1961 operated in a desultory fashion in the Dembos mountains in the north. For the most part, though, their stance was defensive and their concern was with mere survival rather than the prosecution of an effective guerrilla war. In October 1961, barely six months after the northern rising, the governor-general of Angola, General Venâncio Deslandes, pronounced the 'war' finished, with only police action required to re-impose imperial authority throughout the territory.[28] The subsequent course of the armed struggle in Angola from 1961 to the collapse of the Lisbon regime in 1974 can be viewed within three broad periods. These coincide approximately with the rise and fall of the fortunes of the two principal nationalist movements in relation to each other. The first phase, between 1961 and the end of 1963, was one in which the UPA/FNLA appeared to be in the ascendant. The MPLA in contrast was in considerable disarray at this time, disorganized internally and with only very limited external support. The second phase, from 1964 until about 1970, was one in which the FNLA was increasingly subject to leadership disputes and doubts as to the real extent of its guerrilla campaign. During this period the MPLA, now reorganized, was active on new fronts, had secure bases in neighbouring countries and was attracting substantial foreign help. The period from about 1970 to 1974 was one in which divisions within the MPLA began to re-emerge with a consequent fall in its military effectiveness. While the guerrilla capacities of the FNLA did not undergo any major improvement at this time, it was receiving ever-greater and more significant support from outside Africa. If any party was in the ascendant in this period it was the Portuguese military.

Favoured in Congo-Léopoldville by the post-Lumumba government of Cyrille Adoula, Roberto had considerable resources and freedom of manoeuvre in 1961–62. The MPLA, although permitted to open an office in Léopoldville, was regarded with considerable suspicion by the regime there, a suspicion that Roberto was happy to exploit. Conscious of its vulnerability and debilitated by arrests among its leadership both before and after its February 1961 actions in Luanda, the MPLA sought accommodation with the FNLA in 1961 and 1962.[29] But Roberto, with the upper hand, saw no reason to court what might be future challenges to his position. Violent clashes between the two movements in northern Angola in 1961 and 1962, including the annihilation of an MPLA column infiltrating across the border to relieve their comrades in the Dembos mountains, ended these early attempts at unity.[30] Pressing his political advantage over the MPLA, Roberto reorganized the UPA into the FNLA in March 1962 and brought a few small groupings of other ethnicities than Bakongo into the mainstream of the movement. This attempt to escape from the ethno-nationalist image he had acquired before and during the violence of 1961 also involved the elevation of non-Bakongo elements to positions of ostensible leadership. Although these moves were largely cosmetic and Roberto's control of the movement remained autocratic, they contributed to the growing perception of the FNLA outside Angola as the dominant nationalist movement.[31] This impression was reinforced a few weeks after the formation of the FNLA with Roberto's establishment of the Angolan Revolutionary Government in Exile (GRAE: Governo Revolucionário de Angola no Exílio). This public relations work won a number of diplomatic points for Roberto. Meeting in Dakar in 1963 the Organization of African Unity (OAU) decided to recognize FNLA/ GRAE as Angola's sole legitimate liberation movement. The Kennedy administration in Washington, anxious to assert its anti-colonial credentials but suspicious of the ideological character of some anti-colonial movements, was reassured by Roberto's evident 'western' orientation, and money was channelled to the FNLA through the CIA.[32]

The MPLA, meanwhile, was in deepening crisis. Blocked off from any significant activity in northern Angola by the hostile dominance of the FNLA and separated from its Mbundu power base and from urban support around Luanda by a largely impermeable Portuguese security curtain, its morale was also worn down by weak leadership and inefficient organization. The attack on the central prison in Luanda had itself been in part a response to the effectiveness of PIDE operations against the movement in 1959 and 1960 to which the MPLA, as a primarily urban organization, had been uniquely vulnerable. The wave of repression which followed inevitably raised questions about the quality of its remaining leadership. Among the victims of the pre-1961 sweeps by the security police had been Agostinho Neto, one of the most prominent among the founder members of the organization. Of Mbundu origin, Neto had trained as a doctor in Lisbon where he had been prominent in anti-regime politics.[33] After his arrest in June 1960 he had been held in Lisbon and Cabo Verde before being returned to Portugal and placed under restriction. In 1962 his escape from Portugal was engineered by the underground PCP and he eventually arrived at the MPLA office in Léopoldville in July of that year.[34] A show-down with the existing leadership followed. Viriato da Cruz, who had been secretary-general, was expelled from the movement in July 1963 'for acts of indiscipline tending to undermine the movement's unity and inspired by personal ambitions for power'.[35] Unrepentant, he left the movement along with a group of supporters of loosely Maoist outlook and after an unsuccessful attempt to establish an alternative MPLA leadership his faction joined the FNLA. Mário de Andrade, less radical than da Cruz but still suspicious of Neto's pragmatism and his somewhat imperious style, stood down from the presidency of the movement but remained within it.

The MPLA's problems were not instantly solved by this leadership coup. A sequence of events followed in which the hand of Roberto was not difficult to discern. In September 1963 Neto was arrested in Léopoldville along with his political lieutenant, Lúcio Lara, and in November the MPLA office was closed and the movement expelled from Congo-Léopoldville. Displacement from Léopoldville, although a bitter experience at the time, was ultimately to work to the MPLA's advantage. The movement sought a refuge in the capital of the former French Congo, Brazzaville.[36] Although geographically less well positioned as a base for guerrilla activity in Angola, the Brazzaville regime was more in sympathy with the MPLA's radicalism. And, however close Congo-Léopoldville might have been to the northern frontier of Angola, access would have remained vulnerable to FNLA obstruction at this time.

For all of Roberto's diplomatic success and the security of his foreign base in the Congo, the military achievements of the FNLA were less than impressive after the loss of initiative to the Portuguese following the initial convulsion of March 1961. By the end of the year Portuguese assessments put the number of UPA guerrillas in the Dembos area at about 2000 with perhaps 10,000–12,000 across the border in the Congo.[37] Despite this impressive numerical strength, FNLA activity was restricted to intermittent and relatively ineffective localized attacks.[38] This underlying military weakness would contribute to a sharp decline in the FNLA's fortunes in the second half of the 1960s, a period in which MPLA prospects revived.

In January 1964 at a meeting in Brazzaville the MPLA, now firmly under the control of the Neto faction, 're launched' itself with a more centralized decision-making structure which concentrated considerable power in Neto himself. Although this restructuring would later feed accusations of 'presidentialism', at the time it met the transparent need for greater efficiency after the weaknesses of the Viriato–Andrade leadership. On the military side the obvious difficulties of mounting a sustained campaign in northern Angola from Brazzaville were openly acknowledged. It was therefore decided to open a front against the Portuguese in the Cabinda enclave.

Cabinda, a small triangle of land some 11,000 sq. km in area with a population of about 80,000, lies on the Atlantic coast in a niche between what were in 1964 the two Congo republics. It had been ceded to Portugal at the Berlin Conference in 1884 as a consolation for the loss of the Congo hinterland to Belgium. Although untouched by the territory of Angola at any point, it was nevertheless administered by the Portuguese as part of the larger colony. While access to northern Angola was obstructed by Congo-Léopoldville, Cabinda was more easily accessible to the MPLA through Brazzaville. A patchwork of different ethnicities, Cabinda was eyed with a view to possible annexation by both Brazzaville and Léopoldville.

Although largely unaffected by the internal politics of Angola up to the 1960s, Cabinda did have its own nationalist organization. A fragmented and fissiparous 'independence' movement had been in existence from the mid-1950s. This had consolidated itself, though uneasily, in 1963 as the Front for the Liberation of the Cabinda Enclave (FLEC: Frente de Libertação do Enclave de Cabinda), though the inherent instability of FLEC continued to be fed by the rival manoeuvrings of the two Congos.[39] The Cabinda campaign was important to the MPLA as a means of validating its guerrilla identity and providing *some* arena of 'armed struggle' rather than for any tangible political or military achievements. These, in truth, were sparse. There is no real evidence of widespread popular support for the MPLA in the enclave at this time and the escape route to Brazzaville was clearly crucial.[40] But the operations in Cabinda allowed the MPLA to maintain armed activity and provided a means of asserting and consolidating the movement's identity both in Angola and abroad. Ultimately the MPLA's early presence would also help to ensure the continued status of the enclave as part of independent Angola after the establishment of the People's Republic in 1975. This would be of a significance unforeseen in 1964: two years before the discovery of Cabinda's huge off-shore oil deposits by Gulf Oil.[41]

The year 1964 proved to be successful for the MPLA diplomatically. In November OAU recognition was extended to the movement, although it had to be shared with the FNLA. In 1964 too, Neto was respectfully received in Moscow during a visit apparently organized on behalf of the MPLA by the PCP.[42] About this time the movement was visited in Brazzaville by Che Guevara who was then on an extended African tour, and it may be supposed that it was from this point that the first Cuban aid to the movement began.[43] The renewed vigour of the MPLA also raised its credit with regional neighbours beyond Brazzaville. In 1964 and 1965 respectively MPLA offices were opened in Dar es Salaam and Lusaka. The relationship with Zambia proved particularly important as it opened the possibility of military operations by the MPLA inside Angola proper. A new front in the eastern district of Moxico was accordingly planned and was to be supplied from bases in western Zambia.

While the MPLA was showing a new cohesion and effectiveness in these years, the position of the FNLA, dominant at least politically after 1961, began to decline. Its standing in Léopoldville (Kinshasa after 1965) was still secure. Indeed Roberto's personal position was assured by his marriage to the sister-in-law of General Mobutu Sese Seko, who became president of what was shortly to be renamed as Zaire in 1965. But many of the non-Bakongo elements brought into the movement in 1961 and 1962 to create a more 'national' image began to drift away as resentment grew at the continued domination of the Bakongo and the extent of Roberto's personal control.

One of the most significant defections came in 1964 when the 'foreign minister' of GRAE, Jonas Savimbi, departed following an unsuccessful power struggle with Roberto. Unable to shake Roberto's personal grip on the FNLA, Savimbi now denounced his former leader as a stooge of the United States and ridiculed the FNLA's military incapacity.[44] Aside from his considerable charisma and political astuteness, Savimbi's strength lay in the fact that he was from the largest of Angola's ethnic groups, the Ovimbundu. About two million-strong (around 35 per cent of the African population of Angola), the Ovimbundu populated the central highlands and parts of southern Angola. Savimbi's departure, while removing a danger to Roberto's own grip on the movement, thus threatened to deprive it of an enormously important ethnic and geographical constituency. Savimbi evidently sought to link up with the MPLA after his split with Roberto.[45] Clearly an ambitious individualist, however, he was given little encouragement from a movement in the process of centralizing under a unified leadership. Eventually, in March 1966 after a period of recruitment and organization among the Ovimbundu, Savimbi launched his National Union for the Total Independence of Angola (UNITA: União Nacional para a Independência Total de Angola). The establishment of UNITA completed the tripartite structure of Angolan nationalism which was to remain in place until the Portuguese collapse and which would, subsequently, form the geometry of protracted civil war.

From 1966 the focus of the armed struggle in Angola shifted from the north of the country and from Cabinda to the sparsely populated grasslands of the east and south-east where both the MPLA and UNITA were now active. Neither movement could be said to have posed an especially critical challenge to the Portuguese there, but both took all available opportunities to enhance their political images in a war in which external perception was becoming as important as concrete military achievement.

The MPLA, following the examples of Frelimo and the PAIGC,

declared 'liberated zones'. The sparseness of population in eastern
Angola made the concept rather less meaningful than in Mozambique
and Guiné-Bissau and the Portuguese were relatively unconcerned
by the development. But there were obvious political advantages in
the gesture. In March 1968 the MPLA was able to hold a congress
inside Angola which managed to suggest to the outside world a level
of settled 'occupation' of the national territory which did not truly
exist. Public relations aside, though, significant political developments were confirmed at the congress including the movement's
fundamental Marxist orientation and its decision to convert itself
into a 'vanguard party'.[46]

With only about 800 untried fighters UNITA's beginnings were not
auspicious. Savimbi's position at the head of the external relations of
GRAE had, however, provided him with considerable experience as
well as important international contacts. These were to prove more
valuable to UNITA in its later incarnations, but even in the mid-1960s
they were exploitable. In 1964 he had visited Beijing on behalf of
GRAE and had been received by Mao Zedong. This initial contact
facilitated a later visit as head of UNITA in 1968 when he won some
limited material support. In the intervening period he had cultivated
something of a pro-Chinese image for UNITA and was able to turn
his poverty of resources into Maoist virtues. With only the most
limited base facilities in Zambia Savimbi could proclaim UNITA's
uniqueness among the movements as the one 'fish which swam
among the people'. Similarly, the absence of foreign backers meant
that UNITA could supply itself only with what it could take from the
enemy (either Portuguese or MPLA), which of course was another
example of good Maoist practice.[47]

Savimbi showed less political acumen in prosecuting the armed
struggle itself. Following a series of attacks on administrative posts in
the last months of 1966, UNITA's main activity appeared to be
restricted to occasional and bloody skirmishes with the 4500-strong
MPLA force on the eastern front.[48] The one target against which
UNITA attacks did appear to make an early impact was the 1500 km
Benguela railway which ran through eastern Angola to the Atlantic.
Here UNITA's military 'success' redounded to its severe political
disadvantage. Symbol of imperialism the railway may have been, but
it was also the outlet for about half of the copper exports of Zaire and
Zambia and UNITA's attacks resulted in 1967 in its expulsion from
the latter. While of limited military significance, this deprived
UNITA of both a safe refuge and the opportunity to work for the
MPLA's marginalization in Lusaka.[49]

So unavailing was UNITA's campaign against the colonial forces, and so preoccupied did Savimbi become with his conflict with the MPLA, that in 1972 UNITA actually sought a truce with the Portuguese. The terms of the agreement (made locally with the Portuguese military commander in Angola) were essentially that the colonial army would leave UNITA alone as long as it maintained its attacks on the MPLA and where possible extended them to the FNLA.[50] The arrangement lasted until the beginning of 1974. The revelation of the deal came with the (perhaps calculated) loosening of military tongues after the Lisbon coup and was a considerable blow to UNITA's external credibility in the critical period of inter-movement manoeuvring leading up to the negotiations over the transfer of power.[51]

The beginning of the 1970s saw the MPLA at a relative high-point of effectiveness. The FNLA, on the other hand, was weakening, partly due to its poor leadership and lack of any clear political direction and partly as a result of defections, most notably that of Savimbi. UNITA, the outcome of this defection, was militarily weak, ideologically uncertain and barely functioning as a nationalist movement. But the three or so years prior to the Portuguese coup were ones of general decline for all three movements. The slump in fortunes was most obvious in the MPLA which had the furthest to fall and less so in the FNLA whose slide was partly arrested by increased Chinese aid in 1973.[52] But the overall curve of nationalist achievement was a falling one. There was no single reason for this atrophy. As much as anything else it came from the demoralization inherent in a fundamentally stagnant conflict.

In analysing the movements in terms of their political and military aspirations and claims, there is a danger of losing sight of a basic truth: that the nationalists posed no critical threat to the Portuguese presence in Angola during the armed struggle. After 1961 the major centres of European population were virtually untouched by the conflict. Throughout the thirteen years of the war 3455 Portuguese troops died in Angola, of which only 1369 were killed in action. By the standards of most 'wars' an average toll of little over a hundred deaths in action a year is remarkably light. Virtually all sectors of the Angolan economy experienced sustained growth throughout the period of the conflict.[53] Coffee production in northern Angola, at the epicentre of the violence of 1961, actually increased over the following decade.[54] The settler presence, far from diminishing in these years, virtually doubled between 1960 and 1970. The apparent immovability of the colonial state – and its evident invulnerability to significant military damage in the short-term – was a demoralizing reality, whatever material support and political solidarity might be offered from abroad. It was a reality which inevitably engendered internal disunity within and between the nationalist movements.

In common with the other African territories Angola was subject to a series of Portuguese offensives in the early 1970s. American tactics in Vietnam were an obvious influence on the colonial military. Napalm and herbicide bombs were widely used, the latter to clear forest cover and prevent cultivation in areas with a significant guerrilla presence. *Aldeamentos*, a Portuguese version of General Westmoreland's 'strategic hamlets', were established as part of the policy of 'rural reorganization' (*reordenamento rural*). By the end of the war they held more than a million people or about a quarter of the rural population.[55] Africans (mostly Ovimbundu) were recruited into commando units – the Special Groups (GEs: *Grupos Especiais*) and Special Paratroop Groups (GEPs: *Grupos Especiais Paraquedistas*) – which had considerable success against the MPLA on the eastern front. A major programme of Africanization begun in the mid-1960s meant that by the end of the war African troops numbered 28,000 out of a total of just less than 66,000.[56] Psychological warfare was also used with some effect to open and maintain social and ethnic divisions among the nationalists. The considerable *mestiço* membership of the MPLA was presented as a threat to Africans, and the Bakongo domination of the FNLA was likewise played upon.

It was the MPLA which proved most vulnerable to renewed internal division. In 1972 conflict flared between its military leader in the eastern region, Daniel Chipenda, and Agostinho Neto. This was soon followed by the re-opening of ideological differences between Neto and Mário de Andrade. The immediate impact on the MPLA was a sharp reduction in Soviet aid as Moscow came to question the potential returns to be achieved from its beneficence.[57] The gravest consequences of this three-way split in the movement, however, came in the period after the Portuguese collapse when it complemented and complicated the larger divisions between the MPLA and the other movements. In this way the anti-colonial struggle in Angola ended in 1974 in conditions of disunity little changed from those at its beginning.

TABLE 2.1   *The Portuguese armed forces and the wars (1961–73)*[58]

	Africa	Angola	Guiné	Mozambique
Average strength	105 000	54 000	20 000	31 000
War duration	13 years	13 years	11 years	10 years
% European/African	71/29	69/31	84/16	60/40
Total deaths	8 831	3 455	3 136	2 240
Combat deaths	4 280	1 369	1 342	1 569
Average annual combat deaths	384	105	122	157

The War in Guiné-Bissau

The war in Guiné-Bissau contrasted sharply with that in Angola. The dominance of a single movement pursuing a strategy based on relatively clear politico-military precepts gave a cohesion to the armed struggle in Guiné which was absent elsewhere. Guiné-Bissau was wholly different from Angola in both geography and social profile. Tiny in comparison (36,120 sq. km as against 1,246,700 sq. km), Guiné had only about one-tenth of Angola's population (about 550,000 as against 5,500,000). In common with the west African colonies of other European empires, the number of long-term European residents in Guiné-Bissau was infinitesimal. There were never more than about 2000 European civilians in the territory throughout the war and the vast majority of these were colonial administrators rather than colonists. Guiné-Bissau's anti-colonial struggle was uncomplicated by any 'settler dimension'. Guiné's economic importance to the metropole was also much less than that of the larger colonies and, in the absence of a significant settler population, it provided a very limited market for metropolitan exports.

Although Guiné's armed struggle properly speaking began as we have said in January 1963, there had been a preliminary phase of a year and a half of so-called 'direct action' involving acts of sabotage and civil disobedience.[59] This coincided with a period of intense political mobilization among the peasantry of the south of the country carried out by PAIGC cadres from the party's headquarters across the border in Conakry. The PAIGC's military victories came quickly. In July 1963, within six months of the beginning of the war, the Portuguese defence minister, General Gomes de Araújo, startled other members of the regime and foreign observers alike by admitting publicly that the PAIGC controlled a significant proportion of the territory.[60] In February 1964 the PAIGC's domination of the south was confirmed – and Portuguese morale was severely damaged – when a major counter-attack against the fortified island of Como, which the PAIGC had occupied early in its campaign, was repulsed after a battle lasting some two and a half months. Henceforward Portuguese strategy was based on the defence of fortified positions and the use of air power rather than any serious attempt to engage the PAIGC on the ground. Pessimism pervaded the local Portuguese command. Called to Lisbon during the first months of the war to give an assessment of the situation to the colonial ministry, the military commander, Brigadier Louro de Sousa, reported simply that 'the war was lost'.[61]

It was not only access to the Guinea-Conakry border which made the south of the colony an appropriate focus for the nationalists' early campaign. The Balanta people of this region had a history of opposition to the Portuguese and had been the last to be 'pacified' in 1915. But while this tradition of resistance predisposed the Balanta to mobilization by the PAIGC it also created certain difficulties in the first stage of the war. Central to Cabral's vision of national liberation was the doctrine of political primacy over military action. In the opening year of the war this had yet to be fully asserted. The issue dominated the PAIGC's first congress which was held at Cassaca in February 1964, a mere 15 km from the battle then raging for Como island. The congress laid down the basic political principles, strongly informed by Maoist thinking, which were to guide the protracted struggle.[62] Cabral's insistence that the PAIGC were 'armed militants and not militarists' had been disregarded by a number of Balanta fighters who had ignored political directives in their enthusiasm for physical attacks on the Portuguese.[63] The assertion of party discipline was ruthless and apparently involved a number of executions. Seen as necessary at the time, this approach served to aggravate African suspicions over the dominance of Cabo Verdean *mestiços* within the leadership.[64] This cleavage was to persist up to and beyond independence and frequently led to internecine violence.

By the mid-1960s, after the dramatic PAIGC advances of the early phase, the pace of the war began to stabilize. The PAIGC claimed to control something over half of the territory and continued to expand its presence but at a less dizzying pace than initially. The south and the central northern districts – adjacent to the Guinea-Conakry and Senegalese borders respectively – were in nationalist hands. Only the Moslem Fula people in the north-east remained loyal to the colonial regime, their conservative instincts reacting against the radicalism of the PAIGC.[65] The appointment of former interior minister and Salazar loyalist Arnaldo Schultz as governor-general and military commander in May 1964 did nothing to retrieve the situation for Lisbon. A force of over 30,000 was unable to contain, let alone reverse the gains, of about 5000 PAIGC fighters.

In May 1968 Schultz was replaced by Brigadier António de Spínola, a cavalry officer of traditional *haute bourgeoise* stamp who brought considerable prestige from his recent successes as a regional commander in Angola. During Spínola's period in Guiné (which lasted until August 1973) Portuguese tactics were significantly different from those pursued hitherto. Unceremoniously ordering back to Lisbon those civilian and military officials he regarded as lacking in proper commitment, he soon gathered round himself a group of young, absolutely loyal, military followers.[66] These 'Guiné boys' (*rapazes da Guiné*), as they became known, would individually and collectively play a major part in the 1974 revolution and its aftermath – though their personal ideological trajectories would be very different.[67]

The basis of Spínola's politico-military project was summed up in his key slogan *por uma Guiné melhor* (for a better Guiné).[68] A firm adherent of the Vietnam-inspired orthodoxy of the period – that guerrilla campaigns cannot be defeated by purely military means – he set about constructing a multifaceted political, social and psychological approach to the war. In an extensive 'civic action programme' military resources were directed to public works and military personnel were involved in the provision of education and medical services. In one respect Spínola went further than his American military counterparts. Using his proconsular powers to their limit, he established formal consultative bodies along parliamentary lines. His *Congressos do Povo* ('People's Congresses') were designed to compete directly with the 'legislative' arrangements being established by the PAIGC in its 'liberated zones'.[69] He was particularly assiduous in courting the powerful Fula chiefs who were happy to utilize the *Congresso* structure as a vehicle of their authority.

A true assessment of Spínola's impact on the war in Guiné is difficult to arrive at. His undoubted charisma as well as his subsequent role in the Portuguese revolution have had a refracting effect on analyses of his record in Guiné. Certainly, he brought a fundamentally new style to Portugal's war efforts in the colony and he introduced a number of new initiatives both military and political.[70] Yet these initiatives were uniformly unsuccessful in achieving their basic objectives. On a moral level too, it should be borne in mind that the innovations of his period, like the establishment of supposedly representative *Congressos* and the social action programmes of the military, took place against a background of continued bombardment, frequently with napalm, of villages in the liberated areas and the wholesale killing of their civilian populations. Spínola's political and diplomatic judgement was also questionable, common sense frequently being subordinated to buccaneering adventurism. In December 1970, in one of the most dramatic incidents of the war, Portuguese forces invaded neighbouring Guinea-Conakry with the twin aims of toppling the Sekou Touré regime on behalf of dissident elements more amenable to Portugal and destroying the PAIGC headquarters. The plan, according to one of Spínola's closest aides, Fabião, also involved the assassination of both Sekou Touré and Amílcar Cabral.[71] Reluctantly approved by Lisbon on condition that Portuguese tracks were firmly covered, 'Operation Green Sea' (Operação Mar Verde) as it was called ended in complete disaster. Failing in their initial objectives of destroying the Guinean air force on the ground and seizing the radio station, the invaders withdrew leaving plentiful evidence of their identity and intentions. The result was a diplomatic catastrophe for Portugal.[72] The main consequence of the débâcle was to provide Sekou Touré with a justification for inviting Soviet warships to patrol off the West African coast.[73]

Another of Spínola's unsuccessful initiatives was to be rather more portentous for Portugal's ultimate disengagement from Africa. No less dramatic than 'Green Sea' but rather less pyrotechnical, his secret talks with the Senegalese president Léopold Senghor in May 1972 and their obstruction by Lisbon were to have far-reaching consequences for both Africa and Portugal. Initially with Lisbon's approval, Spínola met Senghor inside Senegal on the Guiné-Bissau border. A comprehensive peace proposal was discussed by which Senghor was to mediate a cease-fire with the PAIGC. This would have been followed by a round-table conference without preconditions which would have involved not just the PAIGC but also its old nationalist rival FLING. If the outcome of these talks had been successful there would have been a ten-year period of internal self-government during which the form of future relations with Portugal would have been determined. The options would have included total independence, participation in a lusophone community, or a federal relationship with Portugal.[74] Lisbon, however, changed tack in the course of the negotiations and ordered Spínola to end contact with Senghor.

The broader significance of the affair for the future of Portugal in Africa as a whole will be explored in the next chapter, but its immediate effect was to point up the lack of policy cohesion between metropole and colony and a fatal uncertainty of prerogative between military and civilian leaderships. Guiné, in the intensity of its armed struggle and in its peculiar social and economic position in comparison to the other colonies, exposed the cracks not just in the regime's African policies but in its basic structure.[75]

Whatever impact Spínola's period in Guiné may have had on the diplomatic aspects of the war, and whatever his contribution to Portugal's image as a colonial power, his command had little effect on the PAIGC's military effectiveness. By 1970, two years after Spínola's arrival, the PAIGC had intensified the war by the deployment of ever heavier weapons, including artillery, which accelerated Portuguese losses of both men and territory.

The most fateful year of the war for both Portugal and the PAIGC, however, was 1973. The year began disastrously for the nationalists with the assassination of Amílcar Cabral in Conakry on 20 January. Theories and counter-theories abound as to the circumstances of his death and the identity of the 'real' culprits. The various hypotheses differ principally in the proportion of blame laid at the door of the Portuguese. At one end of the spectrum of explanation is the theory that Cabral was assassinated by PAIGC dissidents directly at the behest of the colonial power. Another view is that he was killed unintentionally during a botched abduction attempt by PAIGC renegades who had been commissioned to hand him over to the Portuguese, either across the border in Guiné-Bissau or at sea. Other explanations point to the continuing tensions within the PAIGC between Guinean Africans and Cabo Verdean *mestiços* and the violent resentments going back to the imposition of party discipline at the Cassaca congress in 1964. Some Guineans evidently believed that Cabral was killed on the orders of Sekou Touré who was jealous of his growing reputation as the leading West African radical.[76]

Spínola, for his part, consistently denied any part in Cabral's death, suggesting at one stage that the Soviet Union, in pursuit of a more malleable leadership, may have been responsible.[77] It is conceivable, given the nature of sectional relationships within the Lisbon regime, that the Portuguese security services were involved without the knowledge of the governor-general. But it is perhaps significant that the PAIGC's own official history of Guiné and Cabo Verde published in 1974 is entirely silent on the circumstances of Cabral's death. The loss of Cabral, although leading to considerable and continuing problems within the PAIGC leadership, did not noticeably affect the war effort. Another of the Cabo Verdean founders of the movement, Aristides Pereira, took over as secretary-general of the PAIGC, sharing the leadership with Cabral's half-brother, Luís, who became party president. The momentum of the PAIGC's political offensive was thus maintained.

In March 1973, just a few weeks after Cabral's death, a decisive and for the Portuguese devastating new element entered the war: the PAIGC deployed with immediate success Soviet surface-to-air missiles. Portugal's control of the skies, essential in a war being fought from isolated fortifications, disappeared at a stroke.[78] As aircraft losses began to mount, the prospect of outright military defeat now confronted the Portuguese. It was, however, a prospect which Spínola himself did not have to contemplate at close quarters. In August 1973 he returned to Lisbon, and was replaced by the more conventionally hard-line General Bettencourt Rodrigues.

On the diplomatic battlefield too, 1973 was a bleak year for Lisbon. In April of the previous year, to the indignation of the Portuguese government, a mission from the United Nations decolonization committee had spent a week in the 'liberated area' of Guiné and reported that the PAIGC should be acknowledged as 'the sole and authentic representative' of the Guiné-Bissau people.[79] The recommendation was accepted by the full UN General Assembly in October 1973. International politics as well as increasingly sophisticated weaponry were now battering at the defences of the Portuguese 'overseas province' of Guiné-Bissau. Well aware of the diplomatic mood of the time, the PAIGC now delivered a major blow which Portugal's enfeebled international position could neither absorb nor parry. A month after Spínola's departure, on 24 September 1973 at Madina do Boé in the east of the territory, the PAIGC declared the independence of the Republic of Guiné-Bissau under the presidency of Luís Cabral. Within weeks it had been recognized by over eighty states.[80]

The principle of '*aguentar como se fosse possível*' ('hold on as best you can') was now as close as the colonial state could come to a consistent strategy in Guiné. Now, as Carlos Fabião put it: 'PAIGC pressure . . . on the dispersed and demoralized Portuguese garrisons intensified so that only the 25 of April intervened to prevent a complete military disaster'.[81]

TABLE 2.2   *Percentage of African troops in the Portuguese armed forces during the wars* [82]

Year	Angola	Guiné	Mozambique
1961	14.9	21.1	26.8
1964	28.7	15.3	43.9
1967	25.0	14.9	33.3
1970	34.5	16.0	41.5
1973	42.2	20.1	53.6

The War in Mozambique

Between the fragmentation of Angola's anti-colonial war and the vigorously imposed discipline which characterized that in Guiné lay the experience of Mozambique. Frelimo began its armed struggle with deep unresolved divisions and ended it with a formidable military and ideological unity. The contrivance of Frelimo in 1962 at the behest of the CONCP, Nyerere and Nkrumah only inadequately pasted over the divisions between its component organizations. Mondlane's initial failure to use his personal prestige (or even continued presence) to build on the momentum of the new movement's creation contributed to the persistence of these divisions. His strong American connections, including his wife and a coterie of opportunistic Afro American 'activists' which appeared in his wake, became a focus of discontent.[83]

Further difficulties were caused for Frelimo by the initial reverses suffered in its military campaign. By the end of 1965 the momentum of the armed struggle in the north had faded and attempts to extend it further south to Tete and Zambésia failed. At the same time PIDE activity had devastated Frelimo's embryonic organization in the towns of the south, forcing it, like the MPLA and the PAIGC before it, to focus its activities in the countryside. The first year of the war saw a series of defections which culminated in the formation in 1965 of a rival movement based in Lusaka. This was the Mozambican Revolutionary Committee (Coremo: Comité Revolucionária de Moçambique) which under the leadership of former Frelimo cadre Paulo Gumane conducted an independent though scant guerrilla campaign in the central areas of the country in the late 1960s and early 1970s.

This 1965 split did not end the divisions within Frelimo, indeed disunity increased in the later 1960s. Conflict was now focused on the developing radicalism of the leadership's programme. In its first years the war was fought mainly in Cabo Delgado province adjacent to the safe haven of Tanzania. The Makonde, the historically defiant ethnic group of the area, provided the major part of Frelimo's front-line fighters. The micro-nationalist ambitions of elements in the Makonde leadership soon began to chaff against the ideological constraints placed on the struggle by the radical Mozambican nationalism of the Frelimo central committee. The posture of the most powerful of the dissident 'Makonde faction', Lázaro Kavandame, became increasingly aggressive in the period leading up to Frelimo's second congress in 1968. The problem faced by Frelimo was similar to that of the PAIGC in the face of Balanta resentment. In Guiné objections to centrally imposed restrictions was heightened by ethnic suspicions of the Cabo Verdean dominated leadership; in Mozambique similar resentment was felt towards Frelimo's predominantly southern leaders. Unlike that of the PAIGC, however, the Frelimo leadership was not in a position to contain the problem by calculated ruthlessness. Although the second congress, which was held inside Mozambique in July 1968, was a victory for the leadership in that it adopted programmes which reinforced the movement's emerging Marxist identity, it did nothing to heal internecine divisions.

While Kavandame continued to attack the direction of the movement in ever more violent language, a further challenge to the leadership emerged. A significant faction of students in the Mozambique Institute, which had been set up by Frelimo in Tanzania to train potential cadres, rebelled against the movement's austere collectivist discipline. They were supported in this by colleagues who had been sent for education in the United States. In the midst of the ideological 'victory' of the second congress, therefore, Frelimo was facing a critical, potentially terminal threat to its very existence as a national liberation movement.

The disastrous culmination of these divisions came in February 1969 with the parcel bomb assassination of Eduardo Mondlane in Dar es Salaam. The circumstances of Mondlane's killing are only slightly less opaque than those surrounding the murder of Amílcar Cabral. Once again, dissidents within the movement were clearly in the forefront of the conspiracy, with most fingers pointing to Kavandame. Suspicions that he had acted either at the behest of the Portuguese or with their assistance hardened two months after the assassination when he announced his defection to the colonial state.[84] That the Portuguese were deeply involved in the technical aspects of the attack is in little dispute, but the extent to which it was undertaken at their initiative is less clear.

One of the striking features of the aftermath of Cabral's murder was the capacity of the PAIGC to maintain its political and military momentum without significant falter. This was not within Frelimo's capability. In terms of seniority Mondlane's successor should have been the vice-president, Uria Simango, a Protestant pastor who had originally been leader of Udenamo before the amalgamation which created Frelimo. Simango was, however, widely mistrusted among the more radical elements in the leadership who were suspicious of his 'bourgeois tendencies'. The succession therefore took the form of an uneasy triumvirate of Simango, Marcelino dos Santos (the veteran *mestiço* activist who had close personal and political contacts with both the MPLA and the PAIGC), and Samora Machel who had been military commander since 1966. In all, Frelimo faced the 1970s burdened with much greater problems of disunity and dissension than it acknowledged in its extensive foreign propaganda campaigns of the period.

Beyond the murderous internal conflicts there was the not wholly negligible problem of the Portuguese armed forces to be confronted. After the Angolan and Guinean outbreaks the Portuguese seemed surprisingly unprepared for the beginning of the guerrilla campaign in Mozambique. They were not greatly disadvantaged by this, though. Lacking the initial violence of the Angolan conflict and posing nothing like the military threat of the war in Guiné, the first phase of the armed struggle in Mozambique was viewed with cautious equanimity by Lisbon. The divisions among the nationalists, the apparent containment of their military campaign away from the main areas of population and, perhaps, the sense of security offered by the existence of white regimes in neighbouring South Africa and Rhodesia bolstered this official confidence.

Although troop numbers were dramatically increased from about 4000 in 1964 to a wartime average of between 40,000 and 50,000, major military engagements were rare in the first years. As in Angola and to a lesser extent Guiné, the Portuguese in Mozambique employed psychological operations which emphasized the domination of Frelimo's leadership by southern Rongas and Tongas, 'alien' to the areas of conflict. They also attempted with some success to create divisions between the animist Makonde in Cabo Delgado and their traditional local rivals, the Moslem Makua. The same tactic was employed in the other main area of conflict, Niassa, where the pro-Frelimo Protestant Nyanja were played off against the Yao, also Moslems.[85]

In the later 1960s, however, the Portuguese adopted more obviously offensive tactics. The new approach was determined in part by developments which seemed to call for a show of imperial power and in part by a calculation that the exercise of this power was likely to have tangible success. In 1966 plans were put forward in Lisbon for the construction of a huge hydroelectric scheme based on the construction of a dam at Cabora Bassa on the Zambezi. The scheme would produce more electricity than either the Aswan or Kariba dams and the power generated would be exported to South Africa. Eventually, it was predicted, Cabora Bassa would provide about 70 per cent of the requirements of Johannesburg and Pretoria. A collateral effect of the scheme would be the irrigation of nearly four million acres of new agricultural land. Following lengthy negotiations a treaty was signed between Portugal and South Africa in September 1969 by which Pretoria would provide 20 per cent of the funding and the balance would be raised by an international consortium. This company, Zamco, was constructed from interests in West Germany, France, Britain and Italy. In contrast to Angola, external investment in Mozambique during the 1960s had been small. Cabora Bassa would redress the imbalance in one grandiose gesture.[86]

The Portuguese saw in the Cabora Bassa project an accretion of benefits, both tangible and intangible. It would be a major and continuous source of revenue when in operation in the mid-1970s. In the meantime it would offer rich contracts for Portuguese suppliers. It would consolidate a southern African infrastructure, already in existence in the railway and port system, which would further integrate Portugal in to the political economy of the (white-dominated) region. Conversely, it would tie the most important west European powers in to a commitment to Portuguese Africa by creating, through Zamco, a commonality of economic interests. The huge tracts of new land opened up for cultivation would be given over to the development of *colonatos*, mixed European and African agricultural enterprises which would bring in up to a million new settlers. This would reorientate the pattern of white settlement away from the cities and provide a major security block to the spread of nationalist agitation in central Mozambique.[87]

The project in both its scale and its intentions could only be taken as a direct challenge by Frelimo.[88] On the other side, the construction and operation of such a complex multinational scheme demanded that the Portuguese demonstrate their grip on the colony as a whole. Mere containment of Frelimo would no longer be sufficient – and its obvious internal divisions seemed to make it vulnerable to final extirpation.

Responsibility for this ultimate assertion of Portuguese authority was given to General Kaúlza de Arriaga, an unreconstructed Salazarist *ultra*. Kaúlza was regarded with wary respect by the new prime minister Marcello Caetano who had succeeded the old dictator in September 1968. Appointed military commander in Mozambique in March 1970, Kaúlza began to plan a major and, in his expectation, final campaign against Frelimo. The plan was to begin with a military sweep through the Frelimo affected areas of northern Mozambique. This was to be Operation Gordian Knot (Operação Nó Górdio). The military drive would be followed up by a longer-term scheme, Operation Frontier (Operação Fronteira), which would secure the border with Tanzania through the development of a civil-military infrastructure including a network of *aldeamentos* and *colonatos*.

Initially Kaúlza had the full support of Lisbon; only his plan for raids inside Tanzania and its political destabilization was vetoed.[89] Operation Gordian Knot got underway in May 1970 with paratroop attacks on Frelimo bases in the 'liberated zones' of Cabo Delgado and Niassa followed by a sweep by about 30,000 ground troops. The operation had some initial success. Frelimo strongholds were over-run and the guerrillas dispersed with relatively low Portuguese casualties. Kaúlza, though, perhaps having been over-influenced by American tactics in Vietnam, had failed to understand the fundamental nature of Frelimo's war. Melting before the onslaught, the bulk of the guerrilla forces escaped either north across the Rovumo to Tanzania or south through Malawi and back into Tete province – the location of Cabora Bassa.[90] By the beginning of 1971 Lisbon was balking at the cost of the force levels necessary to sustain the initial impact of Kaúlza's offensive and Frelimo was soon able to seep back into Cabo Delgado and Niassa as well as maintaining an enlarged presence in Tete.[91]

Despite the Gordian Knot having come seriously loose, however, Frelimo was never to make any significant military in-roads on Cabora Bassa. Its supporters have claimed that the point of the campaign against the dam was to keep large numbers of Portuguese troops tied up.[92] But it was also the case that the defence of Cabora Bassa involved its garrisoning by a considerable contingent of South

African troops.[93] In this way Frelimo's attacks helped achieve a key part of Portugal's overall purpose in the Cabora Bassa project: the development of ever closer relations with the white minority regimes of the region. Ironically, Frelimo's campaign may merely have accustomed the South African military to the cross-border activity which would prove so devastating after independence.

In May 1970, after further bitter wrangles led to the removal of Uria Simango from the leadership triumvirate, Samora Machel was named by the central committee as the new president of Frelimo with Marcelino do Santos as his deputy. Simango, soon expelled from the movement, switched his loyalty to Coremo. Machel was both an extremely effective military tactician and a hard-headed, even ruthless political operator. Under his leadership the radical Marxist orientation of the movement was consolidated, though with some creative obfuscation between a politico-military doctrine owing a great deal to Maoist precepts and an emerging diplomatic orientation towards the Soviet bloc.[94]

On the military front Frelimo claimed to have about 10,000 fighters in total at this time.[95] The guerrilla campaign was intensified in 1972 and 1973 with attacks being mounted in new regions of the centre of the country in the Manica and Sofala provinces between the country's second city Beira on the Indian Ocean coast, and the Rhodesian border in the west. This 'narrow waist' of Mozambique included of considerable European settlement and the general impact of Frelimo's attacks was correspondingly heightened. A settler community which had been encouraged to view Frelimo as isolated and disorganized terrorists operating in the far wilderness now came to a shuddering realization of its own vulnerability. Metropolitan emigration to Mozambique had, as with Angola, expanded dramatically in the 1960s with the European population growing from about 80,000 to a quarter of a million at the end of the decade. The security that this mainly urban-based population had taken for granted was now looking increasingly fragile. The white reaction to this sudden awareness of threat was directed against the supposed shortcomings of the armed forces. On its side, the military's regard for the settlers, which had never been high, declined even further and morale deteriorated accordingly.[96]

Another blow to the mood of the military came in 1973 with disclosures of massacres of civilians by the colonial forces. Foreign missionaries reported the killing of several hundred villagers in December 1972 in the Wiriyamu district of Tete province by locally recruited special paratroop forces (GEPs) under the control of the

Directorate-General of Security (DGS: Direcção-Geral de Segurança). There is no reason to believe that these killings were unique in Portugal's suppression of guerrilla-affected areas in Mozambique or elsewhere in Africa. Their revelation by *The Times* in London on the eve of an official visit to Britain by Caetano, however, inflicted particular damage. The impact of the news of the massacres on Portugal's western allies was considerable. The international credibility of the entire Portuguese position in Africa suffered as great a blow as after the reprisal massacres in Angola in 1961.[97] In Portugal itself the affair, though not publicly debated, could only contribute to the growing impetus against the regime.

The Economic Impact of the Wars

The African wars engaged a metropole with a population of less than nine million and with the least developed economy in western Europe in protracted conflict for a period of thirteen years. The economic impact of the wars on Portugal has been the source of some debate. The wars coincided with years of quite remarkable economic development both in the metropole and in Angola and Mozambique, and the relationship between the phenomena was a complicated one.

The economic policy of the *Estado Novo* from the early 1930s until the beginning of the 1960s was virtually defined by ultra-protectionism. This policy, and the rigid monetarism with which it was applied, hopelessly fettered the development of any extensive industrial sector in Portugal. As late as 1960 only 1.5 per cent of investment in industry came from abroad, and more than half of the work-force was still engaged in agriculture. Although the countryside underwent extensive depopulation through out-migration, two out of three migrants sought work abroad rather than in the urban sector in Portugal. While this emigration contributed to the national economy by keeping unemployment low and aiding the balance of payments through remittances, it did not provide the labour reserves to serve a significant expansion of the 'modern' sector in Portugal.[98]

In the 1960s the economic situation changed significantly – in Angola and Mozambique as well as in the metropole – as a consequence of the relaxation of the regime's economic policy. The significance of this change in direction has led Portuguese observers to date the demise of the *Estado Novo* from the early 1960s.[99] Foreign capital, in the form of lines of credit and direct investment, became more welcome in the metropole and in Africa foreign companies were permitted to have 100 per cent control of the mineral extraction sector.

The imperial economy as a whole, and most markedly that of Angola, experienced a period of considerable boom during the wars. The Cabora Bassa scheme in Mozambique was the most grandiose foreign-financed project, but it was only part of a much broader pattern which saw Angola's external trade grow threefold during the 1960s.[100] A common explanation for these economic developments is that they were necessary to pay for the wars.[101] By the early 1970s military spending was eating up about half of the Portuguese budget. At 7 per cent of GNP it was proportionately higher than that of the United States and seven times that of neighbouring Spain.[102] It has been argued too that the relaxation of protectionism and the consequent inflow of foreign investment was also designed to sustain public acquiescence to the wars in the metropole by providing a booming economy as a *quid pro quo* and to mute international condemnation of them by entrapping external capital in the Portuguese economy.[103] But the economic changes of the period can be seen as part of something wider than a policy response to a particular national contingency.

In 1960, before the wars had begun, Portugal became an early member of the European Free Trade Association (EFTA) in what might be seen as the first step towards the 'Europeanization' of its economy. The patterns of Portuguese trade altered fundamentally during the following decade, moving away from the colonies and towards Europe. The 1960s were years in which the international forces in operation would impinge on Portugal's national economic policies regardless of either the demands of the war or the ideology of imperial integration. Two decades later this process would be described as 'globalization'. Its inexorability, however, was not fully acknowledged even as it wore away at Salazar's luso-monetarist defences.

While the metropolitan economy was succumbing to this larger movement in the international economy, attempts to further integrate the economies of the metropole and the colonies were proving far from successful. The easing of exchange controls in the early 1960s as part of a graduated move towards the creation of an escudo zone in fact damaged the metropolitan economy. The rapid development in Africa which followed relaxation led to considerable colonial deficits which the metropole was required to cover.[104] Such negative consequences from attempts at imperial economic integration were more grist to the mills of those pressing for the Europeanization of Portugal's political economy. The experiment was no more successful in Africa as an affirmation of imperial unity. Lisbon's determination to impose fiscal discipline in the later 1960s and early 1970s placed considerable strains on the colonial economies. Mozambique in particular suffered a foreign reserve crisis which contributed greatly to the debilitation of its post-independence economy.

TABLE 2.3   *Direction of Portuguese trade (1959–73)*[105]

| Year | Destination of Exports from Metropolitan Portugal (%) | | |
	1959	1969	1973
EFTA/EC	40.3	50.9	60.5
Colonies	29.8	24.4	14.8

| Year | Source of Imports to Metropolitan Portugal (%) | | |
	1959	1967	1973
EFTA/EC	51.7	56.4	56.9
Colonies	14.2	14.3	10.1

The sea change in Portugal's economic orientation could soon be observed at the heart of the corporatist machine. As we have noted, the *Estado Novo* and the economic nationalism which underlay it had fostered the development of a number of large monopolies which benefited from protection at home and unhindered access to areas of operations in the colonies. The major ones included the group of companies established by António Champalimaud which was particularly active in Mozambique and Angola. Then there was the Espírito Santo family conglomerate which was also active in southern Africa. The largest of the 'oligopolies' was the Companhia União Fabril (CUF) which had more than 180 associated enterprises with particular interests in Guiné-Bissau as well as the larger colonies. These companies, whose proprietors and senior managers were closely interlinked with the political and military elite of the regime, were at the economic centre of Portuguese imperialism.

The protected nature of the monopolies and the discouragement of foreign capital has been central to a particular theoretical model of Portuguese imperialism. Rooted in neo-Marxist 'dependency' and 'world system' theories, this perspective explains the apparent contradiction of Portugal's position as both the weakest and the most enduring of the European imperial powers. State protection of the national monopolies was, the argument runs, indicative of the fundamental weakness of Portuguese capitalism. Without this protection the monopolies would be hopelessly vulnerable to the depredations of more effective foreign enterprises. A central part of Salazar's 1930 Colonial Act which put this protection in place, it will be recalled, had been the abolition of foreign concession companies in Portuguese Africa. The end of the empire would mean the end of this protection and the consequent loss of any economic benefit from Africa. In short, Portugal could not decolonize, the dependency theorists argued, because unlike Britain and France it could not hope to 'neo-colonize'.

With this perspective in mind, the corporate attitudes of the monopolies towards the empire in its final years is instructive. By the early 1970s they had become divided in their assessments of their interests in Africa. While Espírito Santo appeared to favour the maintenance of the *status quo*, the others were shifting ground significantly.[106] Both Champalimaud and CUF were questioning the future of the empire as an integrated entity. They were diversifying, particularly towards western Europe, and their future operations in Africa were being seen increasingly in a neo-colonial rather than a formal imperial context.[107] The movement in these tectonic plates of the national economy were soon to shake the political superstructure which they supported.

Diplomacy and Solidarity: the International Dimensions of the Wars

We began this exploration of the wars in Africa by emphasizing their distinctness from each other. Yet as they developed, the outside world began to perceive a more unified conflict. Internationally the friends and enemies of both sides adopted positions not on the individual armed struggles and their moral and political merits or demerits but on the generality of either 'Portugal's African problem' or 'Africa's Portuguese problem'.

Portugal's relations with its western allies throughout the period of the wars were always ambivalent and frequently uncomfortable. They did not, though, place any great constraints on Lisbon's colonial policies. Not as deeply compromised with the Axis powers as

Spain had been, and with the counter of the geo-strategically important Azores to offer the western alliance, Portugal had been welcomed into the North Atlantic Treaty Organization at its foundation in 1949. Throughout the 1950s the cold war pressures on the western alliance tended to mute criticism of Lisbon's African policy among its partners.

For a number of reasons, though, the Angolan uprising in 1961 upset for a while this diplomatic complaisance. Firstly, the violence of the Portuguese reaction to the rebellion exposed the viciousness lurking under the myth of benevolent decadence. Secondly, the decade then beginning was one in which imperial withdrawal from sub-Saharan Africa became widely regarded as right and inevitable; the Salazarist rhetoric of permanent empire had come to sound more and more eccentric as the winds of change gathered force. Thirdly, cold war calculation now provided a *realpolitik* underpinning to the emerging moral consensus behind decolonization. The prize of the growing Afro-Asian bloc in world politics was now up for contest between east and west, and the imperial tradition of the latter was increasingly burdensome. Finally, the Kennedy administration, which took office virtually simultaneously with the Angolan uprising, was anxious to present its foreign policies as guided by a new liberal morality in contrast to that of its predecessors.

The new approach to Portugal and Africa in Washington was indeed in sharp contrast to that of President Eisenhower and his secretary of state John Foster Dulles throughout most of the 1950s. Salazar, who in truth had never much enthusiasm for anything American other than its anti-communism, now found himself presiding over a deteriorating relationship. Salazar's attitude to the United States throughout his remaining years in office might reasonably be described as 'Gaullist' if its origins had not in key respects pre-dated that phenomenon. While de Gaulle feared an Anglo-Saxon political and cultural hegemony, Salazar's anti-Americanism derived as much from a hostility to the expansion of United States influence in Latin America in the nineteenth century and the consequent threat to the millenarian dream of a Luso-Brazilian community. Kennedy's 'liberalism' was therefore not merely to be regretted for being *liberal* but resisted as a device to displace European influence in Africa as it had been in Latin America a century previously.[108]

In March 1961 Kennedy instructed his UN ambassador, Adlai Stevenson, to vote with the Soviet Union in the UN Security Council for reform in Angola and for a UN enquiry into the uprising and its aftermath. A few months later he banned the sale to Portugal of American arms which might be used in Africa.[109] Perhaps more worryingly for Lisbon, contact was established through the CIA with both Holden Roberto in Angola and Eduardo Mondlane in Mozambique and limited American financial aid began to be directed to them.[110] 'The current American government', Salazar railed in 1963, 'is a case of the lunatics taking over the asylum . . . American policy is even more revoltingly imperialist than that of the Soviet Union.'[111] As an expression of his concern and anger he rattled the one sabre with any edge in his diplomatic armoury: lease renewals on the key American air base at Lajes in the Azores would be negotiated only on short-term agreements.

Following Kennedy's assassination in November 1963, the American relationship improved somewhat. Lyndon Johnson did not share his predecessor's interest in African issues and Lisbon's worst fears were allayed. But the dilemma for America of maintaining a *diplomatically* necessary anti-colonialism while at the same time safeguarding *strategically* necessary assets in the north Atlantic remained. Washington's response was to draw up a comprehensive scheme for the phased decolonization of Portuguese Africa. A plan was devised between the State Department and the US ambassador in Lisbon, Admiral George Anderson, which was presented to Salazar's foreign minister, Franco Nogueira, in September 1965.

The 'Anderson Plan', as it came to be known, invited both Lisbon and the African liberation movements to agree a timetable for self-determination. This envisaged a transition period of eight to ten years which would be followed by an internationally supervised referendum. The choices on offer would be: total independence; inclusion in a lusophone 'commonwealth'; or the continuation of the imperial *status quo*. The package was to be sweetened for Portugal by an American commitment to oversee the transition period and to supply Portugal with arms in the event of the guerrillas breaking the agreement. Washington would also encourage the provision of external development aid for the African territories.

The plan was not dismissed outright by Salazar and discussions continued intermittently between Washington and Lisbon into the following year. But in March 1966 Portugal formally rejected the initiative. Its stated reasons were lack of confidence in American capacity to retain control of a protracted timetable in the face of external pressures and worries that the process in the territories themselves could spin out of control during the transition.[112] The Anderson Plan, for all its imperfections and risks, was to be the last serious opportunity for the regime to extricate itself from Africa and the wars by negotiation.

The next point at which American pressure might have had some impact came with Salazar's replacement by Marcello Caetano in September 1968. By then, though, Richard Nixon was already on the threshold of the White House and American policy on Portuguese Africa, overseen by the new national security adviser Henry Kissinger, was about to undergo a shift to the right. Caetano, who might even have welcomed American pressure for change in Africa as a lever against the more reactionary elements in the regime, was now offered the dubious benefit of American support for Portugal's imperial project. A secret US National Security Council memorandum in January 1970 concluded that the white regimes of southern Africa were destined to remain. The region's growing strategic significance therefore required amicable relations with Lisbon.[113] US navy vessels could, through access to Angolan and Mozambican ports, assert American strategic interest in the South Atlantic and Indian Oceans in the context of long-standing NATO relationships and without the embarrassment of military contacts with South Africa.[114] From now until the collapse of the Lisbon regime in April 1974 the United States aided the Portuguese war effort by the supply of aircraft, ammunition and defoliants and with the training of some 2000 troops in counter-insurgency techniques in US army camps in the Panama Canal Zone.[115]

Western pressure on Portugal in the last decade of the empire was most sustained among those with least leverage, most notably Sweden and other Nordic countries. Those with greater potential influence in Lisbon showed no obvious inclination to use it over Africa. In addition to their shared anti-Americanism, Salazar and de Gaulle had similar world-views in the sense that both wished to pursue a particular 'Euro-African' project. Although the French one was infinitely more subtle than the Portuguese, underlying sympathies persisted between the two countries. France was Portugal's largest single arms supplier during the war and one of the least fastidious about placing limits on the use of what was supplied. The most visible (and for France lucrative) equipment were naval vessels, armoured cars and helicopters. West Germany too was a considerable supplier, providing much of Portugal's combat aircraft as well as ammunition and napalm. In return Bonn was leased the Beja air base in southern Portugal. Britain, historically Portugal's oldest ally, was also an arms supplier, though relations cooled somewhat after Rhodesia's unilateral declaration of independence in 1965 and Lisbon's material support for the rebel regime *via* Mozambique.

At the multilateral level pressure on Portugal was no more obvious or availing. Despite repeated denunciations in the United Nations General Assembly and its systematic disregard of resolutions, Portugal could usually look to its friends for protection. Britain, France and the United States, as the three western powers with permanent seats on the Security Council, either collectively or individually frustrated the attempts of the Assembly to engineer meaningful measures against Lisbon throughout the 1960s and early 1970s.[116] In short, whatever doubts western neighbours and allies may have had about the African wars, Portugal was consistently given the benefit of them. This was as much the case under European governments of the left as those of the right.

If the outside world tended to view the armed struggles as a single undifferentiated war, it did so not merely on the encouragement of Portugal. The liberation movements were, as we have seen, anxious to present a similar picture for their own purposes. There was, of course, the real similarity of their shared ideological orientation. The MPLA, the PAIGC and Frelimo appeared committed to the same revolutionary project both in pursuit of independence and in the process of nation-building which would follow it.

What determined the adoption of the distinctive Marxist analyses and programmes of the three movements? Global, African and, ironically, peculiarly Portuguese factors were at work in this. The armed struggles were framed chronologically by the Cuban revolution and the victory of North Vietnam. They took place during the period in which the 'Third World' was asserting its place in the international system in an increasingly radical voice. During these years the discourse of 'anti-colonialism' and 'national liberation' was inseparable from radical social and economic critiques. 'Nationalism' of itself was in disfavour. Marxism therefore was part of the very *zeitgeist.* Then there was the fact of Portugal's membership of – and sustenance by – the western alliance. In a polarized world, with the enemy supplied militarily and protected diplomatically by its NATO allies, the international political orientation of the liberation movements was in some senses inevitable.

Beyond this, Africa itself encouraged the search for new and radical development strategies. By the mid-1960s the initial optimism that surrounded the first wave of sub-Saharan decolonization had faded. Faith in 'developmentalist' ideas of an accelerated modernization leading to rapid integration into the global political economy was increasingly difficult to sustain. African independence appeared to mean merely the replacement of formal colonial rule with a more insidious economic neo-colonialism. In this analysis the post-colonial state was itself complicit in the exploitation of its people. Against the background of, for example, systematized inter-ethnic conflict in Nigeria and the shameless kleptocracy of Zaire, the need for a new model of national liberation seemed self-evident.

Also present in the construction of the lusophone movements' ideology, however, was a strand of transferred political culture from metropole to colony. The leaders of the liberation movements were, inescapably, the products of a particular social formation. Just as figures like Hastings Banda and Kenneth Kaunda were marked in their different ways by the culture of British imperialism, so Neto, Andrade, Cabral, Mondlane and dos Santos were shaped by essentially 'continental' modes of thought in which theory held a more central position and the Marxist tradition was dominant in the programmes of the left.

Once adopted by the three movements, their shared stance was fortified by interdependence. The work of the CONCP was immensely important in this, particularly at the United Nations General Assembly which, in September 1972, admitted delegations from the three Marxist liberation movements as observers. The external perception of unity between the movements brought shared benefits. One of the sharpest political blows inflicted on the Lisbon regime, for example, was the joint audience granted by the Pope Paul VI to Amílcar Cabral, Neto and dos Santos in July 1970. Such diplomatic coups not only legitimized the wars, they endorsed the interrelationship of the different national movements. In this way each struggle sustained the others and enhanced their impact: a revolutionary synergy was established.

Another shared resource was the considerable coterie of western journalists and academics enlisted as supporters by the liberation movements. In a period when the major opinion formers in the western democracies tended to be of the left, this support was of great importance.[117] Frequently, critical judgement would be suspended for the good of the cause, and propaganda dignified as fact. The support of the western Communist Parties for the movements could be assumed. What was rather more significant, though, was the way their message resonated with the less traditional revolutionary discourse developing within the European 'student movement' in the later 1960s. The attraction of revolutionary violence seemed much greater for this generation than subsequent ones, and the African liberation movements quickly took their place with the Paris Commune, the Spanish Civil War and Che Guevara among its heterodox collection of icons. Within this general climate it was significant that the more educated youth of Portugal itself, whose society was slowly, painfully but inexorably modernizing in the 1960s, was rapidly assimilating itself into this transnational culture.

The irony here is that while a fair assessment can be made of the *international* support the liberation movements were able to attract, estimates of their support among their own populations are virtually impossible. No such exercise could have been seriously undertaken during the wars and any retrospective ones in the post-independence setting would hardly have been more reliable. Certain realities are inescapable, however. Firstly, in Angola and Mozambique the wars barely impinged on the areas of largest population concentration. Secondly, despite the class analysis which the three Marxist movements put at the centre of their programmes, their support was to a great extent ethnically determined. Finally, whatever the extent and nature of the 'liberated areas' in the three territories, none of the major movements was ever able to repatriate its headquarters from abroad. In short, with the possible exception of Guiné, there can be no convincing evidence that the liberation movements carried a majority of their 'nations' behind them. The importance attached to such factors, however, was not so great in the prevailing political mood of the 1960s and 1970s as it has become in a world more concerned with individualism and its expression through 'democratization'. In the period of the transfer of power the key formulation was 'revolutionary legitimacy'. To have conducted an armed struggle was itself deemed to legitimize the political claims of each liberation movement. It was a formulation which was at once both romantic and pragmatic. Conveniently, it was also one which met the complementary needs of each side in the negotiating process.

Notes

1 Mário Soares, *Portugal's Struggle for Liberty* (London: George Allen and Unwin 1975), p.175.

2 Joel da Silveira, 'As guerras coloniais e a queda do império', António Reis, ed., *Portugal Contemporâneo*, vol.V (1958–1974), (Lisbon: Alfa 1990), p.80.

3 Michael A. Samuels, 'The nationalist parties', David M. Abshire and Michael A. Samuels, eds, *Portuguese Africa: A Handbook*, (London: Pall Mall 1969) p.390.

4 Basil Davidson, *For the Liberation of Guiné* (Harmondsworth Middlesex: Penguin 1968), p.87.

5 Samuels, 'The nationalist parties', pp.399–400.

6 According to Kenneth Maxwell, Cabral was actually involved in the establishment of the MPLA. 'Portugal and Africa: the last empire', P. Gifford and W.R. Louis, eds, *The Transfer of Power in Africa: Decolonization 1940–1960* (New Haven CT: Yale University Press 1982), p.355.

7 For a concise account of Cabral's theoretical position see Patrick Chabal, 'The social and political thought of Amílcar Cabral: a reassessment', *Journal of Modern African Studies* 19(1) 1981, pp.31–56. A more detailed treatment is given by the same author in his *Amílcar Cabral as Revolutionary Leader* (Cambridge: CUP 1983).

8 Allen Isaacman and Barbara Isaacman, *Mozambique: From Colonialism to Revolution, 1900–1982* (Boulder CO: Westview 1983), p.80.

9 Frelimo's first president, Eduardo Mondlane, gives his account of the formation of the movement in *The Struggle for Mozambique* (Harmondsworth: Penguin 1969), pp.116–21.

10 Malyn Newitt, *A History of Mozambique* (London: Hurst 1995), p.522.

11 According to Mário de Andrade, writing several years later, the attacks were mounted because of reports that MPLA prisoners in Luanda were about to be transferred out of Angola. João Paulo Guerra, *Memória das Guerras Coloniais* (Porto: Afrontamento 1994), p.176.

12 There is some evidence that the authorities had advance warning of the attack. A.H. de Oliveira Marques, *History of Portugal*, vol.2, *From Empire to Corporate State* (New York: Columbia University Press 1972), p. 236.

13 In 1962 the International Red Cross calculated that 200,000 Angolan refugees had fled across the border to the Congo (Zaire).

14 PAIGC, *História da Guiné e Ilhas de Cabo Verde* (Porto: Afrontamento 1974), p.148.

15 Newitt, *History of Mozambique*, p.523.

16 See Robert D'A. Henderson, 'Relations of neighbourliness: Malawi and Portugal, 1964–74', *Journal of Modern African Studies* 15(3) 1977, p.437.

17 Thomas H. Henriksen, *Mozambique: A History* (London: Rex Collings 1978), p.189.

18 This shift in attitude was noted by Salazar's successor in his *apologia* written from exile. Marcello Caetano, *Depoimento* (Rio de Janeiro: Record 1974), p.25.

19 Douglas Porch, *The Portuguese Armed Forces and the Revolution* (London: Croom Helm 1977), p.30.

20 In August 1961 a prior but less serious imperial humiliation was suffered when newly independent Dahomey annexed the tiny Portuguese enclave of São João Baptista de Ajudá after Lisbon had ignored requests for negotiations.

21 So shaken was the regime by the Delgado challenge that he was eventually murdered after being lured to Spain in February 1965. See Soares, *Portugal's Struggle for Liberty*, pp.139–67.

22 António de Figueredo, *Portugal: Fifty Years of Dictatorship* (Harmondsworth Middlesex: Penguin 1975), p.209. Soares considered the ideological positions of the two groups too incompatible for this to be likely. *Portugal's Struggle for Liberty*, p.127. Mário de Andrade later claimed that the Santa Maria affair was significant in the opportunity it offered MPLA was to capitalize on the presence of the large number of foreign reporters gathered in Luanda in expectation of the *Santa Maria's* arrival. Guerra, *Memória das Guerras Coloniais*, p.176.

23 The fullest recent analysis of civil–military relations at this crucial point is José Medeiros Ferreira, *O Comportamento Político dos Militares: Forças Armadas e Regimes Políticos em Portugal no Século XX* (Lisbon: Estampa 1992), pp.255–73.

24 This was Caetano's interpretation, *Depoimento*, p.27.

25 Among the conspirators removed from their posts was the under-secretary for the army, General Francisco da Costa Gomes, who as chief of the general staff at the beginning of 1974 would be a dominating figure in the overthrow of the

regime. During the crisis he published a letter in the Lisbon daily *Diário Popular* pointing to the 'complex of problems' over Africa in which military control was 'far from being the most important one'. Francisco da Costa Gomes, *Sobre Portugal: Diálogos com Alexandre Manuel* (Lisbon: A Regra do Jogo 1979), p.11.

26 Caetano, *Depoimento*, p.27.

27 Although closely associated with Moreira himself, the reforms had in fact begun a few weeks before his appointment under his predecessor. Between 1 April and 15 May 1961 forty-nine new legislative orders were issued by the colonial ministry. Guerra, *Memória das Guerras Coloniais*, p.45.

28 Silveira, 'As guerras coloniais', p.88.

29 Kenneth L. Adelman, 'Report from Angola', *Foreign Affairs* 53(3) 1975, p.563.

30 Keith Somerville, *Angola: Politics Economics and Society* (London: Pinter 1986), p.29.

31 F.W. Heimer, *The Decolonization Conflict in Angola: An Essay in Political Sociology* (Geneva: Institut Universitaire de Hautes Etudes Internationales 1979), p.27.

32 José Friere Antunes, *O Factor Africano* (Lisbon: Bertrand 1990), p.61 and fn.5.

33 In the late 1940s Neto was a member of the central committee of the MUD. Maxwell, 'Portugal and Africa', p.354.

34 The circumstances of Neto's escape from Portugal were unclear until 1981 when the veteran PCP leader, Álvaro Cunhal, described the involvement of the PCP to a visiting MPLA delegation. Alex MacLeod, 'Portrait of a model ally: the Portuguese Communist Party and the international Communist movement, 1968–1983', *Studies in Comparative Communism* 17(1) 1984, p.48.

35 MPLA statement quoted by Basil Davidson, *In the Eye of the Storm: Angola's People* (Harmondsworth Middlesex: Penguin 1972), p.225.

36 Immediately after its expulsion from Léopoldville the MPLA had been thrown back on its office in Conakry, established in 1959 with the support of Sekou Touré.

37 Charles K. Ebinger, 'External intervention in internal war: the politics and diplomacy of the Angolan civil war', *Orbis* 20(3) 1976, p.671.

38 Thomas H. Henriksen, 'Portugal in Africa: comparative notes on counterinsurgency', *Orbis* 29(2) 1977, p.396.

39 The tortuous development of Cabindan micro-nationalism in the 1950s and 1960s is explored by Ebinger, 'External intervention in internal war', pp.674–7.

40 Heimer, *The Decolonization Conflict in Angola,* p.28. Heimer also points to the lack of any solid information on the representativeness of FLEC and the fact that many Cabindans who had originally been FNLA fighters later went over to the Portuguese army, p.31.

41 By the time of the Portuguese collapse in 1974 Gulf was extracting 150,000 barrels of oil a day in Cabinda.

42 MacLeod, 'Portrait of a model ally', p.48.

43 Basil Davidson, 'Portuguese speaking Africa', Michael Crowder, ed., *The Cambridge History of Africa*, vol.8, *From c.1940 to c.1975* (Cambridge: CUP 1984), p.786.

44 Davidson, *In the Eye of the Storm,* p.229.

45 Heimer, *The Decolonization Conflict in Angola,* p.30.

46 Somerville, *Angola*, p.37.

47 John A. Marcum, 'Lessons of Angola', *Foreign Affairs* 54(3) 1976, p.411.

48 UNITA's most damaging operation against the Portuguese, in which it inflicted significant casualties, was mounted on 26 April 1974 – the day following the Lisbon coup.

49 Ebinger argues that contrary to contemporary reports it was not UNITA but the FNLA which was responsible for the attacks on the Benguela Railway and that the real reason for UNITA's expulsion was its connections with dissident sects in western Zambia. 'Report from Angola', p.682. Either way, UNITA appeared to have lacked political judgement.

50 The most detailed account of what the Portuguese called 'Operation Madeira' is given by Pedro Pezarat Correia in his *Descolonização de Angola: A Jóia da Corona do Império Português* (Lisbon: Inquérito 1991), pp.37–40.

51 The first revelations were made in the Lisbon weekly *Expresso* on 8 July 1974. Two days later a detailed article was published in the French periodical *Afrique–Asie*.

52 According to the Portuguese military, FNLA activity at this time was increasingly based on conventional rather than guerrilla tactics and thus tended to play into the hands of the Portuguese army. Silveira, *'As guerras coloniais'*, p.103. It is possible that this was a result of a new Chinese training regime.

53 Franz Ansprenger, *The Dissolution of the Colonial Empires* (London: Routledge 1989), pp.283–4.

54 Malyn Newitt, *Portugal in Africa: The Last Hundred Years* (London: Hurst and Co. 1981), p.232.

55 Davidson, 'Portuguese speaking Africa', pp.776–7.

56 Guerra, *Memória das Guerras Coloniais*, p.397.

57 Adelman, 'Report from Angola', p.569.

58 Table based on Portuguese general staff figures given in Guerra, *Memória das Guerras Coloniais*, pp.379–81. The Portuguese armed forces during the wars were made up on average of 90 per cent army with the air force and navy constituting the other 10 per cent. The figures do not include 'auxiliary' forces (local militias which were about 23,000–strong throughout Portuguese Africa by 1974) or operatives of the PIDE/DGS.

59 PAIGC, *História da Guiné*, p.149.

60 In a statement on 18 July 1963 the minister conceded that: 'large well-armed groups trained in North Africa and the communist countries have penetrated a zone of Guiné of about 15 per cent of its total area'. In something of a damage limitation exercise the Armed Forces Information Service responded with a statement insisting that 'in 85 per cent of the province life is entirely normal'. Quoted by Guerra, *Memória das Guerras Coloniais*, p.214.

61 Joaquim da Silva Cunha, *O Ultramar, A Nação e o "25 de Abril"* (Coimbra: Atlântida 1977). Silva Cunha, later to become colonial minister, was the official to whom the brigadier reported.

62 The new party structure consisted of a twenty member politburo and a sixty-five member central committee divided into functional departments such as external affairs, security and economy and finance. See Davidson, *For the Liberation of Guiné*, pp.79–80.

63 Guerra, *Memória das Guerras Coloniais*, p.207.

64 Joshua B. Forrest, *Guinea-Bissau: Power, Conflict and Renewal in a West African Nation* (Boulder CO: Westview 1992), p.36.

65 The regime went to the extent of financing pilgrimages to Mecca for the Fula chiefs in order to keep them loyal to Catholic Portugal. Henriksen 'Portugal in Africa', p.406.

66 Carlos Fabião, 'A descolonização da Guiné-Bissau. Spínola: a figura marcante da guerra na Guiné', *Seminário: 25 de Abril 10 Anos Depois* (Lisbon: Associação 25 de Abril 1984), pp.305–6.

67 Prominent among this group were figures such as Carlos Fabião, Otelo Saraiva de Carvalho, Manuel Monge, Dias de Lima and Nunes Barata, all of whom would have significant roles both in the revolution and the decolonization process.

68 *Por uma Guiné Melhor* was also the title of a descriptive study of his approach which he published in 1970.

69 The *Congressos* continued to function up until the eve of independence and were seen by Spínola even after the 25 April revolution as a potential counter-weight to the PAIGC. António de Spínola, *País sem Rumo: Contributo para a História de uma Revolução* (Lisbon: Scire 1978), p.274.

70 From 1970 the Spínola administration in Guiné was reportedly responsible

for the construction of 15,000 new houses, 164 schools and 40 health posts. Porch, *The Portuguese Armed Forces*, p.54.

71 Fabião, 'A descolonização da Guiné-Bissau', pp.308–9.

72 In 1993 Spínola claimed, incredibly, that the objective of Mar Verde had not been to destroy the PAIGC but to capture Cabral, return him to Bissau and appoint him secretary-general of the administration. Interview in *Expresso Revista*, 16 January 1993.

73 Friere Antunes, *O Factor Africano*, pp.87–8.

74 Interview with Carlos Fabião in Maria João Avillez, *Do Fundo da Revolução* (Lisbon: Público 1994), p.179.

75 Spínola later claimed that after the abandonment of the Senghor initiative he had been approached through intermediaries by Cabral himself seeking negotiations, *País sem Rumo*, pp.43–4. Also, interview in *Expresso Revista,*, 30 April 1994.

76 Forrest, *Guinea-Bissau*, pp.37–9.

77 Interview in *Expresso Revista*, 16 January 1993.

78 It has been suggested that the increase in the range and quality of weapons reaching the PAIGC at this time was a result of the winding down of the Vietnam war, with North Vietnam now able to redistribute part of its stockpile. Porch, *The Portuguese Armed Forces*, p.58.

79 Forrest, *Guinea-Bissau*, p.68.

80 At the beginning of November 1973 a UN General Assembly resolution condemned the 'illegal occupation' of the Republic of Guiné-Bissau by Portuguese forces. The resolution was passed with sixty-five in favour, thirty abstentions including Japan, France and West Germany, and only seven against – Portugal itself, Greece (then under the right-wing 'Colonels' regime), Brazil, South Africa, Spain (under Franco), Britain and the United States.

81 Fabião, 'A descolonização da Guiné-Bissau', p.311.

82 Table based on Portuguese general staff figures given in Guerra, *Memória das Guerras Coloniais*, p.397.

83 Newitt, *History of Mozambique*, p.523.

84 Kavandame evidently hoped for Tanzanian support for Makonde secession from Mozambique. It was not forthcoming. Henriksen, *Mozambique*, p.178.

85 Isaacman and Isaacman, *Mozambique*, p.102. Both the Makua and the Yao were to contribute a large part of the 'Africanized' Portuguese forces in the later part of the war.

86 A full account of the project is given by Keith Middlemass, *Cabora Bassa* (London: Weidenfeld and Nicholson 1975).

87 The *colonato* concept had already been attempted, with mixed success, after the construction of a smaller dam on the Limpopo in the mid-1950s.

88 Cabora Bassa evidently confronted Frelimo with a dilemma as it had made a practice of avoiding attacks on development schemes which, after all, would be inherited by an independent Mozambique. The particular 'political' nature of the Zambezi project though made it a 'legitimate target'. Henriksen, *Mozambique*, p.191.

89 Newitt, *History of Mozambique*, p.531. It seemed that Tanzania was off-limits in this regard in a way that Guinea-Conakry was not. This may be explained by Tanzania's Commonwealth connections and the widespread international prestige of Julius Nyerere.

90 This fundamental weakness of the plan was later acknowledged by the colonial minister of the time, Silva Cunha, *O Ultramar, A Nação e o "25 de Abril"*, p.345. The white minority regime in Rhodesia was also extremely concerned at the effect of Kaúlza's strategy in dispersing guerrillas to border areas. Guerra, *Memória das Guerras Coloniais*, pp.245–76.

91 Kaúlza insisted, long beyond decolonization and independence, that Portugal had been poised on the edge of total victory in Mozambique. Kaúlza de Arriaga, *Guerra e Política* (Lisbon: Referendo 1987), pp.273–9.

92 See, for example, Barry Munslow's partisan *Mozambique: the Revolution and its Origins* (London: Longman 1983) pp.114–16.

93 Mondlane, *The Struggle for Mozambique*, p.162.

94 Henriksen has pointed out that while Chinese models were applied by Frelimo during the armed struggle, after its Third Congress in February 1977, which laid down the general direction of post-independence political and economic development, the Soviet example became dominant. T.H. Henriksen, 'Marxism and Mozambique', *African Affairs* 77(309) 1978, p.433.

95 Henriksen, *Mozambique*, p.204.

96 Friere Antunes, *O Factor Africano*, p.89.

97 The English priest who alerted the press to the original reports by Spanish missionaries later published an account of the massacres: Adrian Hastings, *Wiriyamu* (London: Search Press 1974).

98 Rodney J. Morrison, *Portugal: Revolutionary Change in an Open Economy* (Boston: Auburn 1981), p.10.

99 See, for example, Manuel Porto, 'Portugal: twenty years of change', A.M. Williams, ed., *Southern Europe Transformed: Political and Economic Change in Greece, Italy, Portugal and Spain* (London: Harper and Row 1984), p.87.

100 Angolan exports in 1973 were worth: Oil $US230m; Coffee $US206m; Diamonds $US80m; Iron Ore $US49m. Christopher Stevens, 'The Soviet Union and Angola', *African Affairs* 75(299) April 1976, p.149.

101 See, for example, Eric N. Baklanoff, 'The political economy of Portugal's old regime: growth and change preceding the 1974 revolution', *World Development* (1979), p.801.

102 Ben Pimlott, 'Socialism in Portugal: was it a revolution?', *Government and Opposition* 12(3) 1977, p.336.

103 Porto, 'Portugal: twenty years of change', pp.91–2.

104 Gervaise Clarence-Smith, *The Third Portuguese Empire 1825–1975: A Study in Economic Imperialism* (Manchester: University Press 1985), p.195.

105 Table based on Grupo de pesquisa sobre a descolonização portuguesa, *A Descolonização Portuguesa: Aproximação a um Estudo*, vol.1 (Lisbon: Instituto Democracia e Liberdade 1979), p.123.

106 Maxwell, 'Portugal and Africa', p.342.

107 Clarence-Smith, *The Third Portuguese Empire*, p.212.

108 Figueredo, *Portugal: Fifty Years of Dictatorship*, p.211.

109 Friere Antunes, *O Factor Africano*, p.62.

110 Maxwell, 'Portugal and Africa', p.350.

111 Quoted in Friere Antunes, *O Factor Africano*, p.64.

112 A full account of the Anderson Plan is given by Michael A. Samuels and Stephen M. Haykin, 'The Anderson plan: an American attempt to seduce Portugal out of Africa', *Orbis* 23(3) 1979, pp.649–69.

113 Tad Szulc, 'Lisbon and Washington: behind the Portuguese revolution', *Foreign Policy* Winter 1975–76, pp.20–1.

114 Maxwell, 'Portugal and Africa', p.346.

115 Isaacman and Isaacman, *Mozambique*, p.105.

116 Throughout the wars Portugal was in breach of the key General Assembly resolution 1514(XV) of 14 December 1960 which committed all members to work towards independence for all non-self-governing territories.

117 As Malyn Newitt put it, 'the battle for Mozambique was sometimes fiercer in the western media than on the ground'. *History of Mozambique*, p.528.

CHAPTER THREE

Lisbon: The Decline and Fall of the Regime

Marcello Caetano – The Politics of Indecision

In September 1968 Salazar suffered a disabling stroke and was succeeded by his finance minister Marcello Caetano. The change of leadership brought widespread expectations of reform both in the metropole and in Africa. The 62-year-old Caetano, a former rector of Lisbon University, had been associated with the regime in some capacity or other since the early 1940s. He had not, however, been Salazar's choice as successor; there had been none. The anticipation of change that Caetano's appointment provoked derived in large part from his past opposition to imperial integrationism and his support for increased devolution of power to the colonies. Although he had served as colonial minister between 1944 and 1947, Caetano's career had failed to prosper after the decisive rejection of colonial autonomy in the 1951 constitutional reform. External perceptions of his oppositionist stance had led both British and American intelligence assessments to single him out as a possible reformist leader during Botelho Moniz crisis in 1961.[1] His past position on Africa and his reputation as an economic modernizer raised the hopes of the new middle class which emerged with the economic liberalization of Salazar's final years.

Whatever his own political instincts, however, Caetano's position was circumscribed from the beginning by the presence in the regime of powerful elements committed to the continuation of Salazar's policies, particularly on Africa, in both the government and military. They were most obviously represented by the president of the Republic, Admiral Américo Thomáz, who had been selected by Salazar himself in 1958 for his loyalty to the cause. Immediately on

Caetano's appointment Thomáz sought guarantees over the continuation of existing policy in Africa and warned of military intervention if any attempt were to be made to change them.[2] Evidently aware of the vulnerability of his position, Caetano took the opportunity of his first speech to the national assembly in November 1968 to allay the fears of the integrationist right. These first weeks of Caetano's period in office more or less defined the character of his leadership up to the collapse in April 1974.

Regarded with suspicion on the right and with growing exasperation on the left, he lacked the personal prestige and qualities of leadership to exploit the internal divisions in and around the regime as Salazar had with such success for almost forty years. Although attempting to sustain a reformist image within the constraints imposed on him, Caetano's impact on the metropolitan situation was not far-reaching. The notorious PIDE was re-christened as the 'Directorate-General of Security' (DGS: Direcção-Geral de Segurança) and some attempt was made to bring its more obvious excesses under control, in the metropole at least. The ruling party also underwent a change of name, from National Union (UN: União Nacional) to the marginally less fascistic Popular National Action (ANP: Acção Nacional Popular) and some political exiles were allowed to return home. None of these 'reforms' ever struggled far beyond the cosmetic, however.

In Africa Caetano sought to make some adjustments to the mechanisms of colonial administration. In April 1969 he undertook a week-long tour of the three principal African territories (Salazar, despite his belief in the sacred unity of the empire, had never set foot in Africa). By Caetano's own account this trip convinced him of the rightness of Portugal's determination to hold its ground. The territories were largely peaceful, in his judgement, and the liberation movements unrepresentative. He was 'convinced that it would be an ignoble tragedy for the people and our mission if we talked to small groupings which, through mere adventurism and only with foreign help, disturb the peace here and there in the vast territories of Angola and Mozambique against the will of the majority'.[3]

Yet change was proposed. The introduction of *some* degree of reform was the only means by which he could attempt to accommodate the forces pressing him from beyond the regime. Pressure on Portugal from the United Nations General Assembly was considerable, even if Portugal's friends in the Security Council could normally be relied upon to prevent its translation into meaningful sanctions. In the colonies themselves a new class of settler entrepreneurs was showing renewed interest in achieving a greater degree of political and economic devolution. In many ways this represented a recrudescence of the pressure for settler autonomy first felt under the pre-*Estado Novo* republic in the 1920s. As in that earlier period, it was most marked in Angola which had the fastest growing of the colonial economies. Somewhat disarmed by the security imperatives of the uprisings in 1961, devolutionist ideas were again attracting support as the nationalist threat appeared to have been contained.

Evidently aware of this mood and anxious to capitalize on it during his tour, Caetano, in a gesture replete with symbolism, laid a wreath at the statue of Norton de Matos in the Angolan town of Nova Lisboa. In doing so he was acknowledging the autonomist position of the old high commissioner and associating himself, however indirectly, with one of Salazar's enemies. He was at the same time, though, underlining his own dedication to the colonial tradition.[4] But imperial reform was also a means of winning over another growing sector of the colonial bourgeoisie, one whose emergence would have been incredible to Norton de Matos. The rapid development of the colonial economies in the 1960s had created a new urban African middle class. Distanced both physically and ideologically from the guerrillas, this stratum of colonial society was identified by Caetano as a potentially powerful ally in the defence of Portugal's continued presence in Africa.

In Lourenço Marques during the Mozambican phase of his tour, Caetano delivered a speech in which he outlined his concept of 'progressive autonomy' (*autonomia progressiva*). As elaborated here, and in the national assembly on his return to Lisbon, the doctrine was to consist of the devolution of certain bureaucratic and legal responsibilities to colonial administrations. Crucially, however, the exercise of these responsibilities would always be subject to the ultimate authority of Lisbon. In this way colonial legislative assemblies would have the right to make legislation and elected 'consultative committees' (*Juntas Consultativas*) would be established to advise governors-general. But governors-general would still be appointed by Lisbon and their rule by decree could supersede any local decisions. Control of legal processes would pass to the colonies but the supreme court in Lisbon would retain ultimate authority. In Africa as in the metropole Caetano's reforming efforts were characterized by revised nomenclature. Angola and Mozambique ceased to be 'Overseas Provinces' (*Províncias Ultramares*) and became 'States' (*Estados*) which would form 'autonomous regions within the Portuguese state'.

Overall, the effect of the reforms was limited politically but potentially more significant socially. By creating a much larger 'political class' in the colonies and by engineering the increased participation of Africans in it, the entire social, and ultimately political, culture of the colonies might have undergone considerable change in the longer term. This was certainly the claim of Caetano himself.[5] But a 'longer term' was no longer available. The reforms which became law in August 1971 had barely been introduced by the time of the Lisbon coup. The effect the changes may have had in Africa – and in international perceptions of Portuguese colonialism – if they had been fully implemented can only be guessed at. Drawn from the jaws of a political vice, however, they failed to satisfy anyone when they were first promulgated. The integrationist right saw in them ominous resonances of de Gaulle and Algeria, while they failed to convince the so-called liberal wing (*ala liberal*) in the Lisbon national assembly of Caetano's commitment to genuine change. Nor did they have any effect in stilling the disquiet in the more thoughtful sections of the military about the long-term prognosis for the wars.

While anxious to placate the right in the military – by giving wide latitude to Kaúlza de Arriaga in Mozambique, for example, and showing an almost exaggerated respect for Thomáz – Caetano simultaneously courted these more progressive elements in the officer corps. In 1970, while working on the progressive autonomy reforms, he had commissioned from António de Spínola (then still governor-general and military commander in Guiné-Bissau) a paper on the future of the African colonies. In this report – 'Some Ideas on the Political Structure of the Nation' – Spínola advocated the concept of a federally organized 'Luso-African-Brazilian' community as a way out of the deepening military and political impasse. Although the idea would have been anathema to the integrationists, Caetano nevertheless regarded Spínola as a political ally.

Later, in September 1972, General Francisco da Costa Gomes was appointed chief of the general staff. Costa Gomes, although of impeccable military pedigree, had been one of the conspirators with Botelho Moniz in 1961. His career had been little affected by this, however, and he had been appointed deputy military commander in Mozambique in the mid-1960s and then commander-in-chief in Angola from 1969 until 1972. The advancement of both Spínola and Costa Gomes was facilitated by their prestige in the military, particularly among junior officers. Their standing in the country as a whole was relatively high as well, in consequence of their much publicized 'successes' in Africa. Caetano thus appeared to be building a counterweight to the right in the military high command. Yet he seemed unwilling to develop and exploit his relationship with the reformist elements in the regime to the point where the Salazarist *ultras* could have been faced down.

Caetano's motivations and aims remained unclear up to and beyond the overthrow of his regime in 1974. By 1971 or 1972 he could have been in a position to forge a working alliance with the more liberal elements within the military, the *ala liberal* in parliament and with those business leaders who increasingly saw Portugal's economic future as lying in western Europe. Yet he failed to make any decisive move to drive national politics in this reformist direction. This position – or more correctly lack of one – may have been due simply to a profoundly indecisive and vacillating personality. A less psychologically determinist explanation, however, might point to the fundamental impossibility of managing reform within structures created by and for the *Estado Novo*. In support of this more political view Lawrence Graham has suggested that Caetano 'was locked into a system so dominated by the cumulative weight of institutions and choices made by his mentor over the previous 40 years that he soon became its captive rather than its leader'.[6] But whatever the balance between the personal and the structural basis of Caetano's politics, his vacillation was a key element in the unfolding of events in 1973 and 1974 and, ultimately, in the dissolution of the empire.

The dizzying pace of events triggered by the military coup of April 1974 has tended to distort perceptions of the political relationships which pre-figured it. Some of this distortion has been the result of deliberate obfuscation. Many personal histories were quickly re-written to adapt to the rapidly changing political environment after April 1974. In part though the confusion merely reflects the difficulty of maintaining a clear focus through such fundamental upheaval. With this in mind it is important to an understanding of the Portuguese revolution and its African aftermath to emphasize that in the early 1970s Caetano, Spínola and Costa Gomes were more united in their politics than divided by them. All three had risen within the regime and despite occasional episodes of dissent (as in 1961) they defined themselves as loyal servants of the regime.

Spínola, although more charismatic than the routine in a regime which seemed almost to make a virtue of personal dullness, was in essence a fairly typical scion of the upper middle class which had prospered under the *Estado Novo*. In common with most of his fellow officers, he maintained close connections with business even while on active service. His father-in-law had founded the steel company Siderúrgia of which Spínola became 'chief administrator'. This had been absorbed by the Champalimaud group in the 1950s and Spínola thus became closely associated with one of the biggest of the monopolies. Additionally, during his time as governor-general of Guiné-Bissau he formed a close relationship with CUF, the dominant economic player in the territory.[7] As Ben Pimlott put it, despite his being unorthodox in some respects, Spínola 'was never other than a committed and unrepentant member of a national super-elite whose interlocking business, political and family connections had dominated the management of Portuguese affairs for generations.'[8]

With both Champalimaud and CUF beginning to look beyond Africa in the early 1970s in search of a firmer place in the west European economy, Spínola's business interests merged quite happily with the politics of imperial reform associated with Caetano's early leadership. The parliamentary 'liberals' associated Spínola with attempts to free Caetano of the constraints of the integrationists. In 1972 he was approached by the *ala liberal* leaders with a proposal that he stand against Thomáz as president. The plan was that he would exploit his prestige to force the admiral from the contest. At this point Caetano himself would enter the race, secure the presidency, and in that capacity invite another reformer to head a new government. Spínola declined, not because he objected to the intention but because of the implicit indignity of the role of stalking horse.[9] Later, from the safe political distance of the twentieth anniversary of the April revolution, he recalled welcoming Caetano's appointment as head of government as 'a moment of hope' and insisted that he would have supported Caetano if he had run for the presidency on his own behalf.[10] From exile in Brazil shortly after the revolution, Caetano himself, perhaps with a certain relish, remembered Spínola having declared himself as '*Marcellista*' in the factional politics of the early 1970s.[11]

One telling indication of the extent to which Spínola was regarded as a natural political ally by Caetano was the latter's attempt to make him colonial minister shortly after his return from Guiné in 1973. The offer arose out of a re-shuffle in November of that year in which Caetano's close associate, Joaquim da Silva Cunha, who had occupied the post, was moved to the then more sensitive defence ministry. Spínola declined, later claiming that it was merely a means of silencing him.[12] It is perhaps more likely, though, that the offer was made in good faith as part of Caetano's tentative strategy of building reformist support in the government. A more feasible explanation of Spínola's refusal of the post might lie in his assessment of the regime's survival prospects and his reluctance to be hauled aboard a sinking ship.

This is not to say though that Spínola's suspicions of Caetano's motives were not genuinely held. There had been, it will be recalled, a serious breach between them the previous year over Spínola's negotiations with Léopold Senghor in pursuit of a settlement in Guiné. Subsequent accounts have suggested that this disagreement represented a fulcral point in the unravelling of the reformist consensus on Africa. Caetano saw the continuation of negotiations as a sign of weakness which would be picked up in Angola and Mozambique where Portugal's interests, both economic and human, were much greater than in Guiné. From this 'domino' perspective Caetano thought it crucial that Guiné, while fundamentally expendable, must nevertheless *be expended* only in the event of total military collapse. He later recalled his key conversation with Spínola when he vetoed any further talks with Senghor:

> I made a statement which shocked the general's sensibilities, saying more or less this:
> 'For the larger defence of the overseas territories it is preferable to leave Guiné through a military defeat with honour than through an agreement negotiated with terrorists which would point the way to other negotiations [in other territories].'
> 'Then you would prefer a military defeat in Guiné', exclaimed the general, scandalized.
> 'Armies exist to fight and they should fight to win but it is not essential that they should win. If the Portuguese army was defeated in Guiné after fighting within its capabilities, such a defeat leaves us with the legal and political possibilities intact to defend the rest of the overseas territories. And the obligation of the government is to defend the overseas territories in their totality.'

After this Spínola, according to Caetano, returned to Bissau 'profoundly shocked and anguished'.[13]

Spínola, recalling the affair in 1978, complained that:

> there had been created, and inexplicably rejected, optimum psycho-social conditions for a just political solution. . . . This lack of realism raised the spectre of Goa before the military and at the same time planted in them the conviction of the complete political incompetence of the government.[14]

Looking back from the mid-1990s, Spínola represented the two positions in these terms: '(f)or me it would be the beginning of a solution in the best Portuguese tradition of dignity; for Marcello Caetano it was a threatened loss of control of events . . . A unique opportunity was lost.'[15] According to his protégé of the time, Carlos Fabião, it was at that point that Spínola's thoughts turned to revolution.[16]

However significant the split over Guiné would prove to be, the question remains as to how far it represented a divergence in means as opposed to ends in Africa. Significantly perhaps, Spínola later suggested that Caetano himself had been amenable to his arguments for maintaining contact with Senghor but that Silva Cunha, then still colonial minister and present at the conversation, had swayed him against this.[17] Both Caetano and Spínola saw Portugal's future in Africa (and both without question *did* see Portugal's future in Africa) as based on a relatively high level of colonial autonomy and wider African participation. In this both set themselves against the Salazarist orthodoxy of the civilian and military integrationists although neither contemplated anything amounting to complete decolonization. Untrammelled by the need to manage conflicting political interests within the regime, however, Spínola could afford to give sparse thought to presentation and tactics. By character too, he was unburdened by Caetano's crippling indecisiveness. But as '*Spinolismo*' developed as a doctrine it was never clear that it amounted to much more than *Marcellismo* by other means.

Two decades after the April revolution a surprising new light was cast on the conflict between Caetano and Spínola over Guiné. In March 1994, during the twentieth anniversary commemorations of the coup, the Lisbon weekly *Expresso* published some remarkable revelations. Just three weeks before it was overthrown, the Lisbon government, with Caetano's approval, had opened secret talks in London directly with representatives of the PAIGC.[18] The meeting had been brokered by the British Foreign Office which had put the proposal to the Portuguese foreign ministry. Arrangements were then made (reportedly by the British Secret Intelligence Service, MI6) to bring the Portuguese and PAIGC delegations together.[19] The results of the first round of talks were apparently encouraging and a further session was arranged for six weeks later in May. On 25 April, however, the regime collapsed, in part because of its perceived intransigence over negotiations with the guerrillas. Caetano made no reference to these events in his otherwise quite frank *apologia*, *Depoimento* (*Testament*) published from exile a few months after the coup. To have done so, of course, would have raised questions about his judgement two years previously when he ruled out even talks about talks through Senghor.

Clearly some caution is necessary in assessing the significance of Caetano's apparent conversion and the depth of his commitment to a negotiated settlement in Guiné. Vetoing the initiative of a colonial governor, however prestigious, belongs to a different order of decision-making from snubbing the efforts of a powerful foreign ally. Acquiescence under diplomatic pressure to participate in talks is some distance from the conclusion and implementation of an agreement. But, assuming that he was indeed ready to seek a settlement directly with the PAIGC and to do so without preconditions, he was demonstrating a flexibility on Africa at least as great as that of Spínola. Whether his evident open-mindedness in early 1974 can be traced to his early federalist ideas, long suppressed by the exigencies of power, or whether it was induced by the first SAM 7s fired by the PAIGC the previous year, is problematic. But once again there is a clear indication that the difference in the positions of Caetano and Spínola at this time was essentially one of public pronouncement rather than private conviction. The prime minister could not openly profess views that he almost certainly shared with his less constrained military colleague. Even as his representatives were sitting down with the PAIGC in London, Caetano was maintaining his public position on Africa, insisting in a letter to Spínola that compromise along 'federal' lines could not be countenanced as 'it is merely a stage on the way to independence'.[20] Spínola, although informed of the talks by the diplomats involved shortly after the coup, retained no memory of the issue and later professed a deep sense of betrayal at Caetano's apparent duplicity.[21]

Spínola and Portugal and the Future

Despite having declined the colonial ministry when it was offered to him on his return from Guiné, Spínola was willing to accept a position specially created for him by Caetano, that of deputy chief of the general staff with responsibility for reviewing war policy. This was, of course, a post which placed him in an ideal situation from which to develop his thinking on Africa and it is inconceivable that Caetano was not aware of the political implications of this.[22] By the end of 1973 rumours were circulating in Lisbon that Spínola's thoughts were about to find their way into print and on 18 February 1974

Caetano received a pre-publication copy of Spínola's *Portugal and the Future* (*Portugal e o Futuro*). The book had already been approved for publication after being read by General Costa Gomes who, as chief of the general staff, was Spínola's direct superior.[23] Late on the evening of the twentieth Caetano sat down to read it. According to his later recollection: 'I did not put the book down until the last page, when it was already dawn. As I closed it I understood that a coup d'état, the approach of which I had felt for months, was now inevitable.'[24]

The book was prepared and published under conditions of considerable secrecy as, despite government permission for publication, fears remained of freelance interference by the DGS. A copy of the manuscript was kept in readiness in France for printing there should anything untoward happen in Lisbon. In the event, though, its publication was unhindered and it went on sale throughout Portugal on 22 February. It would eventually run to five reprints with total sales of a quarter of a million. Tellingly, perhaps, its publication had been subsidized by CUF; the ambivalence of the monopolies towards the empire was becoming increasingly evident.[25]

Where did the peculiar potency of *Portugal and the Future* lie? As political analysis the book rarely struggles above the banal. Its anatomization of a moribund empire in need of fundamental reform and restructuring if it is to survive was hardly novel. Many of the key ideas had already been articulated by Spínola in the paper he prepared at Caetano's request during the formulation of the colonial reforms in 1970, indeed it chimed closely with Caetano's own early 'dissident' views. His key concept of a lusophone community evolving Commonwealth-like from the empire after a process of transition was remarkably similar to the ideas of the 'Anderson Plan' which had been presented to Salazar by the American State Department in the mid-1960s. The book's proposal for a protracted transitional period prior to a multi-option referendum on future constitutional arrangements between metropole and colonies was also very close to the American blueprint.[26] It seems that the book was to some extent a cooperative effort, early drafts having been passed round Spínola's military acolytes in Bissau for comment and addenda.[27] But the importance of *Portugal and the Future* lay only partly in its content. It was the author's identity and the timing of publication which gave the book its real political charge.

The professed intention of *Portugal and the Future* was to offer an alternative to the 'sterile dialogue' between those advocating mindless defence of the *status quo* and those calling for the abandonment of Portuguese Africa.[28] Central to its argument was the recognition that at the international level integrationism was a lost cause. The rhetoric of the defence of western civilization had become a diminishing currency even among Portugal's NATO allies. It could no longer be assumed 'that the west will compromise itself in the eyes of Africans merely from sympathy with our "historical tradition" or our "civilising mission" '.[29]

What Spínola proposed was the 'regionalization' of government in Africa. This did not mean the 'Africanization' of the colonies, but neither did it mean white minority rule.[30] This regionalization of powers, he argued, should lead eventually to a community of 'self-governing provinces' or 'federal states'. All powers other than foreign affairs, defence and finance (which would remain the responsibility of the 'federal' or 'central' government) would be devolved to the units.[31] Somewhere in the process of transition there would be an act of 'self-determination': 'a fundamental principle hitherto considered taboo'.[32] But the nature of this act, and the possibility that it might result in an expression of will for something more than the federal model outlined, seems not to have been fully considered by Spínola.

The book's proposals then were hardly revolutionary in the setting of the mid-1970s. This was a period, after all, in which prescriptions for North–South relations and Third World development models were at their radical zenith. It could have no real influence on the liberation movements. Frelimo's Aquino de Bragança represented the general view of the African nationalists when he dismissed the book as a 'neo-colonial tract . . . a plan with a Gaullist flavour, drawn up by a Portuguese Bismarck, historically ten years too late, playing with words to camouflage an operation that was intended to establish the white minority in a hegemonic position in a future state, linked directly to the metropole, whose economic interests would thus be assured'.[33] But as we have said, the book's content was secondary to the circumstances of its appearance.

Despite his subsequent attempts to play down his involvement in the process of the book's approval, it is unthinkable that Caetano, as head of government, was not aware of the political implications of its dissemination and incapable of preventing it.[34] The publication of *Portugal and the Future* was probably favoured by Caetano at least initially as part of his general strategy of creating a momentum for reform within the regime.[35] The hard-line President Thomáz had not been consulted, though later he argued that the book should have been banned, regardless of the political risks involved. He berated Silva Cunha, who was by then defence minister, for not having taken a stronger line against publication. The title for the book, Thomáz observed ruefully from exile, should not have been *Portugal and the Future* but *Portugal without a Future* (*Portugal sem Futuro*).[36] To the unreconstructed Salazarism that Thomáz represented, any suggestion of reform in Africa was a sign of weakness which posed a threat to the nation as a whole.

Spínola himself was to claim that *Portugal and the Future* 'was never intended to bring about an armed revolution'. Its function was merely to point to 'the last door that it was possible to open in order to avoid the collapse'.[37] But integrationist and federalist positions were inherently irreconcilable and in the long term no regime could encompass both. A change of regime – and in the context of Portugal in 1974 this necessarily meant a military coup – was the only means of resolving the problem. It is characteristic of revolutions, however, that they lead to solutions other than those initially planned.

The Armed Forces Movement and the Coup

In the aftermath of the publication of *Portugal and the Future* Caetano could have no doubt that his momentum-building strategy had been miscalculated and that the conservatives in the regime had been dangerously provoked. In a panic-stricken attempt to retrieve the situation both Spínola and Costa Gomes were sacked. This followed their refusal to take an oath of allegiance to the government at a hastily contrived ceremony on 14 March. Having been menaced by rumours of a right-wing military conspiracy centred around Kaúlza de Arriaga as recently as the previous December, Caetano now feared that the situation in the country could career out of control and that power would 'fall into the streets'.

The capacity of the book to create such insecurity in the regime might be judged disproportionate even given the circumstances of its publication but here the question of its timing came into play. The concerns of the book ran separate from but parallel with growing professional discontent within the permanent officer corp of the armed forces. Recent legislation had threatened the enhanced status of junior and middle-ranking career officers in relation to their conscript (*miliciano*) counterparts. The aggrieved officers had come together in a widespread but semi-clandestine 'Captains' Movement' as a focus of protest. The new regulations, commonly referred to as the 'Rebelo Decrees' after their architect, the defence minister General Sá Viana Rebelo, were issued in July 1973. Their effect was to discount the hitherto enhanced status and automatic seniority of graduates of the Military Academy. It was in this sectional concern that the Armed Forces Movement (MFA: Movimento das Forças Armadas) which would carry out the 25 April coup had its genesis.

There was, therefore, an apparent paradox between the political origins of the April revolution and its eventual course and consequences. Its military roots were conservative rather than progressive. The captains' initial concerns were with the maintenance of the traditional prerogatives of the officer caste and seemed wholly unconnected with the modernizing forces at work in the rest of Portuguese society in the early 1970s. But the grievances of the Captains' Movement were only superficially professional in nature. Africa lay at the root of them in that the Rebelo Decrees' equalization of opportunity and status between career and conscript officers was designed to encourage a greater number of the latter to extend their commissions to meet the ever-expanding manpower requirements of the wars.

By publishing *Portugal and the Future* in these first months of 1974 Spínola helped two strands of dissent, linked together by the wars in Africa, to bind together. '(A)lthough the officers originally came together to deal with their sectional problems', General Costa Gomes recalled, 'they soon focused on the more fundamental problems facing the country.'[38] Shortly after the coup the leading MFA radical Major Otelo Saraiva de Carvalho explained the 'Captains' Movement' in these terms: 'In reality the fundamental base was the African war. But the motivation was, without a doubt, the . . . decrees. In the heart of each of them . . . there lay the problem of Africa. We were aware that it was necessary to resolve it urgently, because we felt that the nation had been defrauded over a war with no meaning for us.'[39]

The manpower crisis at the level of the officer corps was indicative of a broader failure of military resources. By the time of the coup in 1974 a quarter of all men of military age were in uniform. The military had grown from about 60,000 in 1960 to over 200,000 in the early 1970s. In an attempt to keep the war machine fed, the duration of compulsory military service had been increased to four years in 1967. By the late 1960s the size of Portugal's armed forces in relation to its population was exceeded only by those of Israel and the two Vietnams. In proportional terms the Portuguese army was five times the size of that of the United States, even at the height of the Vietnam war, and three times that of Britain and Spain.[40] The strains were becoming evident by the end of the 1960s. Carlos Fabião recalled, for example, wartime battalions of 660 men led by only three professional officers.[41]

Although there was no anti-war movement on the scale of that which developed in the United States during the Vietnam years, a military assessment on the eve of the regime's collapse calculated that about 110,000 conscripts had failed to present themselves for service.[42] The shortcomings in quantity were evidently aggravated by a decline in quality in the latter part of the war. General Costa Gomes noted a marked deterioration from about 1968. After this, he later complained, '(t)hey were frightened of creepie-crawlies, lions, everything . . . '.[43] In Fabião's view, by the eve of 25 April things were simply on the point of collapse, with technical incompetence and lack of fighting spirit pervasive: 'as was well known, nobody was disposed to die'.[44]

By March 1974 the MFA had moved far beyond the sectional concerns provoked by the Rebelo Decrees. Africa and the military predicament there had become its dominant concern. An increasingly large section of the junior and middle officer ranks of the military saw their immediate priority to be the overthrow of the regime and the installation of an as widely acceptable as possible post-coup administration. An early move on 16 March, two days after the dismissal of Spínola and Costa Gomes, had been easily stifled by a detachment of troops loyal to the regime. This initial failure, though, did not appear either to encourage the government or discourage its opponents and the decisive move came, after intricate planning, overnight on 24–25 April. The coup was more or less complete by the afternoon of the 25th.

The conspirators, no less than the government they sought to replace, had to consider the management of disparate interests, at least in the short term, if their revolution was to be a bloodless one. To this end they sought to legitimize and entrench their gains by passing political control to established senior military figures. The MFA's original choice for the presidency of the seven-member Junta of National Salvation (JSN: Junta de Salvação Nacional) set up on 25 April had been General Costa Gomes. The plan had envisaged General Spínola becoming chief of the general staff. Costa Gomes declined this political post, however, claiming later that Spínola's experience and expertise gained as governor-general of Guiné made him more suited for the job.[45] He did though resume his position from which he had been removed the previous month at the head of the armed forces.

The attitudes of the two generals to the MFA conspiracy which led to the coup were ambivalent. Despite Spínola's having assured Caetano that he had no connection with the Captains' Movement, it is clear that he was informed of developments within the nascent MFA from an early stage in the process.[46] He later admitted to having had contact with it 'by indirect means' two weeks before the coup. It is, though, highly unlikely that he could have remained ignorant of earlier developments in which loyal subordinates like Carlos Fabião had been intimately involved.[47] Costa Gomes had, apparently, refused to participate in the MFA as to do so would have been incompatible with his position as chief of the general staff. He had also professed a personal aversion to the idea of revolution, despite his involvement in the 1961 conspiracy. If a coup was necessary then in his view it should take place in Africa to minimize the possibility of bloodshed in Portugal. He maintained a position of benevolent neutrality, however, and declined to betray the conspirators.[48]

Whatever the extent of Spínola's involvement with the conspiracy it did not extend to participation in the initial drafting of its 'Programme'. It was over this fundamental statement of objectives that the first divisions opened between Spínola and the MFA on the African problem. The original draft Programme had made a commitment, though a somewhat vague one, to colonial self-determination and autonomy. While this was not in dramatic conflict with the thrust of *Portugal and the Future,* Spínola objected to even the implication that the revolution might portend African independence.[49] The issue remained unresolved until the night of 25 April itself when the success of the coup appeared assured. At this point the Political Commission of the MFA prevailed on Spínola and the other senior officers who had agreed to form the JSN to accept a revised draft in order that it could be published in the following day's press.

The Political Commission (re-styled the 'Coordinating Committee' after 25 April) consisted of seven officers who would become increasingly assertive in the events of the coming eighteen months, the period of the so-called 'revolutionary process'.[50] Three of them in particular would have key roles in the decolonization process. Colonel Vasco Gonçalves, an engineering officer with extensive African experience and a leftist reputation pre-dating his involvement with the MFA, became prime minister in the second provisional government from July 1974. Major Ernesto Melo Antunes, an artillery officer with wide experience in Angola, was the principal author of the MFA Programme and would emerge as the grey eminence of the decolonization negotiations after the eclipse of

Spínola. He would eventually become foreign minister in 1975. Captain Vítor Crespo, who had served during the war as a frigate commander in the coastal water of Mozambique, would oversee the transfer of power to Frelimo as Portuguese high commissioner there during the transitional period in 1974 and 1975. He would then become minister for cooperation with the former colonies.

For the present, however, these officers were willing to accept the dilution of the Programme as the price of the 'legitimacy' conferred on the revolution by the leadership and support of senior military figures. The key alteration dictated by Spínola was to section eight which dealt specifically with the colonial question. A proposed revision retained a commitment to the 'recognition of the right of peoples to self-determination' and 'the accelerated adoption of measures to extend administrative and political autonomy to the overseas territories with the effective and wide participation of the native populations'.[51] This remained unacceptable to Spínola, however. The final, acceptable, version committed the new regime merely to a 'recognition that the solution to the problem of the wars in the overseas territories is political and not military', and to 'the creation of conditions for a frank and open debate at the national level on the overseas territories problem (and) the laying of foundations of an overseas territories policy which will lead to peace'.[52] A commitment, in short, wholly compatible with the terms of *Portugal and the Future.*

After Spínola's resignation from the presidency in September 1974 an assumption emerged, convenient to both his friends and enemies, that the insistence on the dilution of the commitment to decolonization had been his alone. He himself was to claim that, without his knowledge at the time, Costa Gomes had been familiar with and approved of the first, more radical, version of the Programme.[53] This, though, was typical of Spínola's almost obsessive disparagement of his former military chief and successor as president. The Junta as a whole was composed of senior officers considerably to the right of the MFA Political Commission.[54] Spínola's position was certainly no more conservative than that of the majority of the JSN members. He was indeed to the left of some of his JSN colleagues, including General Galvão de Melo of the air force and Brigadier Jaime Silvério Marques of the army.[55] General Costa Gomes was later to admit that he himself had made some alterations to the Programme 'related to the overseas problem'.[56] But as the revolution veered to the left, Costa Gomes and other members of the JSN were quite content to allow the increasingly marginalized

Spínola to take the full responsibility for diverting the original purposes of the MFA on the colonial question.[57]

The symbolic importance of the Programme to the entire process of the revolution should not be underestimated. It provided the quasi-constitutional basis of the new regime's 'revolutionary legitimacy'. Those around the president (who might loosely be described as 'Spinolists'), as well as the MFA and the embryonic political parties, all looked to the Programme to legitimate their increasingly conflicting policies. The language of the Programme was ubiquitous in the formal policy proposals of the first provisional government which were issued as a decree law three weeks after the coup. Even in the acrimony surrounding the end of his presidency, Spínola was anxious to represent his resignation as a protest against the supposed abandonment of the Programme.[58]

While at the height of his prestige in the euphoric week following the coup, Spínola attempted to gloss the terms of the Programme to align them even more closely with the prescriptions of *Portugal and the Future*. A scheme was to be undertaken 'to raise the consciousness of all populations resident in the respective territories in order that they may decide, through a free and frank debate, the future based on the principle of self-determination in such a way as to safeguard harmonic and permanent amity between the various ethnic, religious and cultural groups'. And, significantly, there was a commitment to the '(m)aintenance of defensive operations in the overseas territories, whenever necessary, to safeguard the lives and property of residents of all colours and creeds'. There was also to be '(s)upport for the accelerated cultural, social and economic development of the populations and territories overseas with a view to the active social and political participation of all races and ethnic groups in public administration and other aspects of civic life'.[59] The following two months were to provide the testing ground for Spínola's capacity to implement these ideas in the chaos of an increasingly multidimensional and 'pluricontinental' revolution.

The Decline of Presidential Authority

The post-coup regime encompassed a complex structure of institutions among which power was distributed in a uncertain and changing way. Spínola had a dual role as president of the JSN and, *ex officio*, as president of the Republic. In the circumstances there could be no firm constitutional points of reference to define and delimit his authority. The JSN itself was, as we have seen, composed of senior officers of differing political outlooks, although its centre of gravity lay fairly close to Spínola's own position. As president of the Republic Spínola assembled a personal cabinet of advisers, drawn in large part from his military staff from his Guiné days. Though unquestioningly loyal to Spínola himself, this cabinet had no real policy-making power.

The Council of Ministers (in effect the provisional government) had been sworn in on 16 May and was composed almost entirely of civilians of the centre and the left. After fifty years of military-backed dictatorship, and as yet without strong party structures, the civilian politicians were understandably wary of the temper of the new, still essentially military, regime in which they had been invited to participate. Their confidence would grow, but now, just weeks after the coup, they were unsure of the extent of their policy power and were diffident in their approach to their portfolios. The structure of governance was further complicated by the creation of a Council of State. This was a nominated body which was designed to substitute for the legislative component of the administration pending future parliamentary elections. Composed of both civilian and military nominees of the Junta and the Council of Ministers, the Council of State was in principle responsible for the generation of legislation. In reality, however, its function was one of legitimization through ratification of policy decisions initiated elsewhere.

Finally there was the Coordinating Committee of the Armed Forces Movement, those who had actually made the revolution. This had no formal function but was an inescapable and, for the civilian politicians, a somewhat unsettling presence. Its self-assigned role was, in the words of one of its leading figures, to 'follow the process'.[60] It was in the middle of this mapless terrain of power, in a climate of accelerating social ferment, that the different forces seeking to impose their own revolutions on Portuguese Africa contended with one another.

The principal elements in the metropole and Africa operating against the Spinolist project (as elaborated in *Portugal and the Future*) and in support of total decolonization during the weeks following the coup came from three distinct though frequently interlinked sources. The party-based ministers who occupied the key portfolios concerned with Africa had from the beginning been pro-independence in their outlook on both moral and pragmatic grounds. It was in the parties of the centre and centre-left that the new middle class sought political expression for its

European-orientated world-view. The Socialist Party (PS: Partido Socialista), the Popular Democratic Party (PPD: Partido Popular Democrática and even the relatively conservative Social Democratic Centre (CDS: Centro Democrático Social) which embraced the *ala liberal* of old regime's national assembly, all favoured negotiations for independence.[61] The firm assertion of this view was, as we have said, constrained by wariness about the still opaque intentions of the military. Next there were the African liberation movements, which appeared to have a much greater appreciation than Spínola himself of the extent of the Portuguese collapse in the colonies after 25 April. The nationalist movements were fully aware of the impossibility of the Portuguese military maintaining, let alone expanding, its operational capacity. Finally there was the Armed Forces Movement, maintaining its watching brief but developing its own policies and showing a willingness to state them. These policies, on Africa as in other areas, were increasingly in conflict with the preferences of the MFA's own choice of president. Whatever the complexities and uncertainties of post-coup government in Lisbon, it gradually became clear as 1974 progressed that the resolution of the African problem was ultimately in the hands of the liberation movements and the MFA. Progress on the question would only come when they could engage directly with one another. Before this could happen, however, it was necessary for the MFA to find a general position on which it could meet the African nationalists.

What were the bases of the MFA's stance on Africa? How and from where did its anti-colonialism emerge? The lack of elaboration of its position on the colonies in the MFA's original Programme – and its evident willingness to dilute its commitments on demand – suggest that the African question had not been explored in all its implications. While Africa had been a *leitmotif* in the accretion of discontents within the military, no detailed consideration appeared to have been given to the concrete outcomes that the MFA wished the post-coup regime to pursue in relation to it.[62] After 25 April, however, the influence of the revolutionary military on Africa – and of Africa on the military – was much debated as the MFA moved to the left.

Discussion was frequently accompanied by a heavy seasoning of revolutionary romanticism. The notion of 'revolutionary contagion' gained wide currency. The soldiers' radicalism, it was said (frequently by the soldiers themselves), had been fired by the example of the African guerrillas and the recognition of the relevance of their political analysis to Portugal.[63] From within the MFA, for example,

Otelo Saraiva de Carvalho claimed that his own 'political awareness . . . was due to the contacts I made with the enemy and their political propaganda'.[64] Such claims were never entirely convincing, however. The radicalization of the MFA did not pick up momentum until well into 1974. If it had been influenced by any existing doctrines (other than that of the Portuguese Communist Party) they were probably those of the various ultra-left groups which flowered colourfully but ephemerally in the wake of the coup.[65] These in turn took their ideological models from Trotskyist and Maoist groups in other west European countries.

The latent radicalism of the young in Portugal which gradually revealed itself in the year following the coup was in many respects a delayed manifestation of the street politics which had already run their course in Britain, France and West Germany six or seven years previously. Young conscript officers who had been educated in institutions touched by 'the spirit of sixty-eight' but prevented by the state apparatus of repression from participating in it, now found themselves not merely free of the secret police but at the head of political events. Once pariahs to their counterparts abroad as the brutal instruments of imperial domination, they were now transformed into revolutionary heroes. Some romanticization of their ideological provenance, both on their own part and by their admirers, was only to be expected.[66]

It is perhaps from these *milicianos* rather than the African guerrillas that a form of contagion began to infect the career officer corps and accelerated the mutation of its initially sectional discontents into a broader ideological stance. Luís Moita, for example, has argued that the *milicianos* 'provided the point of contact between political consciousness and military awareness'.[67] Even Otelo qualified his assertion of revolutionary contagion from the guerrillas by acknowledging the importance of 'associating with brother officers who were not professionals'.[68] This cross-infection not only communicated a political perspective, it closed the cleavage between *miliciano* and career soldier which had originally brought the Captains' Movement into being and cemented a unified Armed Forces Movement.

Another explanation of what might be described as the MFA's 'Africanism' which likewise rejects the idea of contagion by the guerrilla movements, sees developments in the broader context of the culture of the Portuguese military. In this view the MFA was not a dramatic new phenomenon emerging *ab initio* from the circumstances of 1973 and 1974. It was, on the contrary, a link between the corporatist *Estado Novo* and an uncertain future. The MFA leftists were, in this view, radical nationalists determined to protect the nation from 'the lure of western cosmopolitanism' and to regenerate a recently corrupted but basically worthy corporatism, though within a progressive rather than a reactionary framework.[69]

From this perspective decolonization was not designed to free Portugal to pursue a modern political and economic destiny in western Europe. Its purpose was to purge the relationship between Portugal and Africa of its unequal distribution of power in order to create the conditions for a new Luso-African community of radical states. In short, what was advocated was a species of 'Spinolism' based on a radical leftist relationship rather than the neo-colonial one proposed by the General. Certainly, in the period after 1975, as Portugal consolidated its pluralist democracy and the outlines of its post-revolutionary foreign policy were debated, a clear division was evident between 'Europeanists' and 'Third Worldists'. It was a cleavage which closely followed the lines of division between the civilian politicians of the centre parties and the residue of military revolutionaries still within the structures of the state.

Whatever the longer-term implications for Portuguese foreign policy, in the weeks after April 1974 the MFA's emerging Third World consciousness brought the movement into more or less open alliance with its one-time nationalist enemies. It was an alliance between the two most substantial locations of power during 1974 which closed off any option for Portugal other than the unconditional transfer of sovereignty to the guerrilla movements. This was, however, a political reality better comprehended in retrospect than in prospect. In the meantime other interests still insisted on pursuing alternative agendas.

Early Negotiations: The Quest for Cease-Fires

The most pressing problems for the provisional government in Africa were firstly Guiné-Bissau and secondly Mozambique. Angola, divided internally by its three competing and relatively inactive liberation movements, was a nightmare in waiting for 1975, while the archipelagos of Cabo Verde and São Tomé & Príncipe had remained untouched by the wars on the mainland. In Guiné and Mozambique, however, where guerrilla activity had remained high up to April, the provisional government's first priority was to negotiate cease-fires. These would provide the necessary space 'to raise the consciousness of all populations resident in the respective territories' which had been proposed in the provisional government's programme. For Spínola and his supporters the object of this was to prepare for '*consultas*' in the form of the referendums proposed in *Portugal and the Future*. It would also allow, either by natural development or engineered process, the emergence of the 'third force' parties (that is between the guerrillas and the Portuguese) which, Spínola hoped, would act as advocates and agents of the federal solution.

There was, however, an enormous gulf between Spinolist theory and African reality, here. Neither the PAIGC nor Frelimo had anything to gain by ending their military operations. On the contrary, to do so would be to act directly against their political interests. Nor, it soon became clear, would there be any great cost to them in maintaining or even intensifying the armed struggle. Unit after unit of the colonial army was reverting to a posture of minimal self-defence when not actively fraternizing with the enemy. Spínola was later to express incomprehension that 'units of the armed forces of my fatherland . . . would cover themselves in disgrace by total and spontaneous surrender to the enemy'.[70] But the psychological effect of 25 April had been to raise expectations in the military of an immediate cessation of fighting. Whatever the intentions of the revolution's leaders in Lisbon, to the military in the colonies its main objective should be to end the wars and not merely to re-define their purpose. General Costa Gomes, visiting Mozambique to assess the military situation, quickly discerned this. In Lourenço Marques on 11 May he was ready to acknowledge that the armed forces had little fight left in them.[71] The situation in Guiné was, if anything, worse in this respect. The problem for the Portuguese negotiators in both cases was in essence quite simple: Lisbon demanded cease-fires as a prerequisite for a political solution while the liberation movements demanded the political solution of guaranteed independence as a prerequisite for cease-fires. It was the impossibility of squaring this circle which delivered the *coup de grâce* to Spínola's already beleaguered vision of a transformed Portuguese Africa.

The main burden of the early, doomed attempts to negotiate an outcome short of independence fell for the most part on politicians either in or closely associated with the Socialist Party. These already had scant political sympathy with the mandate imposed on them by Spínola. There were three major actors in this. The Socialist Party leader Mário Soares was appointed minister for foreign affairs on his return from exile in Paris and took the lead role in the early decolonization negotiations.[72] A new portfolio, 'interterritorial coordination' replaced the colonial minister (*ministro do ultramar*) and was occupied by António de Almeida Santos who had been prominent in the Lourenço Marques-based 'Democrats of Mozambique' movement of white leftist intellectuals. Almeida Santos was close to the Socialists but not initially a member of the party. His appointment was probably proposed by his old Coimbra professor, Veiga Simão, who although having been education minister in the Caetano regime was nominated by Spínola as Portugal's UN representative.[73] The third significant figure in the process was Soares's secretary of state, Jorge Campinos, another returned exile and PS member.[74]

What might be described as the semiotics of Lisbon's negotiating platform added to the already deeply confused setting. The fact that the lead role was taken by the foreign minister might have been taken as a signal of Portugal's acceptance of independence and the creation of new states as the ultimate outcome. The minister with specific responsibility however was notably *not* the 'minister for decolonization'. The formulation 'interterritorial coordination' carried obvious federalist – that is, Spinolist – connotations.[75] The confusion was compounded by the pronouncements of the ministers themselves. Initially Soares was open about the differences between the PS line on Africa which was 'independence pure and simple' and that of Spínola.[76] When questioned by *Der Spiegel* in early May – just before his appointment to the provisional government – about Spínola's ideas for a continuing political community in Africa he replied: 'I can only speak for my party which wants independence for the colonies'.[77] Almeida Santos was more guarded. Although not rejecting totally the possibility of a federation, he was cautious about its feasibility. He was also anxious to examine the key aspect of the Spinolist commitment to 'self-determination' that the General himself appeared reticent to explore. Self-determination could have many outcomes, Almeida Santos insisted, other than the acceptance of federation: '(a)mong these, obviously, is independence'.[78] Nowhere in *Portugal and the Future* was this potential outcome of a genuinely free and fair *consulta* contemplated.

The first contacts with both the PAIGC and Frelimo sharply underlined the weakness of Lisbon's position. It was clear at the initial meeting with the PAIGC, which was held in London at the end of May, that the nationalists saw little to negotiate beyond a date for the formal transfer of power. Guiné-Bissau had after all already declared itself independent the previous September and was now recognized by a substantial proportion of states in the international system. Frelimo was no more open to the idea of a cease-fire prior to negotiations. Although its physical lodgement in Mozambique was much less extensive than that of the PAIGC in Guiné it was fully aware of the extent of Portugal's weakness. Far from accepting a cease-fire Frelimo seized the military initiative against its rapidly disintegrating opponent and intensified its guerrilla operations.

Soares, in the constitutionally opaque circumstances of these weeks answerable to Spínola and the JSN, was now forced to rehearse the Spinolist line in public while continuing to reject it in private.[79] Meanwhile Spínola did nothing to ease his negotiators' difficulties. The way forward in Africa, he insisted at his investiture as president on 15 May, was for the liberation movements to revert to political activity.[80] Implicit in this was the assumption that this activity would involve competition with whatever 'third force' groupings might emerge by whatever means.

Despite the increasing distance between Spínola and his civilian ministers on Africa and the growing restiveness of the MFA, he still had a considerable power base. Within the JSN he could count on the support of the two air force representatives, Diogo Neto and Galvão de Melo, and of Jaime Silvério Marques, the army chief of staff. Costa Gomes and Pinheiro de Azevedo (respectively future president and prime minister) were somewhat to the left of Spínola but only Captain (later Admiral) António Alva Rosa Coutinho of the navy seemed to share the accelerating radicalism of the MFA Coordinating Committee. Beyond the Junta, Spínola's strongest ally was the prime minister, the patrician liberal Adelino da Palma Carlos, who was at one with Spínola on the colonial issue. As late as July 1974, therefore, Spínola still had grounds for optimism about his African plans, at least in the setting of the Lisbon regime.

The divisions between the president and the MFA were, however, becoming overt. On 13 June Spínola attempted to assert his authority over the movement at an assembly in the Lisbon Military Maintenance headquarters (*Manutenção Militar*). The outcome of the encounter was confused. Spínola left with the impression that he had pulled the MFA behind him but this seemed to be largely self-delusion. The MFA Coordinating Committee had a different view of the meeting. Its position, outlined at the assembly, was that Spínola could gain the cooperation of the movement only by committing himself to the full implementation of its Programme. Given the vagueness of its terms, not least on Africa, implementation could only follow interpretation and that would lie, the Coordinating Committee insisted, with the MFA itself.[81]

The following month the Spínola camp suffered an even greater blow. On 9 July Palma Carlos resigned. This followed the rejection by the provisional government of his proposal to postpone constituent assembly elections and bring forward those for the presidency. The origins of the scheme plainly lay in the Spínola camp, and it was probably motivated by the widening breach with the MFA. If successful – and if he had been returned in the election – Spínola's position would have been enormously enhanced. The presidency would have been the only institution of state with a popular mandate. The reinforcement of his authority which would have followed the successful completion of this manoeuvre would have extended to Africa where his grip on the colonial military was slipping as that of the local MFAs tightened.[82] The manoeuvre did not succeed, however, and the limits of his power base were now fully exposed.

Constitutional Law 7/74 and the Commitment to Decolonization

The immediate consequence of the *crise Palma Carlos* for Africa was a clearing of the negotiating log-jam as the beleaguered Spínola was forced to concede ground. Typically, in this peculiarly legalistic revolution, this took the form of a new constitutional law. The central importance of Law 7/74, promulgated on 26 July, was to make explicit what had been ignored in *Portugal and the Future* and evaded by Spínola since the revolution: that 'self-determination' encompasses 'independence'. The new Law recognized *inter alia*: 'the right to self-determination, with all of its consequences, *including the acceptance of the independence of the overseas territories . . .* ' (emphasis added).[83] The promulgation of the law had been the outcome of growing MFA pressure. It reflected the ascendancy of the left in its metropolitan leadership and the growing frustration of its African sections with the *impasse* on Africa.

In essence, Law 7/74 represented the reinstatement of the more radical commitment to decolonization which had been part of the original draft of the MFA Programme. The Law was not strikingly revolutionary in its terms and proposed no detailed procedure for the exercise of self-determination which might lead to independence. But the process of cease-fire followed by referendum, central to the Spinolist scheme, was nowhere referred to. Its last article merely authorized the president, in consultation with the JSN, the Council of State, and the provisional government, to conclude agreements related to the right of the colonies to independence.

This did not, of course, *rule out* the possibility of plebiscites in all or any of the territories. But in relation to Guiné and Mozambique the signal was clear: the way was now open for bilateral agreements for the transfer of power from Lisbon to the PAIGC and Frelimo respectively. In the view of Almeida Santos, Law 7/74 did not preclude referendums, but they were foreseen neither in the MFA Programme nor in the programme of the provisional government. 'This *could* vary from territory to territory' (original emphasis). However it 'could come down to a simple text of agreement between the Portuguese state and the liberation movements . . . '.[84] And, following a somewhat Jesuitical line of reasoning, the ethics of concluding agreements with individual liberation movements could not be questioned. The Lisbon regime itself was founded on 'revolutionary legitimacy'. If the validity of this concept was extended to Africa then, Almeida Santos argued, acts of 'self-determination' had already been made in Guiné and Mozambique. The simple fact of the armed struggles affirmed the legitimacy of the PAIGC and Frelimo as the sole legitimate representatives of their respective nations.[85]

Meantime in the wider world pressure for a clear Portuguese commitment to decolonization had been growing. The secretary-general of an increasingly restive United Nations was due to make an official visit to Lisbon at the beginning of August. This visit, which was of some importance to the international legitimization of the revolution, was put in jeopardy by the lack of movement on Africa. On 9 May the CONCP had persuaded the General Assembly's decolonization committee to demand from Lisbon a clear statement of its intentions in Africa. A month later the OAU at its annual summit in Mogadishu had added to the pressure by making a commitment to decolonization a precondition for the establishment of diplomatic relations between its members and Portugal.

While the Third World bloc in the UN and the states of Africa were laying down their markers on decolonization, Portugal's western allies were notably unforthcoming on the issue. Taken strangely by surprise by the events of 25 April and slow to work out the broad political, strategic and economic implications of a clutch of new, Marxist-orientated states in Africa, the west kept its council. On 19 June Spínola met President Nixon in the Azores on the latter's return journey from a Middle East visit. Discussions, however, seem to have concentrated on Portugal's role in NATO and the implications of the Lisbon coup for western security. Specifically, Nixon was concerned to secure an agreement to continued American use of the Lajes air base in the Azores which had recently assumed a new importance in relation to American interests in the Middle East.[86] Africa seems not to have figured with any prominence during this first high level US–Portuguese encounter. Spínola, whose project for Africa would have required powerful international support, could elicit virtually no response, either supportive or hostile from Europe or the United States. As José Medeiros Ferreira, a future Socialist foreign minister was to put it, 'the Portuguese decolonization process demonstrated conclusively the non-existence of a western policy regarding (Portuguese) Africa'.[87] In the absence of any clear orientation from the west, the diplomatic initiative on decolonization remained firmly in the grasp of those states and organizations most hostile to Spínola's position.

By the end of July therefore Spínola was virtually without resources to enable him to persist with his federal project for Africa. The loss of Palma Carlos had delivered a double blow. The failed attempt to concentrate power in Spínola's hands which had precipitated his resignation left the provisional government more conscious of its own policy responsibilities and increasingly wary of Spínola's intentions.[88] But as well, Palma Carlos's successor, Colonel Vasco Gonçalves, was close to the MFA left and deeply unsympathetic to the Spinolist position on Africa. While Spínola retained support within the JSN, the authority of the junta itself was diminishing. There were now, despite Spínola's best endeavours, pro-independence 'governors' in each of the three major colonies.

Ironically, the promulgation of Law 7/74 had the immediate effect of reviving Spínola's popularity in the country.[89] His televised address on 27 July was suitably portentous. 'If there is a great hour in the life and the history of the nation, this is it', he declaimed.[90] Throughout the address he attempted to place the Law within an essential 'continuity' (*coerência*) of Portuguese relations with the *ultramar* which stretched back to the supposed liberal humanism of the Monarchy and First Republic.[91] Having been interrupted by the previous regime, this proud tradition was now being re-established.[92] The Law was also, it appeared, in line of continuity with Spínola's own vice-regal policies as a colonial governor:

> Constitutional Law No.7/74 . . . creates the framework of legitimacy for the immediate initiation of the process of decolonization in the Portuguese overseas territories. Thus, and in direct conformity with

the line of action of my government in Guiné, the moment has arrived for the President of the Republic to solemnly reiterate the recognition of the right of the peoples of the overseas territories to self-determination, including the right to independence.

There should be no doubts about the historical importance of the moment and the clarity of what we are saying; this declaration means that we are ready as of now to begin the process of the transfer of powers to the populations of the overseas territories regarded as suitable, namely Guiné, Angola and Mozambique.[93]

'His address', Almeida Santos announced two weeks later, 'marked the reconciliation of Portugal with itself.'[94] It was also, according to the same observer thirty years later, an acknowledgement that if Lisbon did not move negotiations ahead the armed forces in Africa would themselves hand over power to the liberation movements.[95] The *impasse* having been broken on both Guiné and Mozambique, substantive negotiations with the PAIGC and Frelimo quickly got underway. At the international level Kurt Waldheim's visit to Lisbon at the beginning of August not only went ahead but concluded with a statement affirming Portugal's full compliance with the UN on decolonization, a situation hitherto confused by Spínola's position. Portugal was now, according to a joint communiqué issued with the UN secretary-general, ready to recognize Guiné-Bissau's independence, begin negotiations with Frelimo 'to accelerate the process of independence' and establish contacts with the Angolan movements with a view to early independence negotiations.[96] In just over a week, between the publication of Law 7/74 on 27 July and the meeting with Waldheim on 4 August, Portugal had become committed to the dissolution of its third empire.

On Spínola's initiative a National Commission on Decolonization (CND: Comissão Nacional de Descolonização) was now set up. The CND was based on a blueprint prepared by his close ally, the UN representative Veiga Simão. If the CND was designed, as Spínola himself implied, to regain the African initiative for the Spinolists after the set-back of Law 7/74, it was unsuccessful.[97] Although chaired by Spínola, the CND was composed of the relevant ministers of the provisional government and chiefs of the military staffs. A clear majority of the membership was therefore unsympathetic to the Spinolist project.[98] In practice the CND became a 'ways and means' committee, facilitating rather than obstructing the pace of imperial dissolution.[99] Its very title, of course, was an implicit defeat for the federalist position; the language of 'inter-territoriality' had now given way to that of 'decolonization'. From the end of July 1974 the depletion of Spínola's authority was a virtually daily process until its final evaporation at the end of September.

Indulgence, or more correctly disregard, of Spínola's views on the future of the empire was the price the MFA was willing to pay for the stamp of his authority and prestige on the 25 April coup. Ultimately, though, attempts to realize his vision for Africa ran against the very grain of the revolution. The MFA leader Ernesto Melo Antunes has pointed up the basic contradictions of the Spinolist position. Attacking what he saw as Spínola's re-writing of the history of the revolution in the late 1970s, he rejected the federal solution as thirteen years behind the times. Once the guerrilla wars had begun there was, according to Melo Antunes, no prospect of any solution other than withdrawal.[100] This view of the historical inappropriateness of the project was shared by Costa Gomes who argued that a federal solution would have required a clear political commitment from at least the early 1940s.[101]

Even putting aside the anachronistic nature of Spínola's scheme, the circumstances in which he attempted to implement it were hopelessly difficult. In the most favourable political conditions, which certainly did not pertain in the spring of 1974, the project was based on a gradualism requiring years of incremental reform. 'We would not move suddenly', he wrote in *Portugal and the Future*, 'from the present system to a federal one, so that gradual evolution would militate against an explosive disintegration.'[102] Neither the time-scale nor the necessary stability of environment were available to Spínola.

The fact that *Portugal and the Future* played a role in precipitating the revolution did not make it a revolutionary book. Its discourse was reformist, certainly, but still located firmly within the 'liberal' mainstream of the Caetano regime. In Melo Antunes's view, if the coup had been merely a generals' revolt 'aimed at transferring power from one section of the dominant class to another', then Spínola might have had the chance to pursue his plans, even if they were pre-doomed to failure by forces outside of Portugal. But in the event the coup became a 'revolution with an internal dynamic that no one could resist and which determined . . . the decisions of the political leaders of the time'.[103]

Despite his flawed and inapplicable vision of a Portuguese future in Africa, Spínola's importance both to the revolution and, ultimately, to the process of decolonization should not be underestimated. His standing, indeed identification, with the deposed regime enormously eased the transfer of power and dissipated the threat of counter-revolution. This was so not only in the metropole but in Africa as well where apprehensive and potentially rebellious white settlers had their fears allayed at least in part by Spínola's occupation of the presidency. Law 7/74, however, marked the end of the Spinolist project. From the moment of its promulgation Guiné and Mozambique were set on the way to total independence. Although still capable of muddying the waters on Angola, Spínola was now unable to intervene to prevent the process of decolonization gaining pace there as well. As Almeida Santos remarked with a characteristic mix of tact and realism in 1975, 'General Spínola had his own vision of the phenomenon of decolonization and he advanced it with a sharp authoritarianism. But in my view, if anything was obvious in the final years of our presence overseas it was the greater power of realities over strong convictions.'[104]

Notes

1 *Sunday Times* Insight Team, *Portugal: The Year of the Captains* (London: Deutsch 1975), p.23.

2 José Friere Antunes, *O Factor Africano* (Lisbon: Bertrand 1990), p.75.

3 Marcello Caetano, *Depoimento* (Rio de Janerio: Record 1974), p.32.

4 Friere Antunes, *O Factor Africano*, p.76.

5 Caetano, *Depoimento*, pp.34–8.

6 Lawrence S. Graham, *The Portuguese Military and the State: Rethinking Transitions in Europe and Latin America* (Boulder CO: Westview 1993), p.15.

7 Insight, *The Year of the Captains*, p.59.

8 Ben Pimlott, 'Socialism in Portugal: was it a revolution?', *Government and Opposition* 12(3) 1977, p.333.

9 Interview with Carlos Fabião in Maria João Avillez, *Do Fundo da Revolução* (Lisbon: Público 1994), p.180.

10 Interview in *Expresso Revista*, 30 April 1994.

11 Caetano, *Depoimento*, p.189.

12 *Expresso Revista*, 30 April 1994.

13 Caetano, *Depoimento*, pp.191–2.

14 António de Spínola, *País sem Rumo: Contributo para a História de uma Revolução* (Lisbon: Scire 1978), p.251.

15 *Expresso Revista*, 30 April 1994.

16 Carlos Fabião, 'A descolonização da Guiné-Bissau. Spínola: a figura marcante da guerra na Guiné', *Seminário: 25 de Abril 10 Anos Depois* (Lisbon: Associação 25 de Abril 1984), p.309.

17 *Expresso Revista*, 30 April 1994.

18 *Ibid.*, 26 March 1994.

19 Further details on the background to the talks were provided by the British military attaché in Lisbon at the time, Thomas Huggins, in a subsequent interview in *Expresso Revista* published on 16 July 1994.

20 Quoted in Friere Antunes, *O Factor Africano*, p.89.

21 Spínola had 'no words to express the extent of (his) indignation'. *Expresso Revista*, 30 April 1994.

22 Caetano, *Depoimento*, p.193.

23 Costa Gomes's reading may have been influenced by the circumstances in which it was undertaken – in Mozambique in the aftermath of anti-army demonstrations by settlers following Frelimo attacks in Manica province. Commemorative article on the twentieth anniversary of publication in *Expresso Revista*, 19 February 1994.

24 Caetano, *Depoimento*, p.196.

25 Insight, *The Year of the Captains*, p.43.

26 See Michael A. Samuels and Stephen M. Haykin, 'The Anderson plan: an American attempt to seduce Portugal out of Africa', *Orbis* 23(3) 1979, p.662.

27 Some of Spínola's enemies were later to suggest that his actual contribution to the book was not in fact very great. *Expresso Revista*, 19 February 1994.

28 António de Spínola, *Portugal e o Futuro: Análise da Conjuntura Nacional* (Lisbon: Arcádia 1974), p.25.

29 *Ibid.*, p.144.

30 *Ibid.*, pp.165–6. The South African and Rhodesian model of segregation and white minority rule was peculiarly distasteful to metropolitan traditionalists who were imbued with a belief in Portugal's unique multiracialism. Caetano, *Depoimento*, p.28.

31 Spínola, *Portugal e o Futuro*, pp.217–20.

32 *Ibid.*, p.146.

33 Aquino de Bragança, 'Independence without decolonization: Mozambique 1974–1975', Prosser Gifford and William Roger Louis, eds, *Decolonization and African Independence: The Transfers of Power 1960–1980* (New Haven CT: Yale University Press 1987), p.435.

34 Caetano recalled Costa Gomes's assessment of the book as a 'brilliant' service to the nation, though he acknowledged the unease of defence minister Silva Cunha over publication. *Depoimento*, pp.194–5.

35 Manuel Porto, 'Portugal: twenty years of change', A.M. Williams, ed., *Southern Europe Transformed: Political and Economic Change in Greece, Italy, Portugal and Spain* (London: Harper and Row 1984), p.97.

36 *Expresso Revista*, 19 February 1994.

37 António de Spínola, *Ao Serviço de Portugal* (collected speeches and statements), (Lisbon: Ática 1976), pp.10–11.

38 Francisco da Costa Gomes, *Sobre Portugal: Diálogos com Alexandre Manuel* (Lisbon: A Regra do Jogo 1979), p.17.

39 *Expresso*, 27 July 1974.

40 Porto, 'Portugal: twenty years of change', p.91.

41 Fabião interview, *Do Fundo da Revolução*, p.183.

42 There was some debate as to how much this was the result of 'draft-dodging' as such and how much a consequence of illegal economic migration. Douglas Porch, *The Portuguese Armed Forces and the Revolution* (London: Croom Helm 1977), p.32.

43 *Público Magazine*, 20 February 1994.

44 Fabião interview, *Do Fundo da Revolução*, p.183.

45 *Público Magazine*, 20 February 1994. Spínola later accused Costa Gomes of deviousness in evading the political risks of the presidency while retaining control of the military. *Expresso Revista*, 30 April 1994.

46 Caetano, *Depoimento*, p.197.

47 Carlos Fabião later suggested that Spínola's involvement with the movement had been extensive but kept secret. Interview, *Do Fundo da Revolução*, p.181.

48 This account of Costa Gomes's position is that of Vítor Crespo, who had been at the centre of the conspiracy. *Público Magazine*, 20 February 1994.

49 Whatever Spínola's reservations about MFA intentions on 25 April, his later claim to have realized immediately that he was faced 'with a revolutionary programme with a Marxist basis' was merely self-serving. *Ao Serviço de Portugal*, p.12.

50 This period of 'revolutionary process' was later to acquire the half ironic

acronym 'PREC': Processo Revolucionário em Curso ('Revolutionary Process in Course').

51 Grupo de pesquisa sobre a descolonização portuguesa, *Descolonização Portuguesa: Aproximação a um Estado* (Lisbon: Instituto Amaro da Costa 1982), vol.2, p.4.

52 *Expresso*, 27 April 1975. The left-leaning Lisbon daily *República* unknowingly published the unrevised version on 26 April as the agreed Programme.

53 Spínola, *Ao Serviço de Portugal*, p.13fn.

54 The Junta, presided over by Spínola, was composed of two representatives of each arm of the forces: Brigadier Manuel Diogo Neto and Colonel Carlos Galvão de Melo for the air force; Costa Gomes and Brigadier Jaime Silvério Marques for the army; Captains José Baptista Pinheiro de Azevedo and António Alva Rosa Coutinho for the navy. Diogo Neto, Silvério Marques and Pinheiro de Azevedo were simultaneously appointed chiefs of staff of their respective arms.

55 MFA radical Major Otelo Saraiva de Carvalho later placed the JSN on a spectrum from the left to the right thus: Rosa Coutinho – Pinheiro de Azevedo – Costa Gomes – Spínola – Silvério Marques – Galvão de Melo (Diogo Neto, who was on duty in Mozambique on 25 April and joined the JSN later was not included in the evaluation). Otelo Saraiva de Carvalho, *Alvorada em Abril* (Lisbon: Ulmeiro 1977), p.479.

56 Costa Gomes, *Sobre Portugal*, p.25. He wished to prevent the immediate dismantling of the DGS in the colonies. Saraiva de Carvalho, *Alvorada em Abril*, p.478.

57 The timing and circumstances of the changes to the colonial clause of the Programme are disputed. Interviewed by *Público Magazine* for a commemorative feature twenty years later, Costa Gomes and Crespo insisted that the changes had been agreed about a week before the coup. Spínola, Diogo Neto and Rosa Coutinho in contrast recalled the alterations being made only at the first meeting of the JSN *after* the coup on the night of 25 April itself. *Público Magazine*, 20 February 1994.

58 Spínola, *Ao Serviço de Portugal*, pp.211–15.

59 Decree Law No.203/74, 15 May 1974 (Section 7) reprinted in *O Programa do MFA e dos Partidos Políticos* (Lisbon: Edições Acrópole 1975), p.17.

60 Interview with Rear Admiral Vítor Crespo, Lisbon, 2 March 1995.

61 Vítor Alves, 'Colonialismo e descolonização', *Revista Crítica dos Ciências Sociais* Nos.15/16/17 May 1985, pp.564–5.

62 It was the view of Frelimo's Aquino de Bragança, a close observer of the metropolitan environment as well as the African one, that in general the MFA 'lacked any kind of coherent revolutionary or anti-colonial ideology' and that they were simply desperate for a peace settlement. 'Independence without decolonization', p.432.

63 The argument has been advanced among others by Pimlott, 'Socialism in Portugal', p.339; Insight, *The Year of the Captains*, p.29; Thomas H. Henriksen 'Portugal in Africa: comparative notes on counterinsurgency', *Orbis* 29(2) 1977, p.410.

64 Interview in Hugo Gil Fereira and Michael W. Marshall, *Portugal's Revolution Ten Years On* (Cambridge: CUP 1986), p.115.

65 Phil Mailer's *Portugal: The Impossible Revolution* (London: Solidarity 1977) offers a useful if less than disinterested tour around the bewildering alphabet of organizations, factions and tendencies which the sudden liberation of 25 April brought into being on the far left.

66 Porch makes the telling point that the most left-wing arm of the military was probably the navy – the one least open to 'infection' by the African guerrillas. *The Portuguese Armed Forces*, p.56.

67 Luís Moita, 'Elementos para um balanço da descolonização portuguesa', *Revista Crítica dos Ciências Sociais* Nos.15/16/17 May 1985, p.503.

68 Gill Fereira and Marshall, *Portugal's Revolution Ten Years On*, p.115.

69 Jonathan Story, 'Portugal's revolution of carnations', *International Affairs* 52(3) 1976, pp.427–9.

70 Spínola, *Ao Serviço de Portugal*, p.22.

71 Basil Davidson, introduction to Aquino de Bragança, 'Independence without decolonization', p.429. Spínola was to claim that Costa Gomes's assessment was an intentionally mendacious one, only accepted because of his (Spínola's) personal unfamiliarity with Mozambique. *País sem Rumo*, pp.289–93.

72 Soares later recalled that he had himself to solicit this post, Spínola having planned to appoint him as minister without portfolio. Soares interview, *Do Fundo da Revolução*, p.267.

73 Interview with Vítor Crespo, Lisbon, 2 March 1995.

74 The PCP, although represented in the provisional government by its leader Álvaro Cunhal who was minister without portfolio, had no direct role in the decolonization negotiations.

75 The significance of the replacement of the *ministério do ultramar* with *co-ordenação interterritorial* rather than *descolonização* was later remarked by the MFA leader Vítor Alves. 'Colonialismo e descolonização', p.563.

76 Interview with *Newsweek*, 13 May 1974. Mário Soares, *Democratização e Descolonização: Dez Meses no Governo Provisório* (Lisbon: Dom Quixote 1975), p.39.

77 *Ibid.*, p.35.

78 Press Conference in Lourenço Marques, 21 May 1974. Transcript in Almeida Santos, *15 Meses no Governo ao Serviço da Descolonização* (Lisbon: Representações Literária 1975), p.84.

79 Bragança, 'Independence without decolonization', p.441.

80 Spínola, *Ao Serviço de Portugal*, p.36.

81 For participant accounts of the Manutenção Militar assembly see Gil Fereira and Marshall, *Portugal's Revolution Ten Years On*, p.37 and p.87.

82 As Douglas Porch put it: 'Like the French Fourth republic, the new provisional government was too shaky to resist a *pronunciamento* from its colonial capitals. Spínola's July bid for extended powers and early presidential elections aimed to restore his authority in the colonial army as well as in the country.' *The Portuguese Armed Forces*, pp.114–15.

83 The law was published in *Diário do Governo*, 27 July 1974.

84 Interview with *Província de Angola*, 6 August 1974, *15 Meses no Governo*, p.126.

85 *Expresso Revista*, 3 August 1974.

86 Tad Szulc, 'Lisbon and Washington: behind the Portuguese revolution', *Foreign Policy*, Winter 1975–76, p.25.

87 José Medeiros Fereira, 'International ramifications of the Portuguese revolution', L.S. Graham and D.L. Wheeler, eds, *In Search of Modern Portugal: The Revolution and its Consequences* (Madison: University of Wisconsin Press 1983), p.292.

88 Interview with Dr António de Almeida Santos, Lisbon, 3 March 1995.

89 The publication of the Law brought mass demonstrations in its support to the streets of Lisbon and Porto. *Diário de Notícias*, 30 July 1974.

90 Speech reprinted in *Ao Serviço de Portugal*, pp.145–51.

91 Spínola remained insistent on this essential continuity when recalling events from exile four years later. *País sem Rumo*, p.261.

92 The theme was echoed by Almeida Santos some time after Spínola's fall when, at the investure of new high commissioners for São Tomé & Príncipe and Cabo Verde on 18 December 1974 he recalled the 'autonomizing tendency' of the Monarchy and First Republic and regretted that 'for half a century we were compelled to be false to this tradition ... We were condemned to let the train of progress pass ... ', *15 Meses no Governo*, p.226.

93 Spínola, *Ao Serviço de Portugal*, p.148.

94 *Diário Popular*, 12 August 1974.

95 Interview with António de Almeida Santos, Lisbon, 3 March 1995.

96 Communiqué published in *A Capital*, 5 August 1974.

97 Spínola, *País sem Rumo*, pp.270–1.

98 The Commission was composed of the ministers of foreign affairs, interterritorial coordination, finance and the chiefs of staff of the army, navy and air force, as well as Costa Gomes as chief of the general staff. Vítor Alves, 'Colonialismo e descolonização', p.12.

99 Interview with António de Almeida Santos, Lisbon, 3 March 1995.

100 *Expresso Revista*, 17 February 1977.

101 Costa Gomes, *Sobre Portugal*, p.38.

102 Spínola, *Portugal e o Futuro*, p.203.

103 *Expresso Revista*, 17 February 1977.

104 Interview in *Flama*, 14 February 1975, *15 Meses no Governo*, p.264.

CHAPTER FOUR

Guiné-Bissau, Cabo Verde and São Tomé & Príncipe

Guiné-Bissau on 25 April

The most pressing problem facing the post-25 April regime in Lisbon and the one which first exposed the extent of its divisions over the issue of decolonization was that of Guiné-Bissau. The urgency of the issue was due to both military and political factors. Having fought by far the most successful of the guerrilla wars, the PAIGC was by the beginning of 1974 threatening to inflict simple military defeat on the Portuguese army. The PAIGC's deployment of surface-to-air missiles in March of the previous year had shaken the equilibrium of stalemate which had characterized the conflict from the mid-1960s. Portuguese morale, never high in this most dangerous of African postings, had now dipped to the point of mutiny.[1] The guerrillas, about 10,000 strong according to the later assessment of Luís Cabral, were laying plans for a new two-pronged offensive in the east and south in the coming wet season.[2]

Diplomatically too, the nationalist movement in Guiné was in a much more powerful position than those in Mozambique and Angola. The Republic of Guiné-Bissau, declared by the PAIGC in September 1973, had, by time of the Lisbon coup, been recognized by over eighty states. And, as the PAIGC leadership (though evidently not the Lisbon conspirators) knew, the Caetano regime had already conceded the seriousness of the situation by opening the secret London negotiations a few weeks before the coup. For post-coup Portugal, therefore, the real issue in Guiné was more one of recognition than decolonization and less to do with the transfer of power than the acknowledgement that such a transfer had effectively already taken place. Spínola's refusal to confront this reality in the first weeks after the coup not only hindered a settlement with Guiné itself, but complicated the entire negotiation process in Africa.

The MFA in Guiné was the most widely supported and most politically cohesive component of the movement, not only in Africa but throughout the Portuguese military as a whole. There were various reasons for this. The relative intensity of the war, combined with the absence of a settler community with which the garrison could merge, meant that the military in Guiné was particularly introverted in its activities and attitudes. Additionally, the impact of Spínola's governorship between 1968 and 1973, his fostering of an *esprit de corps* built around loyalty to himself, and the aura of dissent that went with it, had created a uniquely conspiratorial ambience. *Portugal and the Future* had had its genesis in Guiné and had passed in draft, *samizdat*-fashion, round Spínola's staff for comment and refinement. At one stage during Spínola's term, according to Carlos Fabião, there was a grand strategy which if successful would have removed the need for a military coup. The idea was that the 'Guiné boys' would gradually take over positions of power in Lisbon on the springboard of their mentor's prestige and effect a palace revolution which would put the federalist scheme into operation.[3] In a real sense Guiné was, in the words of one of the MFA radicals there, Captain Jorge Sales Golias, 'the cradle of the MFA . . . a scale model for what the MFA in Portugal was later to become'.[4] This climate of dissension persisted after Spínola's return to Lisbon and was sustained by the sharp contrast of approach by his unimaginative, hard-line successor, General Bettencourt Rodrigues. The irony for Spínola was that the spirit of rebellion which he himself had nurtured would be turned against him as the Guiné MFA pressed for a recognition of political and military realities which he was incapable of grasping.

News of the coup in Lisbon reached Bissau at 5.00 a.m. on 25 April. The next twenty-four hours were ones of huddled discussion and wary planning on the part of the local MFA. Although the movement was well-established in Bissau, there was considerable suspicion about the intentions of both Bettencourt Rodrigues and the omnipresent DGS. The decision to move came on the morning of the 26th when an MFA delegation of ten officers with a paratroop escort arrested the governor. Political prisoners were released and their places in jail taken by DGS officers. In effect Guiné-Bissau had its own military coup the day following that in the metropole. Bettencourt Rodrigues was sent back to Lisbon and his functions as governor and military commander taken over by officers who enjoyed the confidence of the MFA. Preoccupied with larger issues in Lisbon, the JSN was in no position to intervene in Guiné in the first days after the coup, even had it been motivated to do so.

Events on the broader political front moved quickly after 25 April. Léopold Senghor, the Senegalese president and Spínola's partner in the abortive 1972 plan for a negotiated settlement, was in France *en route* to China on the day of the Lisbon coup. He immediately sent two separate messages of congratulation and offers of his good offices to Spínola and to Mário Soares.[5] He had befriended Soares during the latter's exile in Paris and although the Socialist leader had as yet no formal standing in the new regime, it was clear that he would soon have a prominent role. Three days later, on 28 April, Spínola despatched Carlos Fabião and another of his trusted staff officers from his Guiné years, Nunes Barata, to see Senghor in Paris.[6] Senghor's advice at this meeting was that the 1972 plan for a gradual transfer of power and continuing formal links between Portugal and Guiné-Bissau was now dead. With scores of countries – including Senegal itself – having recognized the PAIGC's 1973 declaration of independence, Spínola had no room for manoeuvre on the transfer of power. Portugal should now, in Senghor's view, make a virtue of necessity by itself recognizing the Republic of Guiné-Bissau. By doing so it would not only extricate itself from the political and military quagmire of Guiné but also win considerable goodwill in the UN and the OAU which would ease the solution to the other African problems.[7] Spínola, still determined to assert his own control over developments in Africa, declined the advice.

In the meantime, on 6 May, the PAIGC Executive Committee met in Madina do Boé to consider its terms for talks with the new regime in Lisbon. According to the account of Basil Davidson, these were that the JSN should recognize the independence of Guiné declared the previous September and acknowledge the right to independence of the other African colonies. Talks could then begin with or without a cease-fire. To secure a cease-fire, however, Lisbon must in addition order the concentration of its forces at assembly points in preparation for evacuation and all military activity must cease.[8]

On the diplomatic front, Senghor continued to be active, motivated in part no doubt by his continuing rivalry with Sekou Touré of Guinea-Conakry and by a determination to lay the foundations of a special relationship between Senegal and the new Guiné-Bissau. On 17 May Soares, sworn-in just hours previously as foreign minister in the first provisional government, flew to Dakar in Senghor's personal jet to meet Aristides Pereira, the PAIGC secretary-general.

With him went Spínola's own men, in this case the head of his military office Lt. Col. Almeida Bruno and another of his Guiné staff, Major Manuel Monge.[9] The practice of placing his 'minders' at the side of civilian politicians in the African negotiations was to be followed by Spínola throughout his months in power. At this Dakar meeting Pereira agreed to an interim truce (though not, significantly, a 'cease-fire') on condition that it was part of a process leading to Portuguese withdrawal.[10] The British foreign secretary James Callaghan had meantime offered his good offices, and it was agreed in Dakar that substantive talks should begin in London ten days later.[11]

First Talks: London

The London meeting of 25–31 May was the first round of three which extended to the end of August. The vicissitudes of the negotiations parallelled political developments in Lisbon and were determined largely by the shifting balance of power between Spínola and his federalist followers on one hand and the growing alliance of those committed to total decolonization. The fulcral point in this balance – and in the fate of the negotiations – came with Constitutional Law 7/74 at the end of July. In the meantime, however, much scarce time and resources would be expended and much suspicion engendered as Spínola and his followers fought to maintain the possibility of a qualified independence.

The talks in London began in the Hyde Park Hotel amidst considerable optimism.[12] Initially the Portuguese delegation was composed of Soares, Jorge Campinos and Almeida Bruno – described by the Lisbon press as 'Spínola's right arm'.[13] The only intimation of future difficulties was the absence of Aristides Pereira from the PAIGC team which was led by its 'defence minister' and military commander Pedro Pires.[14] The arrangement was probably dictated by the politics of protocol on the part of the PAIGC. Their delegation was, after all, representing the Republic of Guiné-Bissau and not a guerrilla movement. It ought therefore to be led by a figure of equivalent rank to that at the head of the Portuguese delegation, that is to say, a 'cabinet minister'. It was a signal that Lisbon should have taken note of. The PAIGC delegation was also reported to be concerned at the absence of any specific reference to Cabo Verde on the agenda for the talks.[15]

By the second day of the talks the optimism was dissolving. The

PAIGC had declared that Portugal's recognition of the Republic of Guiné-Bissau was the absolute precondition for a cease-fire.[16] By the fourth day agreement was no closer. Aside from the substantive issues in dispute, the negotiating process was complicated by departures and arrivals in the Portuguese delegation. Half-way through the week of talks Soares left to attend to other business and was temporarily replaced at the head of the delegation by Almeida Santos and Almeida Bruno was later replaced by Manuel Monge. These disruptions were symptomatic of one of the principal problems of the Portuguese revolution: the imbalance between tasks of the greatest urgency and the resources of personnel available to meet them. Despite the hurried return of Soares on 29 May, the talks broke up two days later with no agreement and no communiqué. The only concrete results of the talks were the appointment of a PAIGC observer to the Portuguese administration in Bissau and the creation of a radio link between the Bissau authorities and the PAIGC's headquarters in Conakry.[17] A further round of talks was, however, agreed in principle for the following month.

Although thought by observers at the time to be a key point of conflict, it seems that the Cabo Verde issue was not a major stumbling block in the talks. Understandably, it was assumed that a movement which claimed a mandate for the liberation of both Guiné and Cabo Verde and their ultimate unification would resist the disaggregation of the two territories in negotiations. In its declaration of Guiné's independence in 1973, after all, the PAIGC had claimed Cabo Verde to be an integral part of a new 'African motherland'.[18] The issue had certainly caused difficulties at the secret pre-coup talks a few weeks earlier.[19] At the May negotiations, however, the PAIGC adopted a pragmatic approach to the question. In its original statement of position before the talks began it had merely stipulated: 'the recognition (by Portugal) of the Republic of Guiné-Bissau and the right of our people in Cabo Verde to self-determination and independence (and) the recognition of the same right for the peoples of the other Portuguese colonies'.[20] Clearly this fell far short of a demand for coupled negotiations. Immediately after the end of the London talks, the Lisbon weekly *Expresso* reported that a 'very good source' within the PAIGC delegation (possibly Gil Fernandes, the movement's representative in Scandinavia) had indicated that if Lisbon accepted the independence of Guiné there would be no difficulty in reaching a separate agreement on Cabo Verde based on the Spinolist notion of 'self-determination' by referendum.[21]

According to Almeida Santos, the PAIGC's willingness to treat the question of Cabo Verde separately was in part an acknowledgment of unresolved internal difficulties. The only group with unalloyed enthusiasm for the unification of the two territories was the Cabo Verdean element in the PAIGC leadership. Their Guinean counterparts looked forward to a reduction in Cabo Verdean influence (and a corresponding increase in their own) after the status of the two territories had been formally agreed with Lisbon.[22] The fact that one party had mobilized the anti-colonial movement in both territories should not, in this view, lead automatically to unification after independence. So far as it was possible to judge, this thinking was shared by the broader populations of each territory. Spínola probably overstated the case when he argued that the PAIGC had only ever embraced Cabo Verde in its title as a means of legitimizing the dominance of its leadership by Cabo Verdeans, but strong and enduring elements of a unified culture were in truth difficult to locate.[23] Unification remained a formal aim of the PAIGC but it was not one which was pursued with any energy either before or after Portuguese withdrawal. The real problem at the London talks was simply Portugal's refusal to acknowledge the PAIGC state in Guiné and begin the withdrawal of the colonial army.

Léopold Senghor, who had urged just this course of action immediately after the coup, repeated his advice to Soares and his delegation which had travelled to Paris following the London talks.[24] The balance of political power in Lisbon, however, had not yet shifted sufficiently for Senghor's urgings to be heeded. Indeed, far from concentrating minds in Lisbon on the realties of power in Guiné, the failure of the first round of talks led Spínola to propose the abandonment of negotiations until the PAIGC proved more open to his views. He was dissuaded by Mário Soares and leaders of the metropolitan MFA, but conceded no more than a grudging agreement to a further round of talks.[25]

The Algiers Negotiations

In view of Spínola's intractability, the Portuguese delegation arrived in Algiers (the venue for the second round of talks) on 13 June with little expectation of further progress.[26] The normally upbeat Almeida Santos could only summon 'prudent optimism'.[27] Even this proved unjustified and the talks collapsed after one day when Pires left the conference room observing ominously that 'there is no cease-fire. There are truces.'[28] The bullishness of the Guinean delegation in Algiers derived in large part from the PAIGC's growing diplomatic support. After the London talks the PAIGC had launched a major international campaign. More countries were persuaded to recognize Guiné's independence including, to Lisbon's discomfort, some notably non-radical ones like Brazil and Japan. Guiné-Bissau was admitted to the OAU as its 42nd member with Luís Cabral being nominated as vice-president at its annual summit in Mogadishu at the beginning of June. At this meeting the UN secretary-general, Kurt Waldheim, had insisted that Portugal must comply with General Assembly resolutions and recognize the independence of Guiné.[29]

In Lisbon Spínola seemed not to take cognizance of the realities either on the ground in Guiné or in the diplomatic arena. On the contrary, his public pronouncements seemed almost designed to sabotage the negotiations. At Algiers the PAIGC delegation protested at a speech he had made on the eve of the negotiations re-emphasizing the regime's commitment to controlling the process of self-determination in Africa. The offending address had been made at the swearing-in ceremony of new governors-general for Angola and Mozambique. Spínola had insisted that 'decolonization' would involve the creation, implicitly by Portugal, of 'schemes of full democratic participation and an accelerated regionalization of political, social and economic structures [and] recourse to a referendum [*consulta popular*] as the means of realizing these plans'.[30] The federalist project was clearly still alive for the General.

An indispensable prerequisite for pluralism, of course, was a plurality of participants in the type of *consulta* envisaged by the Spinolists. 'Third forces' were required and in Guiné they were frankly thin on the ground. The main non-PAIGC grouping remained the now venerable FLING which had competed briefly for the leadership of Guinéan nationalism in the 1950s and early 1960s. FLING now re-emerged from a more or less dormant exile in Dakar. The smaller, but sporadically active, Liberation Movement of Guiné (MLG: Movimento de Libertação da Guiné) also attempted to mark out its political territory in Bissau as did the Guiné Democratic Movement (MDG: Movimento Democrático da Guiné) which had enjoyed the toleration of the colonial regime during the war.[31] None of these movements, though, was in a position to pose a serious challenge to the PAIGC whose influence was now dominant in more than two-thirds of the country.

The doctrine of 'revolutionary legitimacy' as justification for regarding the guerrilla movements as the sole legitimate representatives of their territories was emerging in Lisbon as a political and intellectual counterweight to the Spinolist scheme and in Guiné only the PAIGC could claim this legitimacy. The Spínola loyalist Manuel Monge attended an MFA assembly in Lisbon held on the eve of his departure to join the London negotiations at the end of May. At this he sought guidance on the line to pursue in the negotiations. The meeting became heated and soon split between those who wished, in Monge's words, 'to show firmness in defence of our interests' and those, represented by Otelo Saraiva de Carvalho, who called for total support for the liberation movements.[32] The dispute illustrated the widening divide between Spinolists and decolonizers in the MFA and, although Monge claimed that his own line prevailed on this occasion, it would not do so for much longer.

Frustration with Spínola's schemes and their deadening effect on the negotiations was felt beyond the MFA. On the eve of the Algiers talks the Socialists, now more confident of their role than in the period immediately following the coup, announced that they would consider abandoning the provisional government if the negotiations collapsed.[33] Increasingly, Spínola and the African nationalists appeared to occupy separate political planets, with the hapless civilian politicians of Lisbon's negotiating team hovering uncertainly in space between them. Beyond their personal preference for a settlement based on the recognition of the PAIGC's state Soares and Almeida Santos were political realists. They were aware that regardless of the preferences of the fragmented centres of power in Lisbon, the Guiné issue had already been decided at the international level. What prospect was there that the states – now rising towards a hundred – which had recognized the independence of Guiné under the PAIGC would withdraw that recognition on the outcome of a referendum organized by the colonial power?[34]

On 8 July Senghor attempted once more to persuade Spínola to accept the inevitable in a secret encounter aboard the Senegalese president's jet at Lisbon airport. Senghor now appealed to Spínola's sense of history and urged him to emulate de Gaulle in Algeria by bowing to the inevitability of the PAIGC's success.[35] Attempts to nurture the third force parties should be abandoned, Senghor insisted (he himself having given expression to this by expelling FLING from its Dakar base). One idea apparently discussed at this meeting was a face-saving device by which the *Congressos do Povo* which had been set up by Spínola during his governorship should proclaim independence jointly with the PAIGC.[36] Such a gesture could, with some creative interpretation, be taken as an act of self-determination sufficient to meet the doctrinal requirements of Spinolist theology.

This particular manoeuvre was not, in the event, pursued but it was becoming clear that Spínola would be unable to hold out much longer. He later recalled Senghor's insistence that the 'self-determination' phase had already passed in Guiné and that independence was 'the only viable solution consistent with the point in history that Portugal was passing through'.[37] The pressure from within the metropole and from the international system that would shortly force Spínola's acquiescence to Constitutional Law 7/74 was steadily mounting.

African Realities: Developments in Guiné

Along with these domestic and diplomatic pressures, events in the territory itself had been moving rapidly since the local MFA's *putsch* of 26 April. Although PAIGC operations had declined after the coup, and had more or less ended completely after the Soares–Pereira meeting in Dakar in the middle of May, its capacity to return to the offensive could be in no doubt.[38] After 25 April an accretion of interrelated factors made the position of the 30,000 Portuguese troops in Guiné different in degree if not in kind from that of their counterparts in Mozambique and Angola. The apparent invincibility of the enemy, desperately low morale, and the absence of any significant Portuguese human or economic resources to be protected, made the demand for immediate unconditional withdrawal which was spreading throughout the colonial military in Africa particularly powerful in Guiné. For the most part the motivation behind this was personal rather than political. But in a garrison predisposed towards political conspiracy and increasingly dominated by junior officers keen to legitimize instincts of self-preservation with the rhetoric of anti-colonial solidarity, the personal rapidly became the political.

Portuguese military action effectively ceased within a few days of the MFA taking control in Bissau.[39] But pressure was soon being exerted even on the MFA itself by self-professed leftist factions in the garrison such as the transiently influential Movement for Peace (MPP: Movimento para a Paz) for ever-stronger expressions of the soldiers' anti-war position.[40] In the two weeks following the coups in Lisbon and Bissau the MFA itself became the colonial administration. After the expulsion of Bettencourt Rodrigues, the

MFA had an army colonel and a naval commodore as governor and military commander respectively. These two worked in cooperation with the local MFA Coordinating Committee in what was effectively a provisional government. The assumption underlying all MFA activity in Bissau was that the structures being created would facilitate an early transfer of power to the PAIGC in the capital and a consequent Portuguese withdrawal.

This did not, of course, coincide with Spínola's plans for his old political springboard. On 7 May the newly promoted Brigadier Carlos Fabião arrived in Bissau as JSN 'delegate' (in effect as governor and military commander) to implement the General's directives. Spínola had chosen Fabião both for his personal loyalty and for his understanding of the local situation.[41] Having undertaken five tours of duty in Guiné from 1955 onwards, he had a unique awareness of the ethnic complexities of the territory and a knowledge of its local languages. During his last posting from 1971 to 1973, which he accepted at Spínola's personal request, he had been in charge of the locally recruited militias. Spínola now required him 'to continue the political process of self-determination (previously) initiated . . . '.[42] This would have involved the resuscitation of Spínola's hearts and minds approach of 1968–73 and the reinvigoration of the *Congressos do Povo*. He was also to stamp out the insubordination of the local MFA and make contact with the PAIGC but maintain a defensive posture until a cease-fire was guaranteed.[43]

The initial encounter between Fabião and the MFA in Bissau was a difficult one.[44] He was, though, sufficiently astute to reach a quick appreciation of the utter incompatibility of Spínola's aspirations with the circumstances in Guiné. As he later recalled, Spínola's prestige in the territory had disappeared even among his one-time African supporters: 'the Lisbon "senhor" was finished with the arrival of the Revolution . . . Now the master was called PAIGC.'[45] To Spínola's enduring sense of betrayal, Fabião 'went over' to the local MFA. 'Brigadier Fabião', the General later complained, 'not only showed himself incapable of controlling the situation; he had also practically transformed himself into a mere agent of the PAIGC, accepting positions and striking attitudes manifestly contrary to his military background and to the undertakings he made on leaving for Bissau'.[46]

Whatever Spínola's opinion of him, Fabião proved to be a pragmatic and effective manager of the situation in the territory. It was his misfortune to be required to achieve the unachievable and to his credit that he quickly recognized this and adjusted his objectives accordingly. For Fabião to have pitched himself directly against the local MFA's *de facto* administration in Bissau would have been dangerous and futile. Working with the MFA was the only feasible means by which he could influence events. The Guiné MFA had, moreover, won the backing of the movement in the metropole after a visit by a delegation of the Lisbon Coordinating Committee at the beginning of June. For Fabião not to have cooperated with the MFA in Bissau would have been to import to the territory the cleavages currently bedevilling politics in Lisbon. With the MFA now holding mass assemblies to demand the recognition of the PAIGC's republic, Fabião had no choice but to disregard his original orders despite the strain this placed on his sense of personal loyalty.[47]

As the deadlocked negotiations in London and Algiers put the general truce agreed by Pereira in Dakar in jeopardy, Fabião sought local agreements with PAIGC commanders to maintain the peace throughout the territory.[48] His initiative was supported by General Costa Gomes but had only the grudging acquiescence of Spínola.[49] As part of this general accommodation, and much against Spínola's wishes, the Portuguese began to evacuate their fortified positions in the operational zones and concentrate in Bissau.[50] Spínola's authority was further undermined when a group of MFA radicals he had ordered to be returned to Lisbon was permitted to go back to Bissau after a few days with the approval of Costa Gomes.[51] To all practical purposes Spínola's influence on events in Guiné had gone by the middle of July.

The Settlement

By the beginning of August not only had the political and constitutional obstructions to the negotiating process with the PAIGC been removed by Law 7/74, but extraneous pressures as well continued to build a momentum towards an early settlement. The issue of Mozambique was becoming urgent, and the resources for maintaining simultaneous negotiating processes were simply not available. Additionally, at the end of July the PAIGC had formally sought the admission of the Republic of Guiné-Bissau to the United Nations with every likelihood of success. The prospect of a series of denunciations of Portuguese imperialism at the September UN General Assembly, the first since the coup, was not relished in Lisbon. Consequently, during the preliminary Security Council discussion on Guiné's application Veiga Simão announced the imminent acceptance by Portugal of the legitimacy of the PAIGC's claims to independence.[52] Law 7/74 was now applicable, after all, and any further delay in reaching a settlement would be pointlessly damaging to Portugal's international standing.

Contacts were quickly re-established with the PAIGC and a third round of talks arranged for Algiers to begin on 22 August with a more or less general assumption of success. Agreement was reached four days later. It was announced that Portugal would relinquish its residual power in Guiné-Bissau on 10 September and that all Portuguese troops would be repatriated by 31 October.[53] The agreement was immediately ratified by the JSN and the provisional government and finally, on 29 August, by Spínola himself as president of the Republic. On 17 September, a year after the PAIGC's unilateral declaration of independence and a week after Lisbon's recognition of it, Guiné-Bissau, sponsored by Portugal, was admitted to the United Nations.

The Portuguese evacuation was effected without serious incident and with the active cooperation of the PAIGC. The tranquillity of the last days of the imperial presence was marred only by an outbreak of lawlessness in Bissau in the climate of uncertainty surrounding the withdrawal. To meet the problem Fabião exercised his characteristic pragmatism for the last time in Guiné by inviting Luís Cabral (whose presidency of the new republic would be formally recognized by Portugal at independence) to provide PAIGC detachments for joint patrols.[54] The one jarring note was to be heard not in Bissau but in Lisbon where Spínola, in one of the final addresses of his presidency, gave vent to his bitterness at the outcome of events in Guiné. In a speech supposedly celebrating the passing of Portuguese imperialism there he spoke in a tone of peevish condescension. Decolonization should not, he complained, mean 'the transfer pure and simple of power to the partisan organizations which maintained the armed struggle against the previous Portuguese regime'. Decolonization had to do with the implantation of pluralism and multi-party democracy. A supposed decolonization which in reality meant merely 'the appropriation of power by certain ideologies and the totalitarian regimes that go with them' should be resisted, and to 'defend the African territories from the risk of this new slavery is an obligation of conscience to which all who support the democratic ideology should be alert'.[55]

Putting on one side the somewhat questionable ethical bases of Spínola's grievance – and in both the national and international climate of the time they appeared scant – the possibility of doing anything about it in practical political terms simply did not exist. In April 1975, reviewing the dizzying pace of events over the previous year, Almeida Santos summed up the Guiné question with a clear-minded realism. There had been altogether too much hesitation over the negotiations between May and August. The choice for Portugal was quite simple: recognize Guiné's independence or renew the war. There was no practical possibility of the latter given the attitude of the Portuguese garrison which 'meant that war, as well as being undesirable, had become impossible. In other words there was only one option – immediate peace.'[56] The final agreement in Algiers had effectively met the original demands laid out by the PAIGC at the first post-coup session in London. The only significant dilution was the acceptance of Cabo Verde as a separate issue for negotiation. The extent to which even this 'concession' was truly a victory for the Spinolists as opposed to the grateful acceptance by the PAIGC of an opportunity to evade a final reckoning with its own internal divisions was, as we have observed, open to question.

Cabo Verde

Removed from the negotiations over Guiné, the issue of Cabo Verde remained to be dealt with in the latter part of 1974. Although disaggregated, the settlements in the two territories were still connected through the preponderant position of the PAIGC in each. Portugal's commitment to negotiate the independence of Cabo Verde was made explicit in the Algiers agreement over Guiné.

The implication of this was that, separate from Guiné or not and regardless of the longer term prospects for unification, the outcome of the process in Cabo Verde would be the independence of an 'African' state. This was not readily accepted by Spínola and his supporters, even after their recognition of the inevitable in Guiné. The geographical position of Cabo Verde and its peculiar social and ethnic composition offered hope to those who still nurtured a belief in some type of federal solution to the problem of the *ultramar*. Separated from Africa by 650 km of the Atlantic and with a Creole population drawing on the genes of innumerable ethnicities, Cabo Verde's 'Africanness' was certainly qualified. It was argued by many, and not just those close to Spínola's general position, that the archipelago could be considered as much European as African. Lisbon had historically treated Cabo Verde as separate from the

African territories. Perhaps most significantly, the 'native statute' had never applied to the archipelago and its inhabitants had thus been 'Portuguese citizens' long before ·the status was extended to the population of the empire as a whole.

In Spínola's view, 'Cabo Verde had reached an advanced stage of cultural development closer to that of the metropole than that of Guiné . . . its origins, in terms of settlement and population, were similar to those of the Azores and Madeira archipelagos, putting in doubt the basis of its classification as a colonial territory . . . '.[57] No specific reference to Cabo Verde was made in his address to the nation on the promulgation of Law 7/74 at the end of July. In this he committed Portugal to 'initiating the process of the transfer of powers to the populations of the overseas territories *recognizably suitable for the purpose,* namely Guiné, Angola and Mozambique' (emphasis added).[58] Even Mário Soares, while remaining guarded on the question during the negotiating process, was later to claim that he 'was always convinced that Cabo Verde had more to gain as a region [of Portugal] than it would have had as an independent African country'. In his view too, Cabo Verde was 'not really Africa'.[59]

Other special factors complicated consideration of Cabo Verde's post-imperial future. One was the strategic importance of its geographical position at a time when, in spite of the general *détente* between the superpowers, naval competition was sharpening in the South Atlantic. The anti-western orientation of the PAIGC during the armed struggle and its political and material debt to the Soviet bloc was universally recognized. Although insisting that such considerations were irrelevant to any agreement, Lisbon's negotiators would have been aware of the sensitivities of a Washington administration still uncertain of the direction of the Portuguese revolution.[60] Quite apart from culture, ethnicity and even global strategy, the harsh practicalities of climate and economy also raised questions about the viability of Cabo Verde as an independent state. Suffering its eighth year of severe drought in 1975, the archipelago was wholly dependant on Lisbon for its economic survival.

The weeks following 25 April in Cabo Verde were ones of frenetic and occasionally violent political activity. Despite the absence of any armed opposition to the colonial authorities in the territory during the course of the war in Guiné, the PAIGC had been operating clandestinely and after the Lisbon coup its front organizations began to emerge publicly. The most important of them was the Broad Front of National Resistance (FARN: Frente Ampla de Resistência

Nacional) which immediately embarked on a large-scale campaign of mobilization.[61] But the PAIGC was far from totally implanted in the territory and the month of May 1974 saw pro-Spínola and anti-PAIGC demonstrations. There appeared to be a genuine and widespread fear at this time that the London talks with the PAIGC would bring an independence conditional on unification with Guiné.[62]

The prospect for the development of viable third force parties in Cabo Verde was much greater than in Guiné. Following the Lisbon coup two significant groupings emerged. The Democratic Union of Cabo Verde (UDCV: União Democrática de Cabo Verde) was an anti-independence party which sought to maintain the link with Portugal, although on a different constitutional basis than hitherto. The People's Union of the Cabo Verde Islands (UPICV: União do Povo das Ilhas de Cabo Verde) was a radical leftist group formed by Cabo Verdean students who had returned from universities in the metropole and could loosely be described as Trotskyist. The UPICV was pro-independence but strongly against unification with Guiné through the PAIGC.

It is difficult to assess the support of these groupings in the period between 25 April and the independence agreement in November 1974. Both parties evidently enjoyed preferential treatment during the period of Spínola's presidency, the UDCV as the torch carrier of the federalist solution, the UPICV as a convenient radical counterweight to the PAIGC. They were, for example, allowed to broadcast from the local radio station, Rádio Barlvento, a facility withheld from FARN.[63] There was undoubtedly considerable suspicion in the islands of the PAIGC's intentions, especially in regard to unification. Local opinion was, moreover, open to influences wider than those of Lisbon and the PAIGC. With an emigrant population somewhat larger than the resident one, political views came back with financial remittances from family and friends world-wide. One of the most significant of the Cabo Verdean communities overseas was in the United States and this was strongly anti-PAIGC.[64] Spínola meanwhile obstructed the entry to the territory of Cabo Verdean PAIGC leaders attempting to return from Guiné to mobilize support.[65]

Yet neither of the third force parties managed to pose a durable challenge to the PAIGC and both had more or less disappeared by the end of the summer of 1974.[66] In mid-1975 Almeida Santos observed that in the six months following the Lisbon coup the situation had been transformed from one of generalized opposition to the PAIGC in Cabo Verde to one of almost total support.[67] This quite dramatic change in political climate derived from a variety of factors. As in all matters of the *ultramar* at this time, the 'official' Portuguese position was difficult to locate. While Spínola was able to exert some influence on events during the course of his presidency, other forces pulled in different directions. His refusal to allow the return of PAIGC cadres, for example, was hotly disputed by both Carlos Fabião in Bissau and General Costa Gomes in Lisbon.[68] Meanwhile, elements in the local MFA were openly supportive of the PAIGC through contacts with FARN.[69] The strongest counter to the Spinolist position was probably the Portuguese governor, Commander Henrique da Silva Horta, who had been nominated by the JSN and sworn in by Spínola himself in July. Left largely alone as other more pressing African issues occupied Lisbon's attention, Silva Horta saw the facilitation of the pro-independence movement as integral to the spirit of 25 April, and hardly concealed his sympathies. He was dismissed by Spínola after barely a month in office but not before exerting considerable influence on events.[70]

Horta was replaced by the more compliant Sérgio Duarte Fonseca, a Cabo Verdean native and a former colonial secretary-general of the territory. At his swearing-in Spínola caused a flutter of apprehension within the provisional government in Lisbon when he spoke of his willingness to use force to prevent any attempt to restrict freedom of political choice in Cabo Verde.[71] The alternative prospects of, on the one hand, Portuguese soldiers firing on PAIGC supporters in Cabo Verde or, on the other, of refusing to do so were equally appalling. Spínola made his remarks, however, with barely a week of his presidency remaining. His instructions to Fonseca and the empty threats of armed force which he used to bolster 'his' governor's authority now merely confirmed the extent of division within the regime. General Costa Gomes objected to Fonseca's extended powers and his direct line of responsibility to Spínola on the grounds that they subverted proper military and political hierarchies.[72] At the same time, Fonseca's 'Spinolist' identity caused difficulties in his relations with the local MFA in Cabo Verde.[73] Hopelessly compromised in the final phase of an increasingly unequal metropolitan power struggle, Fonseca could do nothing to reverse the growing tide of PAIGC support in Cabo Verde.

A further factor in the failure of the third force parties to make any long-term impact on the political process was the PAIGC's largely successful effort to allay concerns over unification with Guiné. PAIGC spokesmen from Aristides Pereira down insisted that although the party had a commitment to unification in principle, nothing would be done without a democratic vote in Cabo Verde.[74] The possibility of effective third force intervention was also weakened by the diplomatic setting in which a solution to the Cabo Verde issue was being pursued. The PAIGC was recognized by both the OAU and the UN General Assembly as the sole legitimate political voice of Cabo Verde.[75] Kurt Waldheim's visit to Lisbon in the midst of the negotiating process at the beginning of August 1974 reconfirmed existing resolutions and the responsibility of Lisbon to negotiate independence agreements within their terms.[76] Once again, the Spinolist project foundered amidst the cross-currents of revolutionary politics in Lisbon and the exigencies of international organizations.

The fall of Spínola at the end of September 1974 gave a decisive thrust to developments. Senior PAIGC cadres, including Pedro Pires, were now able to move freely between Guiné and Cabo Verde. The other parties ceased to operate, lacking, in the words of Almeida Santos, 'motivation, organization or right'.[77] A series of meetings in Lisbon in October 1974 roughed out the form of an agreement. What emerged was essentially a hybrid between the Spinolist idea of a *consulta* and the liberation movements' (and increasingly the MFA's) insistence on the transfer of power to groupings legitimized by revolutionary action. The broad terms of the settlement were outlined by Almeida Santos in a speech to the UN General Assembly at the beginning of December. A transitional government was to be established with a Portuguese high commissioner and five ministers (or 'state secretaries'), three of which would be nominated by the PAIGC and two by the Portuguese president. The transitional government would prepare for the election of a constituent assembly – in which only PAIGC candidates would stand – in June 1975. This assembly would then vote on the issue of independence.[78] On 18 December the high commissioner, Almeida d'Eça, assumed his duties and the transitional government took office on 30 December.

The apparent ease with which the agreement was concluded after the fall of Spínola concealed some difficult negotiations. Talks between Pedro Pires and Almeida Santos were held intermittently between 15 and 22 November and were, according to the latter, in danger of deadlock. The Portuguese position was undermined by the MFA in Cabo Verde which, suspicious of delay in concluding an agreement and increasingly conscious of its own power, had sent an ultimatum to Lisbon threatening simply to transfer authority to the PAIGC and arrange a military withdrawal on its own behalf. Pires, aware of this support, was reluctant to accept even the highly qualified *consulta* prefigured in the proposed agreement. Eventually, however, the condition was accepted and the final agreement was worked out during the course of one afternoon.[79] With the subsequent agreement of Mário Soares and Ernesto Melo Antunes on the Portuguese side and of the PAIGC leadership in Bissau, the plan was finalized in time for Almeida Santos's speech to the UN General Assembly on 3 December.

The period of transitional government passed without significant incident. On 30 June 1975 the constituent assembly elections were held. All fifty-six PAIGC candidates were elected, including Pedro Pires and Aristides Pereira. The PAIGC took 92 per cent of the vote on an 85 per cent turn-out. Following the constitutionally required – but effectively predetermined – vote of the assembly, Cabo Verde celebrated its independence on 5 July. Aristides Pereira became president and Pedro Pires prime minister. The streets of Bissau were, reportedly, deserted on independence day as hundreds of PAIGC militants travelled to Cabo Verde on a ship provided by Cuba to join the celebrations.[80] Revolutionary solidarity notwithstanding, however, little was said of unification and no commitments made for its pursuit. To Almeida Santos it had been 'the most perfect decolonization' of them all.[81]

São Tomé & Príncipe

The island group of São Tomé & Príncipe lying 240 km off the coast of west-central Africa was the smallest of the African colonies to be dealt with after 25 April. The territory had a population which, in the words of Almeida Santos, would have fitted into a football stadium (73,600). It had undergone no armed struggle and, unlike Cabo Verde, had no complicating political linkages with other Portuguese territories. For these reasons São Tomé & Príncipe was left fairly well alone by Lisbon in the immediate aftermath of 25 April. It was assumed in the metropole that the complex but rigid social structure of the islands would be sufficient to maintain stability in the interim. This socio-cultural hierarchy – running from the 'contract' labourers from the mainland *via* different degrees of 'nativehood' and skin-tone to the European cocoa 'plantocracy' which employed them – would, it was hoped, hold firm despite the egalitarian upheavals elsewhere in the empire.

It was an unrealistic expectation. The period after 25 April brought increasing social instability and labour unrest to the islands.

But São Tomé & Príncipe still took a low priority in the stretched resources of the new regime as it sought to manage the transformation of the larger, war-afflicted territories. The governor on 25 April, Colonel Cecílio Gonçalves, remained in post while his counterparts elsewhere were recalled (or ejected) to Portugal. According to Spínola, the lack of activity over São Tomé & Príncipe on the part of the JSN merely reflected an assumption that, given its size and position, there would be no significant change in its constitutional status and certainly no likelihood of independence.[82]

At the end of July Colonel Gonçalves asked to be relieved and was replaced by a pro-MFA officer, Lt. Col. Píres Veloso. The appointment of this leftward-leaning governor served, probably unintentionally, to keep the situation in the territory at least manageable despite the continuing social unrest. Otherwise events were allowed to develop without significant intervention by Lisbon until late September 1974. By then the regime's energies could be re-directed from Guiné-Bissau and Mozambique while the departure of General Spínola removed a major political complication from the decolonization negotiations.

The obvious interlocutor for Lisbon was the Movement for the Liberation of São Tomé & Príncipe (MLSTP: Movimento para a Libertação de São Tomé e Príncipe) which had been established in 1960 and was led by Miguel Trovoada and Manuel Pinto da Costa as president and secretary-general respectively. Although lacking – in the absence of armed struggle – the 'revolutionary legitimacy' of the other movements, the status of the MLSTP was given weight by its participation in the CONCP of which it had been a founder member and which recognized it as the sole legitimate voice of the islands. Similar recognition had been given by the OAU in 1962.[83]

The extent of the MLSTP's support in the territory was, however, very limited as it had operated since its formation only in exile (and not a particularly active one) in the Gabon capital Libreville. Spínola's dismissal of the MLSTP as a 'pseudo-movement (without) the least audience' in the territory was exaggerated, but perhaps not wildly so.[84] After 25 April the MLSTP worked in the colony through a front movement, the Civic Association (AC: Associação Cívica). The relationship between the MLSTP and the AC was broadly similar to that between the PAIGC and FARN during the same period in Cabo Verde. With the generally lower level of nationalist political organization in São Tomé & Príncipe, however, the AC developed a more distinct identity from the MLSTP than FARN ever did from the PAIGC. This separation between the components of the movement was to develop into a troublesome schism during the immediate pre-independence period. The AC became in effect a radical populist faction of the MLSTP, an identity developed and consolidated through its intensive and successful labour agitation after 25 April.

The energies of the AC during the period before negotiations were expended partly on meeting the challenge of an embryonic third force party, the Free Popular Front (FPL: Frente Popular Livre). In truth, the challenge was hardly more than nominal. The FPL was denied the special privileges extended to the UDCV and UPICV by the colonial administration in Cabo Verde, and proved incapable of making a significant impact on local politics. However unequal, though, the contest did contribute to the process of politicization of the territory's population.

The first talks about talks over the future of São Tomé & Príncipe took place at a deliberately low key when a delegation was sent by Mário Soares to Libreville at the beginning of October 1974 to meet Pinto da Costa as well as non-MLSTP interests. So low profile was this encounter that even Almeida Santos seemed to be unaware it was taking place. The meeting grew out of talks Soares had had with Miguel Trovoada in New York during the 1974 UN General Assembly. Pressure, though, was also being applied by the MFA in the territory which had become increasingly alarmed at the deteriorating social situation and the lack of obvious movement on the part of Lisbon.[85] Eventually, at the end of October, Lisbon agreed to move ahead with substantive negotiations. These began on 23 November in the now familiar venue of Algiers with Almeida Santos and Jorge Campinos negotiating with the MLSTP as sole interlocutor.

The agreement that emerged on 26 November 1974 was similar in its essentials to that concluded with the PAIGC over Cabo Verde. It was in effect a compromise which genuflected towards the notion of a *consulta* in the form of a pre-independence election but which, by restricting the candidates in that election to a list drawn up by the MLSTP, amounted to an acceptance of an independent São Tomé & Príncipe under a single-party regime. A transitional government was to be composed of a Portuguese high commissioner, a prime minister nominated by the MLSTP, four other MLSTP ministers and one appointed by Lisbon who would have the role of liaising between the cabinet and the high commission. Pires Veloso was re-appointed as high commissioner and the MLSTP's Leonel d'Alva became prime minister. As in Cabo Verde, the transitional government was to be responsible for the organization of elections for a constituent assembly which would vote on the issue of independence.

The negotiating process too had been similar to that with the PAIGC over Cabo Verde in that the agreement was not reached as smoothly as prior assumptions had promised. This time the complicating third party was not the local MFA but Gabon. With Miguel Trovoada prevented by illness from participating in the negotiations, the MLSTP side was led by Pinto da Costa who was known to be particularly close to the Gabonese government. Sensing an opportunity to avoid even a constituent assembly election, da Costa held out for independence with an automatic transfer of power to the MLSTP. He justified this position on the grounds that no other outcome would be acceptable to Gabon. At critical points in the negotiation, Almeida Santos recalled, Pinto da Costa would leave the table to seek telephone advice from his Gabonese advisers.[86]

Eventually agreement was reached through an unlikely alliance between the Portuguese delegation, the Algerian government and the CONCP observers from the PAIGC, Frelimo and MPLA. Almeida Santos threatened to withdraw from the negotiations and was supported by quiet pressure from the Algerian foreign minister, Abdelaziz Bouteflika, with whom, after the blizzard of Portuguese–African negotiations held in Algiers, he was now on close and friendly terms. The other CONCP movements had little interest in supporting Lisbon *per se* but they were anxious to counter the influence of francophone Gabon, widely regarded among African radicals as one of the most compromised of the continent's 'neo-colonials'.[87] Bowing to this combined pressure, the MLSTP accepted the requirement of the *consulta* and the transitional government took office on 21 December 1974.

The transition period in São Tomé & Príncipe was not to be as tranquil as that in Cabo Verde. The labour unrest which began spontaneously after 25 April and which was later exploited by the AC in pursuit of the independence campaign continued after the Algiers agreement. Only a temporary rise in the international price of cocoa prevented a major economic disaster by offsetting the effects of falling production. Almeida Santos's vision of São Tomé & Príncipe as 'a sort of Atlantic Switzerland of Portuguese language and culture' soon seemed misperceived, to say the least.[88] The territory's difficulties came to a head in late March 1975 when the two AC radicals who had been nominated by the MLSTP for the key portfolios of labour and justice in the transitional government demanded the dismantling of the Portuguese military force in the territory. Their scheme was to convert this unit, which was composed almost entirely of local soldiers, into a 'people's militia'. The plan posed a threat both to the pre-independence *consulta* and to the security of the European agricultural and commercial community which had already been shaken by the labour disputes of the past year.[89] Pires Veloso rejected the demands outright on the grounds that they were in contravention of the Algiers agreement. Threatening to return to Lisbon and advise an immediate Portuguese withdrawal and the cessation of all economic assistance, he managed to stiffen the wavering resolve of the mainstream MLSTP leadership.[90] The dissident ministers left for Gabon and a certain stability was re-established.

The crisis highlighted the special vulnerability of micro-states with small fragmented polities and uncertain social and economic foundations. This political precariousness would bedevil the post-independence politics of the territory but in the short-term the remaining period before the constituent assembly elections on 7 July passed with little incident. Some 25,000 electors were registered – about 97 per cent of those eligible. On 12 July 1975 São Tomé & Príncipe became independent under the presidency of Manuel Pinto da Costa.

The energy expended both in the metropole and Africa during the seven-month period between the first contacts with the PAIGC in Dakar and the conclusion of the Algiers agreement with the MLSTP would have been impressive even if it had been directed only at the negotiation of Portuguese withdrawal from Guiné, Cabo Verde and São Tomé & Príncipe. Yet in many respects these territories were the least of the problems surrounding the liquidation of the Portuguese empire. The outcome in Guiné was inevitable, and only the refusal of General Spínola and his supporters to acknowledge this prevented a more efficiently managed withdrawal. Given the standing of the PAIGC internationally, as well as the economic 'expendability' of Cabo Verde to the metropole, it was unlikely that Lisbon would be either able or willing to obstruct the transfer of power there as well. By extension, after the example of Cabo Verde, it was unlikely that local demand for a similar settlement in São Tomé & Príncipe would be resisted. It is unknown whether Marcello Caetano, now in his Brazilian exile, drew any satisfaction from this apparent vindication of his imperial domino theory.

Notes

1 Jorge Sales Golias, 'O MFA na Guiné', *Seminário: 25 de Abril 10 Anos Depois* (Lisbon: Associação 25 de Abril 1984), p.313.

2 Interview in *Expresso Revista*, 2 July 1994.

3 Interview with Carlos Fabião in Maria João Avillez, *Do Fundo da Revolução* (Lisbon: Público 1994), pp.179–80.

4 Sales Golias, 'O MFA na Guiné-Bissau', pp.317.

5 Senghor interview with Fernando Pires, 2 December 1976, in *Palavras no Tempo* (Lisbon: *Diário de Notícias* 1990), p.174.

6 According to Fabião he himself was chosen for the mission because Spínola had already marked him out to take charge in Bissau, and Nunes Barata because he was known to Senghor from the 1972 talks. Fabião interview, *Do Fundo da Revolução*, p.181.

7 Fabião interview in Hugo Gil Ferreira and Michael W. Marshall, *Portugal's Revolution Ten Years On* (Cambridge: CUP 1986), pp.99–100.

8 Basil Davidson, *No Fist is Big Enough to Hide the Sun: The Liberation of Guiné and Cabo Verde – Aspects of an African Revolution* (London: Zed 1981), p.149.

9 At this stage it appears Soares knew nothing of Senghor's earlier Paris meeting with Fabião and Nunes Barata. Soares interview, *Do Fundo da Revolução*, p.269.

10 *Ibid.*

11 *Diário de Notícias*, 19 May 1974. It remains unclear why London was chosen as the location for the negotiations. It is possible that the venue was related to British involvement in arranging and hosting the secret talks in March 1974 between the previous Lisbon regime and the PAIGC. The nationalists would presumably have retained their contacts in London. Almeida Santos dismisses this possibility, however. Interview, Lisbon, 3 March 1995.

12 *República*, 24 May 1974.

13 *Diário de Notícias*, 25 May 1974.

14 *Ibid.*, 26 May 1974.

15 *Expresso*, 25 May 1974.

16 *The Times*, 26 May 1974.

17 Pedro Pezarat Correia, 'Portugal na hora de descolonização', António Reis, ed., *Portugal Contemporâneo*, vol.VI (1974–1992) (Lisbon: Alfa 1992), p.133.

18 The September 1973 declaration read: 'The state of Guiné-Bissau is a sovereign, republican, democratic, anti-colonialist and anti-imperialist state and has as its primary objectives the total liberation of the people [*sic*] of Guiné and Cabo Verde, and the construction of a union of these two territories in order to build a strong and progressive African motherland. The modality of this union will be established, after the liberation of the two territories, in accordance with the popular will.' PAIGC, *História da Guiné e Ilhas de Cabo Verde* (Porto: Afrontamento 1974), p.182.

19 *Expresso Revista*, 26 March 1994.

20 Cited in *Expresso*, 1 June 1974.

21 *Ibid.* Fernandes had also been one of the PAIGC delegates at the secret London talks with the previous regime.

22 Interview with António de Almeida Santos, Lisbon, 3 March 1995.

23 António de Spínola, *País sem Rumo: Contributo para a História de uma Revolução* (Lisbon: Scire 1978), pp.338–9.

24 *Ibid.*, p.276.

25 Grupo de pesquisa sobre a descolonização portuguesa, *Descolonização Portuguesa: Aproximação a um Estado* (Lisbon: Instituto Amara da Costa 1982), vol.2, p.26.

26 As with the original choice of London, the reasons for the move to Algiers are unclear. The desire of the PAIGC to negotiate on 'friendly territory' is one explanation. Another is the possibility of pressure from Sekou Touré who feared he had lost the initiative on the issue to his 'pro-western' rival Senghor and who now wished to bring the process back to 'radical' Africa. According to Basil Davidson, Sekou Touré had been informed in advance of the London talks and had initially raised no objection. Later, however, he made a number of radio broadcasts critical of the London venue which, in Davidson's view, were deliberately designed to undermine the PAIGC leadership, presumably because of its relationship with Senghor. *No Fist is Big Enough to Hide the Sun*, p.150.

27 Ministry of interterritorial coordination press release, 4 June 1974. Transcript in Almeida Santos, *15 Meses no Governo ao Serviço da Descolonização* (Lisbon: Representações Literária 1975), p.94.

28 *Expresso*, 15 June 1974.

29 *Ibid.*

30 António de Spínola, *Ao Serviço de Portugal* (Lisbon: Ática 1976), p.88.

31 Pezarat Correia, 'Portugal na hora de descolonização', pp.131–2.

32 Interview with Manuel Monge, *Do Fundo da Revolução* p.247.

33 *Descolonização Portuguesa*, vol.2, p.27.

34 The question was posed by an editorial in *Expresso* before even the preliminary meeting in Dakar between Soares and Pereira. *Expresso*, 11 May 1974.

35 *Africa Contemporary Record 1974–75* (London: Rex Collings 1975), p.B680.

36 *Expresso*, 13 July 1974.

37 Spínola, *País sem Rumo*, p.280.

38 Between the Lisbon coup and the end of May there were 102 'incidents' in which five Portuguese soldiers were killed and seventy-nine wounded. Carlos Fabião, 'A descolonização da Guiné-Bissau. Spinola: a figura marcante da guerra na Guiné', *Seminário: 25 de Abril 10 Anos Depois*, p.311.

39 The PAIGC accused the Portuguese of mounting air strikes against civilian targets as late as the middle of May but this was probably either mistaken information or a deliberate propaganda thrust just as the first talks were being planned. *República*, 17 May 1974.

40 Sales Golias, himself an MFA leftist, dismissed the movement as a focus for 'all the opportunists who wanted an immediate and irresponsible return to Portugal'. 'O MFA na Guiné', p.316.

41 Spínola, *País sem Rumo*, pp.273–4.

42 Quoted in Pezarat Correia, 'Portugal na hora de descolonização', p.131.

43 Spínola, *País sem Rumo*, p.274.

44 Sales Golias, 'O MFA na Guiné', p.315.

45 Fabião interview, *Do Fundo da Revolução*, p.182.

46 Spínola, *País sem Rumo*, p.279.

47 Rather poignantly, Fabião remained steadfast in his admiration for his former chief's early 'achievements' in Guiné. 'A descolonização da Guiné-Bissau', p.305.

48 A territory-wide agreement was concluded between Fabião and the PAIGC's José Araújo in the Mejo Forrest in the southern operational zone. Davidson, *No Fist is Big Enough to Hide the Sun*, pp.153–4.

49 Spínola, *País sem Rumo*, p.280.

50 Basil Davidson, 'Portuguese speaking Africa' Michael Crowder, ed., *The Cambridge History of Africa*, vol.8: *From c.1940 to c.1975* (Cambridge: CUP 1984), p.789.

51 Monge interview, *Do Fundo da Revolução*, p.248.

52 *Descolonização Portuguesa*, vol.2, pp.28–9.

53 Translation of the Algiers agreement in *Africa Contemporary Record 1974–75*, pp.C40–1.

54 Luís Cabral interview, *Expresso Revista*, 2 July 1994.

55 'Conceito de descolonização: Comunicação ao país no dia de independência da Guiné, em 11 [*sic*] de Setembro de 1974', Spínola, *Ao Serviço de Portugal*, p.175.

56 Interview with *Século Illustrada*, 26 April 1975, *15 Meses no Governo*, p.320.

57 Spínola, *País sem Rumo*, p.337.

58 Spínola, *Ao Serviço de Portugal*, p.148.

59 Soares interview, *Do Fundo da Revolução*, p.274.

60 Speaking on West German television on 9 October 1974 Soares insisted: '(w)e have set out a policy on decolonization which does not take into account issues of global strategy. We have said and we maintain that the future of Cabo Verde will be whatever the people, freely consulted, wish it to be.' Mário Soares, *Democratização e Descolonização: Dez Meses no Governo Provisório* (Lisbon: Dom Quixote 1975), p.154.

61 Basil Davidson, *The Fortunate Isles: A Study in African Transformation* (London: Hutchinson 1989), p.118. A second PAIGC grouping was the Democratic Action Group of Cabo Verde and Guiné (Grupo de Acção Democrática de Cabo Verde e Guiné).

62 *Africa Contemporary Record 1974–75*, p.B620.

63 Davidson, *The Fortunate Isles*, p.112.

64 Soares interview with *Portuguese Times* of Newark, New Jersey, in *Democratização e Descolonização*, p.53; Almeida Santos interview, *O Século*, 25 March 1975, *15 Meses no Governo*, pp.294–5.

65 *Expresso*, 19 October 1974.

66 The fate of the third party activists in Cabo Verde may have been a hard one. Manuel Monge, who was detained after a Spinolist coup attempt in March 1975, later claimed to have encountered the leadership of the anti-PAIGC parties in a cell in Lisbon's Caxias prison. Interview in *Do Fundo da Revolução*, pp.247–8.

67 Interview with *Sempre Fixe*, 12 July 1975, *15 Meses no Governo*, p.397.

68 Spínola, *País sem Rumo*, p.340fn.

69 Davidson, *The Fortunate Isles*, p.119.

70 Spínola had been angered to be confronted by pro-PAIGC demonstrators at his meeting on Angola with President Mobutu of Zaire which was held on Sal Island in Cabo Verde in mid-September. His anger became incandescent when he discovered the demonstrators had been flown in on the governor's own plane. Pezarat Correia, 'Portugal na hora de descolonização', p.142.

71 *Diário de Notícias*, 23 September 1974.

72 Spínola, *País sem Rumo*, p.343.

73 Davidson, *The Fortunate Isles*, p.117.

74 *Africa Contemporary Record 1974–75*, p.B621.

75 General Assembly resolution A/2918 of 14 November 1972 had designated the PAIGC as 'the sole and authentic representative of the people [*sic*] of Guiné and Cabo Verde'.

76 *A Capital*, 5 August 1974.

77 *O Século*, 23 April 1975.

78 UN Document A/PV.2305, 3 December 1974.

79 Interview with António de Almeida Santos, Lisbon, 3 March 1995.

80 *Descolonização Portuguesa*, vol.2, p.96.

81 Interview with *Sempre Fixe*, 12 July 1975, *15 Meses no Governo*, p.397.

82 Spínola, *País sem Rumo*, p.344.

83 Pezarat Correia, 'Portugal na hora de descolonização', p.144.

84 Spínola, *País sem Rumo*, p.344fn.

85 *Expresso*, 12 October 1974.

86 Interview with António de Almeida Santos, Lisbon, 3 March 1995. A Gabonese presidential aid was evidently lodged in the MLSTP team's official villa. *Expresso Revista* 30 November 1974.

87 *Ibid.*

88 The description was offered in a speech to the United Nations General

Assembly immediately after the decolonization agreement. UN Document
A/PV.2305, 3 December 1975.

89 *Descolonização Portuguesa,* vol.2, pp.98–9.
90 Pezarat Correia, 'Portugal na hora de descolonização', p.146.

CHAPTER FIVE

Mozambique

Mozambique and 25 April

The first months of 1974 had seen an intensification of the guerrilla campaign in Mozambique and on the eve of 25 April Frelimo was increasingly active in the central provinces of Tete, Manica and Sofala as well as its strongholds in Cabo Delgado and Niassa. The containment of the war in the north, a strategy which had been reasonably successful up until about 1970, had now unravelled. The southward expansion of the campaign brought the war ever closer to the main areas of European settlement. Hitherto distanced geographically from the war, the 170,000-strong white population in the territory had accepted the official line of the regime that Frelimo was weak, disorganized and no pressing threat to the territory's stability. As we have observed, the chilling realization by the settlers, particularly in rural areas, that the comforting assurances of the government were fictitious caused considerable problems in civil–military relations and contributed to the further decline of morale in the colonial army.[1]

While Frelimo's challenge to the colonial state was not of the order of that of the PAIGC in Guiné-Bissau, it was a significant one and evidently growing. In the aftermath of the April revolution, widely differing assessments were offered of the military situation in Mozambique. On the right it was claimed that Frelimo had been on the point of defeat until the Lisbon coup came to its rescue.[2] To the left the events of 25 April in Lisbon were almost coincidental to the outcome of a successful guerrilla campaign which was already poised on the verge of victory.[3] A more cautious assessment was offered twenty years later by General Diogo Neto, the air force commander in Mozambique on 25 April and subsequently a member of the JSN, who concluded that the war had been unwinnable by either side at the time of the coup and was likely to slump into stalemate.[4] It is unclear how much further in the short term Frelimo could have expanded its activities beyond the high point of early 1974. Its resources of personnel and material were finite and its supply lines increasingly extended while it still lacked a significant support base in the towns. And, despite the greater cohesion achieved in recent years under Samora Machel's leadership, it continued to suffer schisms and defections.

The substantive question, however, never arose. The political-military circumstances in the territory were transformed by the events of 25 April in Lisbon. The first word of the coup reached Mozambique in the mid-morning of 25 April. The news gave rise to considerable tension within the Portuguese political and military structures in the territory. The junior officers who welcomed the overthrow of the Caetano regime nevertheless feared that the balance of forces in Mozambique was such that the revolution might be resisted by force there. Particular concern was felt about the intentions of the local Public Security Police (PSP: Polícia de Segurança Pública) as well as the senior ranks in the army. The governor-general, General Pimentel dos Santos, was recalled by the JSN shortly after it took office but he initially kept his dismissal secret. Using the authority remaining to him, he planned a somewhat half-hearted counter-action which began with an attempt to close Lourenço Marques airport. Easily outmanoeuvred in this by a detachment of paratroops loyal to the MFA, he was finally removed from office on the evening of 27 April and replaced in the interim by the more reliable Colonel David Texeira.[5] A degree of calm had meanwhile been brought to the colony when the military commander, General Bastos Machado, pledged loyalty to the new Lisbon regime.

The situation in the territory remained unsettled in the weeks following the coup, however, with a significant part of the Portuguese high command in Mozambique remaining unenthusiastic about developments in the metropole. This high-level ambivalence was compounded further down the military structure by restiveness among the colonial army's African troops (about half of the total strength of 60,000 in Mozambique) who were increasingly concerned about where the turn of political events might leave them.[6] This uncertainty within the military could only aggravate the larger apprehensions of the settler communities. A strong and well-organized local MFA might have been successful in neutralizing some of these elements of instability by mobilizing decisive support for the revolution. The MFA in Mozambique, however, was the weakest in the three main African territories with neither the political power of that in Guiné nor the organizational strength of the Angolan movement.[7]

Caught off-guard by the speed and direction of events in Lisbon, Frelimo initially eased its military offensive.[8] But concerned that the predominant position of General Spínola in the new regime prefigured an attempt to impose the prescriptions of *Portugal and the Future*, the leadership remained cautious. On 27 April Frelimo's executive committee issued a lengthy statement. This congratulated the 'Portuguese democratic forces which had for years opposed actively and courageously the colonial war' and pronounced Frelimo's satisfaction in having itself contributed to the return of democracy in Portugal. But, it continued, 'if the Portuguese people has the right to independence and democracy the same rights cannot be denied to Mozambicans'. There followed a warning against any attempt to indulge in any Spinolist experiments:

> It is up to the Portuguese government to draw the totality of the lessons of past experience and understand fully that only the recognition of the right of the Mozambican people to independence, led by Frelimo its authentic and legitimate representative, can put an end to the war. Any attempt to evade the real problem can only end in sacrifices. The way to a solution to the problem is clear: recognition of the right of the Mozambican people to independence. If, however, the objective of the coup d'état is to find new ways of perpetuating the oppression of our people, then the leader of the Portuguese government should be aware that they will be met with our firm determination. The Mozambican people throughout ten years of heroic armed struggle has borne heavy sacrifices and the bloodshed of the best of its children in pursuit of the inalienable principle of sovereignty as a free and independent nation. . . . We cannot accept that democracy for the Portuguese people should serve as a cover to impede the independence of our people. Just as the Caetano period demonstrated plainly that there was no such thing as liberal fascism, it must be clearly understood that there is no such thing as democratic colonialism.[9]

A meeting of the executive committee was hastily convened in Dar es Salaam on 3 May. From this came the decision to exploit the post-coup confusion in Lisbon and Lourenço Marques by resuming the armed struggle with increased force.[10] Activity was stepped up on all fronts with the objective of increasing the psychological pressure on the settler community and improving Frelimo's bargaining position in the inevitable negotiations which would follow.[11] By July the guerrillas had opened a new front in Zambésia province in the central-north of the country and, in an gesture of limited strategic significance but of great symbolic importance, had captured their first town, Murrumbala, near the Malawian frontier.[12]

The ability of Frelimo to intensify and extend its operations between May and July 1974 was in no small part due to the accelerating disintegration of Portuguese military capacity in these months. To Spínola's supporters in Lisbon the federal project may have appeared to be more feasible in Mozambique than in Guiné-Bissau but it was a vision with little support on the ground. While politicized junior officers rejected it on ideological grounds, others, particularly in the non-commissioned ranks, regarded it simply as an obstacle to their repatriation.[13] The slogan *nem mais uma operação; nem mais um tiro* ('not one more operation; not one more shot') became widespread in the garrisons of the territory. Spínola's later assertion that commandos, paratroops and special forces remained disciplined and prepared to fight on had more to do with justifying his early intransigence than offering a realistic assessment of circumstances in the colony.[14]

General Costa Gomes visited Mozambique in the second week of May in order to assess the military situation and, as far as possible, reassure the settler community about its security. His message, tailored to the needs of different audiences, was necessarily ambiguous. Speaking publicly in Lourenço Marques he insisted that the military was fully committed to retain, by force if necessary, the political initiative in Lisbon's hands.[15] He was less confident of this in private, however, acknowledging that in the climate of expectation created by the April revolution, the Portuguese forces had 'reached the limits of psycho-neurological exhaustion'.[16] Partly to lessen the danger of military breakdown and partly as a contribution to the process of settlement, Costa Gomes ordered the Portuguese forces to cease offensive operations and restrict themselves to self-defence and protection of civilians.[17] Just as Frelimo was winding up its military machine, therefore, Portugal's was being wound down.

As the weeks passed without any apparent movement towards a political settlement, individual Portuguese military units on the initiative of their MFA cells began to negotiate local cease-fires with the guerrillas. In mid-June an agreement was reached in the Mueda area of Frelimo's Cabo Delgado heartland and at the end of July a cease-fire was arranged in Tete.[18] The fragmentation of military authority revealed by these *ad hoc* arrangements deeply troubled the Portuguese authorities both in Lisbon and Lourenço Marques. In a telegram to Lisbon on 23 July the governor-general reported that the MFA commissions for Cabo Delgado and Tete had met in Nampula and issued an ultimatum. A unilateral general cease-fire would be declared if Lisbon had not itself negotiated one by the end of the month and helicopter crews would no longer supply garrisons in the operational areas. The governor-general considered the situation to be 'extremely grave and threatening a rapid military collapse'.[19]

On 1 August the first indications of what that collapse might involve came with the surrender to Frelimo of the Portuguese garrison at Omar on the Tanzanian frontier and the evacuation over the border of the company which had manned it as prisoners of war. The details of the Omar affair remain somewhat vague. It is unclear whether the Portuguese soldiers actually surrendered or whether they were participating in a pro-Frelimo propaganda gesture which went rather further than they had expected. Certainly the Frelimo guerrillas that occupied the garrison took the trouble to make a full sound-recording of the incident.[20] Spínola had no doubts about the complicity of the garrison's supposed defenders. To him the affair was 'irrefutable proof of the depths of moral prostitution to which certain Portuguese soldiers had descended'.[21] Another account, from a different political perspective, has been offered by Pedro Pezarat Correia, himself a leading MFA figure in Angola. He suggests that the garrison had been led to believe – wrongly – that a general cease-fire had been agreed and had permitted the guerrillas to enter the base in the new spirit of fraternization. The vector of this misinformation had apparently been the national radio station, Rádio Clube de Moçambique, which in common with all the major information media was now in the hands of Frelimo sympathizers.[22]

Whatever the precise truth of the Omar incident, the issue of press and mass media control became a controversial one in the period from 25 April to the final agreement between Lisbon and Frelimo in September. Vítor Crespo, the future high commissioner, while generally sympathetic to Frelimo, was highly critical of the destructive effect of a partisan and frequently mendacious local media at this time. There was, in his view, a fundamental unreality about a situation in which an unresolved military campaign was being conducted with one side's own sources of information controlled by the other.[23] For Frelimo, though, this capture of the media was a major achievement which was particularly impressive in view of the movement's lack of any significant urban base at the time of the Lisbon coup. Following 25 April the movement had begun to mobilize support in Lourenço Marques through the re-establishment of an older grouping, the Centro Associativo dos Negros de Moçambique.[24] Its main backer in the towns, however, and its principal agent in controlling the media was the largely European leftist grouping the 'Democrats of Mozambique'. Originally a broad front of white opponents to the colonial regime – and the political base of interterritorial coordination minister António de Almeida Santos – the Democrats of Mozambique transformed itself after 25 April into an avowedly Marxist movement. A number of its members would hold ministerial office in the post-independence Frelimo regime, giving concrete expression to the movement's professed non-racialism. In the meantime, the Democrats of Mozambique placed themselves at the disposal of Frelimo's propagandizing efforts and, as a significant proportion of them were working journalists, they effectively delivered the media to the movement.[25]

Important as this control of the press and radio most certainly was in redressing Frelimo's relative weakness in many areas of the country, it inevitably added to the insecurity of the settler community. This insecurity, as we have seen, pre-dated 25 April. It was now hugely increased by the collapse of the Caetano regime, and the military, already in disfavour for its evident failure to deal with the 'terrorist problem', was now regarded with contempt by large sections of the white community and denounced as the agents of colonial disintegration. By the first week in May white demonstrations in Beira and other urban centres were degenerating into violence. This trouble in the towns contrasted with the gradual decline of the guerrilla war in the bush. The geographical impact of the war hitherto was thus inverted.[26]

A further element of instability came from the widespread industrial troubles that followed 25 April. In part a natural reaction to the sudden removal of decades of state repression and in part a calculated attempt to exploit an uncertain political situation for straightforward material ends, a wave of strikes in the weeks after the Lisbon coup paralysed the docks and railways, Mozambique's key economic resources. More worryingly in the longer term, many of the disputes began to assume a racial character, with black employees challenging the positions of white co-workers and managers.[27] The industrial troubles deepened the broader financial crisis provoked in Mozambique before 25 April by Lisbon's recent ruthless attempts to impose fiscal discipline within the empire. By the middle of August

1974 the territory had sufficient foreign currency reserves to pay for only one week's essential imports.[28] On top of these social and economic uncertainties, a report by General Bastos Machado calculated that in mid-May about 3000 armed deserters from both Frelimo and the African units of the colonial army were roaming the bush in central and northern parts of the territory.[29] It was hardly a matter of surprise, therefore, that by August 1974 about 1000 whites were leaving the colony each week.

In the weeks following 25 April it was Mozambique of all the African territories which appeared to be closest to collapse into chaos. Hindsight indicates that greater fears would have been justified in the case of Angola, but in the northern summer of 1974 the western colony remained relatively – if transiently – calm. Mozambique, meanwhile, could be characterized in the Portuguese press with only a little journalistic licence as a 'bubbling cauldron'.[30] While economic crisis, industrial upheaval, racial tension and military disaffection beset the colony, political division afflicted the metropole. It was not an auspicious environment within which to debate the future direction of the Portuguese–Mozambican relationship.

'Self-Determination' and 'Consultation'

As with Guiné-Bissau, early signs of division in Lisbon over Mozambique could be discerned in the pronouncements of the civilian politicians responsible for the management of negotiations. Once again Mário Soares and António de Almeida Santos appeared uncomfortable with their mandate to secure a cease-fire prior to any substantive talks on Mozambique's political future. But they remained cautious in their approach to their military counterparts. Despite their recognizing the federalist project as unfeasible in the face of guerrilla rejection and the indifference of a demoralized army, Soares and Almeida Santos expressed their doubts only in hints and codes until the balance of military power in Lisbon had shifted decisively away from Spínola.

A few days before taking up his post as minister for interterritorial coordination, however, Almeida Santos had published an 'open letter to the people of Mozambique' in the Lourenço Marques magazine *Tempo* in which he did voice serious doubts about Spínola's ideas. 'Is it better', he asked, 'that self-determination for the peoples of Angola, Mozambique and Guiné leads to their independence, or better that it does not? If yes, and I cannot see seriously how to sustain the negative, creating a scheme of self-government seems to me redundant to the point of being useless.' Notions of legitimacy should not be allowed to complicate a process whose outcome was already obvious. The legitimacy of the MFA itself was based on armed revolution: '(w)hen the fight is against tyranny the question is not what is legal but what is just'. The pro-Frelimo tone of the article was underlined by its disdain for the rash of new parties breaking out in the territory at that time with a view to a share of 'self-government'.[31] This was, though, the last pronouncement by Almeida Santos of the Democrats of Mozambique; henceforward Almeida Santos of the Council of Ministers would be markedly more cautious in mediating his views on the Spinolist project.

Lisbon's first approach to Frelimo came, indirectly, during General Costa Gomes's visit to Mozambique in the second week of May. While in the territory Costa Gomes sent a delegation of six former political prisoners known to be pro-Frelimo to Dar es Salaam with a proposal for a general cease-fire.[32] Frelimo, concerned at the continuing talk of 'self-determination' on the basis of a referendum, rejected the approach.[33] Nationalist suspicions had perhaps been heightened by Costa Gomes's public commitment to the road of self-determination via referendum when, prior to his departure for Mozambique, he had insisted that to join the political process Frelimo must declare a cease-fire and convert itself into a political party in line with other groupings before formal negotiations could begin.[34]

A few days after the Costa Gomes visit, Almeida Santos returned to Mozambique as a minister less than a week after leaving it as a former dissident. Much of his three-day visit was occupied by attempts, partially successful, to resolve the labour disputes which had swept the country. But he also provided some early indication of Lisbon's – which at this time meant the JSN's – thinking on the territory's future. Far from being 'redundant to the point of being useless' as he had judged it little more than a week previously, a referendum had now become a concrete commitment and would be held on the basis of universal suffrage within a year.[35] He was, however, ready to pursue the logic of self-determination through referendum rather further than Spínola. Among the options in any genuine act of self-determination, he pointed out, was total independence.[36] It was, moreover, 'unthinkable' that the government would not reach an agreement with Frelimo.[37]

Despite the failure of the Dar es Salaam initiative and the apparent confirmation of the JSN's determination to push ahead with plans for a referendum, efforts continued to establish a dialogue between Frelimo and Lisbon. The fundamental incompatibility between the Spinolist approach to Africa and the demands of the liberation movements brought a pattern of multi-layered 'facilitation' by third parties. There were two main elements in this mediation which were characteristic of the process of Portuguese decolonization in Africa.

In both Guiné and Mozambique this consisted, firstly, of a neighbouring African state sympathetic to, but not too closely identified with, the guerrilla movement. In the case of Guiné this had been Senegal (and *not* Guinea-Conakry). In Mozambique it was Zambia (and *not*, as yet, Tanzania). The Zambian president, Kenneth Kaunda, had approached Lisbon with a view to performing a mediatory role at the beginning of May. A few weeks later he had hosted a meeting in Lusaka of those southern African leaders whose countries were likely to feel the impact of the Portuguese revolution.[38] At this he offered Lusaka as a venue and his own good offices to both Frelimo and Lisbon for a formal meeting.

The second 'facilitating' element was direct contact between the MFA as a 'non-governmental' body, and therefore one untainted by the prevailing 'neo-colonial' line of Spínola's JSN, and the liberation movements themselves. In Guiné this contact had been between the local MFA and the PAIGC on the ground. Over Mozambique, however, it was between the central MFA Coordinating Committee in Lisbon and Frelimo elements already known to the metropolitan opposition to the old regime as comrades in resistance. A key figure in this was Frelimo's Aquino de Bragança who was well-known and widely respected among the newly influential leftist intelligentsia in Lisbon.[39] Informal meetings took place in Lisbon between Bragança, the MFA's Vítor Crespo and Mário Soares in May. From these emerged the basis for a preliminary encounter between Soares and Samora Machel in Lusaka on 5–6 June.[40]

With no sign of Spínola's relenting on his determination to manage the political process in Mozambique according to his own blueprint, there were few grounds for optimism as this meeting approached. Spínola's aim, in the view of Ernesto Melo Antunes, was not to achieve an agreement, but to buy time to allow the emergence and consolidation of a 'third force' in Mozambique more amenable to his federalist ambitions.[41] On the eve of the meeting Almeida Santos damped down expectations by emphasizing that the talks would be merely exploratory.[42]

Once again the civilian politicians were constrained by Spínola's directives from voicing their own doubts about the road of 'self-determination'. Mário Soares, however, was prepared to stretch the boundaries of these constraints by symbolic gesture and elliptical comment. The Lusaka meeting began with what became a much-commented-upon embrace by Soares of a somewhat startled Machel. The *abraço de Lusaca* had a dual purpose: it was an attempt to fix the talks from the beginning in a non-adversarial context; but it was also a means by which Soares could register, by physical gesture, a distance between his own position and that imposed on him by Spínola. During the talks he reinforced this impression by repeatedly emphasizing the limits of his personal authority. Aquino de Bragança, part of the Frelimo delegation at the meeting, recalled Soares's seemingly regretful description of his mandate which was merely 'to make a general appreciation of the situation and if possible to agree on a cease-fire'. He could not 'unfortunately, go any further, for the minister of foreign affairs is not the exclusive holder of power'. There was in Portugal, he cautioned, 'a complex balance of forces which we socialists cannot ignore'.[43] Soares had also refused to include Frelimo's rival movement, Coremo, in the Lusaka talks despite its attempts to be represented at the meeting and its recognition by the Zambian government.[44] It is unlikely that Spínola, assuming he was aware of Coremo's petition, would have been especially well-disposed towards it as it had already rejected any notion of a federalist solution.[45] Soares, however, embellished his exclusion of Coremo with winning words for Frelimo: 'I am here to speak to those fighting inside the country . . . in Mozambique it is only Frelimo which is fighting on the battlefield and we will talk only to them.'[46]

Soares was a skilful politician who knew how far from Spínola's position he could safely diverge. Unhindered by this political training and free of the politician's instinctive wariness of the military, Major Otelo Saraiva de Carvalho, who was also in the Portuguese delegation, was less guarded in expressing sympathy for Frelimo. Ironically, Otelo (who had been born and brought up in Mozambique) had been placed in the delegation by Spínola in order to keep an eye on the civilian politicians. He now began to outbid them in their deviation from the presidential directives. Soares later recalled Otelo's intervention after the limits of the delegation's powers had been outlined to Frelimo:

> suddenly, in front of Samora Machel, Otelo said to me: 'Dr Soares, we could go a lot further, because in the field we are seeing fraternization

by our troops all over the place.' Samora, obviously, was extremely pleased with this intervention by Otelo. I interrupted the talks there and asked for a recess. I told Otelo that he must not say such things as he was . . . undermining me in front of the other party. He agreed I was right but insisted that he knew very well what was happening in the field: the troops were fraternizing, we had to grant independence as quickly as possible. I retorted that I had no such instructions from General Spínola and that I would not accept his position. Otelo again agreed I was right, promising not to speak again.[47]

Otelo's intervention trenchantly illustrated the division that was already opening between Spínola and the MFA over the decolonization process. Although he was in the delegation as Spínola's 'man', he had been a key planner of the April coup and was increasingly representative of the radical wing emerging in the MFA. His local MFA contacts in Mozambique would have given him a particular awareness of realities on the ground and would have encouraged him to confront their political implications. The incident revealed, in short, the willingness and capacity of the MFA radicals to reclaim the revolution from those to whom it had been temporarily entrusted to secure its initial success.[48]

Otelo's own recollection of events ten years later differs strikingly from that of Mário Soares. He had indeed been sent to Lusaka to keep an eye on Soares, but: 'I saw myself, not as a Spínola man, but as a representative of the MFA. I had signed the Programme of the MFA . . . which committed [it] to allow the colonies to have self-rule or total independence, regardless of cost. During the Lusaka negotiations I collided with Soares, who wanted to carry out Spínola's instructions.'[49] But Otelo's criticism of Soares's caution were hardly just in the context of June 1974. The civilian politicians had to find such secure footing as they could in the widening cleavage within the military. Although the Frelimo leadership may have been willing to accept Soares as an ally, it was fully aware that at that juncture the real negotiator was still Spínola.[50] On the evidence of Otelo's interventions, the more perceptive on the Frelimo side may now have realized that when power in Lisbon eventually shifted from Spínola, it would move *within* the military and not, in the short term anyway, in the direction of the civilians.

For all the uncertainty of authority which surrounded them, these initial Lusaka talks were reasonably successful. This is not to say that they moved the situation on in any substantive way; this was impossible in the conditions set by the political geometry of Lisbon at the time. But the simple *fact* of talks was clearly necessary to maintain lines of dialogue and, although Soares returned from Lusaka without the cease-fire he had sought, he brought clarification of the price Frelimo was demanding for this cease-fire. This was, firstly, a recognition by the Portuguese regime of Mozambique's right to immediate independence; secondly, the recognition of Frelimo as the sole legitimate voice of the Mozambican people; and thirdly, the logical conclusion of this, the transfer of power to Frelimo. These were, in fact, the general terms on which the final settlement would be based. But before this stage could be reached a decisive shift in Lisbon's position was required, and the Lusaka meeting was an important factor in advancing this change. Coming on top of the *impasse* between Lisbon and the PAIGC on Guiné, the lessons of the Lusaka meeting were, according to Melo Antunes, decisive in creating the momentum which eventually produced Constitutional Law 7/74 and the consequent leap forward in the decolonization process.[51]

In the meantime, however, Spínola remained determined to impose his referendum plan on Mozambique. In mid-May he had failed in an attempt to have the rightist General Silvino Silvério Marques (brother of Jaime Silvério Marques, the army representative on the JSN) nominated as the new governor-general. The appointment was blocked by Costa Gomes who insisted that the nomination of governors was the prerogative of the provisional government and not the presidency.[52] Undeterred, Spínola set about co-opting the next nominee, Vasco Soares de Melo, to his cause. Soares de Melo, a Mozambican resident, had been a contemporary of Almeida Santos in the Democrats of Mozambique during the previous regime. Like Almeida Santos, he had declined to follow the movement as it moved to its post-coup role of front organization for Frelimo. Despite impeccable liberal credentials, therefore, he faced the immediate hostility of his former comrades and of Frelimo.[53] He was equally unpopular with an anxious settler population which had had its preferred choice snatched away with the failure of Silvério Marques's nomination and which saw him, Soares de Melo, as part of the liberalizing forces that had turned its world upside down.

From the beginning the hapless Soares de Melo was marked by his complicity with the Spinolist prescription for the territory. Briefed by Spínola at the time of his appointment, he undertook to arrange and administer the projected referendum and shortly after taking office on 11 June he set about planning an accelerated programme of 'political education' to facilitate its success. Unsurprisingly these plans angered Frelimo which had its own perception of 'political

education' and which saw any such programme conducted by
Spínola's nominees as a direct challenge. In a speech broadcast on
25 July on its radio station Voz da Frelimo ('Voice of Frelimo'),
Machel denounced Soares de Melo as head of 'nothing more than a
colonial administration' representing 'foreign interests, the interests
of colonialism'. Lisbon's refusal to recognize Mozambique's right to
total independence was, according to Machel, 'criminal and . . .
designed only to delay the end of the war and permit . . . the
installation of 'third forces' in the pay of imperialism'.[54]

The governor-general, caught between the anger and frustration
of Frelimo and rising tensions among sections of the white
population, was also without effective authority over the increasingly
undisciplined armed forces. His administration would have found it
difficult just to maintain itself in office amidst the growing anarchy of
these weeks, let alone put in train preparations for a major and
unprecedented electoral exercise. On 27 July he tendered his
resignation.[55] The crisis that his departure might have precipitated
in the territory was however overshadowed by a larger political
development on the same day: the promulgation of Law 7/74. The
entire basis of the negotiating relationship was now changed and the
process of decolonization in Mozambique could move ahead. Talk of
referendums was now abandoned. For better or worse, Frelimo had
succeeded in evading the means of its own electoral legitimation.[56]

The 'Third Force' Groupings

Even if its popular support had proved less than overwhelming under
electoral test, Frelimo's success in any referendum would probably
have been assured simply by the fragmentation of the opposition.
The ideal outcome for the Spinolists would have been a victory for a
unified anti-independence movement capable of negotiating and
implementing some species of federal relationship with the
metropole. But the sudden sense of release which came with the
removal of prohibitions on political activity and the prospect,
however faint, of access to the spoils of the post-colonial state,
brought a surge of parties and groupings in the weeks after 25
April.[57] The emergence of a cohesive anti-Frelimo platform from
among them was made virtually impossible by the range of
incompatible interests they represented on a spectrum from white
separatism to ethno-nationalism.

The federalist camp may have been encouraged by the fact that a
significant 'third force' movement appeared already to exist in

Mozambique prior to 25 April. Coremo, which in its claims for total independence was of little interest to those anxious to construct a post-imperial federation, had not been the only anti-Frelimo force in the territory in the last phase of the Caetano regime.[58] More promising for the Spinolists were, firstly, the activities of a politically minded Beira-based businessman, Jorge Jardim, and, secondly, the Mozambique United Group (Gumo: Grupo Unido de Moçambique), an autonomist movement which had enjoyed a degree of tolerance under the old regime.

Jardim was a long-term Portuguese resident of Mozambique who had a wide range of financial interests in the territory. He belonged to a particular species of European entrepreneur which had its natural habitat in southern and central Africa in the 1960s and 1970s. The political instincts of these latter-day merchant-adventurers were determined by commercial advantage rather than ideology and they operated with scant attention to national frontiers. Originally close to Salazar, whom he had advised on African affairs, Jardim had by the early 1970s concluded that the integrationist position had no future and shifted his backing to Caetano's ideas of 'progressive autonomy'. Unlike Caetano, though, Jardim was free to carry this thinking forward into more radical ideas for future relationships between Mozambique and the metropole. In 1973, exploiting his close relationship with the Malawian president Hastings Banda (he was Malawi's honorary consul in Beira), Jardim had made contact with Kenneth Kaunda. Having enlisted the cautious support of the Zambian president, in September 1973 he produced the so-called 'Lusaka programme'. This proposed the installation of multi-party self-government in Mozambique in which, significantly, a major role was envisaged for Frelimo. This administration would, at some date in the future, be empowered to opt for total independence but would, in the medium term, remain organically linked to the Portuguese metropole.[59]

The plan was rejected by both the Caetano regime and Frelimo. Caetano, ever cautious under the suspicious gaze of the Salazarist *ultras*, reacted as he had to the similar Spínola–Senghor proposals for Guiné the previous year. Frelimo, now enjoying an improved degree of internal cohesion and ideologically committed to leading Mozambique down the revolutionary road as its single party, denounced the plan as neo-colonialist. Jardim remained a potent force in Mozambique, however, and with the Lisbon coup and the emergence of Spínola at its head it appeared that his hour and that of the Lusaka programme might have arrived.[60]

The establishment of Gumo, the second strand of this pre-25 April third force configuration, had been approved, with some misgivings, by Caetano in the latter part of 1973 after a meeting with its president, Máximo Dias.[61] The group had a multiracial leadership, prominent among which were Joana Simeão, a Makua schoolteacher, and a white businessman, Jorge Abreu. Despite Lisbon's acquiescence in its formation, Gumo had been subjected to some harassment by the rightist governor-general, Pimentel dos Santos, in the months before the Lisbon coup. It could therefore claim a degree of legitimacy as an 'anti-colonial' movement.[62] Its defining objective, according to a statement issued immediately following the coup was 'progressive political autonomy within existing political institutions in the Portuguese ambit pending [the creation of] new structures'. It was committed to the service of a 'luso-Mozambican community through the maintenance and strengthening of historical, cultural and economic relations'.[63] It presented, in short, a programme which might have been written by General Spínola himself, and immediately on receiving news of the coup, Gumo telegraphed him offering its full cooperation.[64]

Sensing perhaps that working through an individual was less vulnerable to critical attention than identifying with an existing party, Spínola sought to establish a political relationship with Jardim. When it still appeared that Spínola's nominee, Silvino Silvério Marques, would be appointed governor-general, Jardim was received by Spínola in Lisbon and encouraged to make contact with General Costa Gomes.[65] Silvério Marques himself recalled having talks with Spínola and Jardim in which the Lusaka programme of the previous year was the main topic.[66] In the view of Almeida Santos, Spínola had marked Jardim out as someone with whom business could be done. The relationship, however, had no opportunity to develop. Not only did Costa Gomes veto the appointment of Silvério Marques, which removed Jardim's main *entré* to the regime, he also concluded that the MFA in Mozambique would not tolerate any dealings with Jardim.[67]

Henceforward impressions of Jardim's movements and motives become confused, not least because of the increasingly firm grip of the left on the media in both the metropole and in Mozambique itself. Rumours circulated of his raising mercenary forces variously in Malawi, Zaire and western Europe in preparation for a unilateral declaration of independence by white settlers. At the beginning of June the Lisbon regime, nervous of his intentions after the rejection of his overtures, ordered him not to leave Mozambique, an instruction he defied by travelling to Portugal where he took refuge in the Malawian embassy.

Although no concrete evidence of subversive or terrorist activity was ever laid against him, Jardim became a major bogey for Frelimo and its supporters in the period up to independence and beyond. With the passage of time and events his reputation has undergone some rehabilitation, in Portugal at least. Almeida Santos, himself part of the pre-1974 political class in Mozambique and therefore more familiar than many in the metropole with Jardim and his motives, was reluctant even during the decolonization process to join in the generalized demonization. His view was, and remains, that Jardim possessed considerable intelligence and originality of thought but found himself in circumstances where these talents could have no outlet.[68] He had, after all, proposed a radical – even subversive – solution to the war in his Lusaka programme before the MFA itself had worked out a cohesive line on the *ultramar*. His fate in the short term, though, was similar to that of Spínola himself. What had been perceived as radical even weeks before 25 April, whether the prescriptions of *Portugal and the Future* or the proposals of the Lusaka programme, soon became transformed into neo-colonial conspiracies.

Gumo too found itself overtaken by the pace of revolutionary events. Although it lost little time in mobilizing for the promised referendum campaign, its early efforts bore little fruit. It was beset by fierce, frequently violent opposition from both left and right. During May when the prospect of a referendum was still alive, Gumo meetings in Lourenço Marques and other parts of southern Mozambique were disrupted by Frelimo supporters while mobs incited by white racists broke up its gatherings in Beira.[69] Just as debilitating were its internal divisions. The tensions inherent in what was in essence a front of linked interests rather than an ideologically cohesive party were soon pulling the movement apart from within. In the second week of June Joana Simeão was expelled from the movement on the initiative of her one-time mentor Jorge Abreu amidst accusations that she was over-playing the Makua ethnic card against Frelimo's perceived Makonde identity.[70] At about the same time its president, Máximo Dias, began to make public overtures to Frelimo. By the beginning of July, now sure of the way the political wind was blowing and anxious to go with it, he announced Gumo's imminent dissolution. The movement, he stated, was 'ceasing all political activity in order to concentrate its efforts along with Frelimo in accelerating the process of the liquidation of colonialism'.[71]

The demise of Gumo removed the most serious single challenge to Frelimo. It was the only grouping which had the potential to present substantial opposition to Frelimo in any electoral contest which might have been imposed prior to independence. Henceforth only the most fragmented political resistance remained.

Following the promulgation of Law 7/74 at the end of July, when the prospect of a referendum receded, a certain desperation overtook the remaining anti-Frelimo forces. While the leading personnel remained the same, the process of formation, disintegration and re-formation of groupings began to accelerate. Unwilling to retire from the battlefield after her expulsion from Gumo, Joana Simeão moved towards Frelimo's long-standing rival, Coremo. She then joined with the Frelimo renegades Uria Simango and Lázaro Kavandame to form the Mozambique Common Front (Frecomo: Frente Comum de Moçambique) in an attempt to consolidate the fragments of non-Frelimo 'nationalism'. Simango had already moved to Coremo after his expulsion from Frelimo, while Kavandame, since defecting to the Portuguese, had founded his own Makonde ethnic grouping, the Union for Peace among the Peoples of Mozambique (Unipomo: União para a Paz do Povo de Moçambique). This group was based in Porto Amélia, the provincial capital of Cabo Delgado, and laid claim to a non-violence not previously associated with Kavandame, professing a commitment to 'independence but by peaceful means'.[72] This, of course, was a position calculated to appeal to those around Spínola still committed to arresting the slide towards total independence and the transfer of power to Frelimo. It was now proposed by the leaderships of the two movements that Frecomo should become the internal wing of Coremo which would remain based in Zambia – as Frelimo did in Tanzania – until a final settlement was reached.[73]

The last real effort to form an effective African anti-Frelimo front came in August 1974 with the establishment in Beira of a single party, the National Coalition Party (PCN: Partido Coligação Nacional) with Uria Simango as president and the Coremo veteran Paulo Gumane as vice-president.[74] Its key objective, reflecting the rapidly changing political realities of the situation, was not electoral – the prospect of a referendum now having disappeared – but simply to secure a place at the independence negotiations along with Frelimo.

In addition to these essentially (though not exclusively) African third force movements, the white community produced its own spectrum of anti-Frelimo groupings. In general these could be described as either Spinolist or as white separatist, as even the most conservative of the settler community had accepted that the integrationist position had been rendered utterly irrelevant after 25 April.

The Federalist Movement (os Federalistas) and Democratic Convergence (Convergência Democrática) which emerged shortly after the Lisbon coup had essentially Spinolist aspirations. The strongest of the white movements, at least momentarily, was FICO (meaning literally 'I stay').[75] Claiming to be multiracial – and indeed boasting a few token Africans among its membership – FICO's leadership under its president Gomes dos Santos was entirely non-African. Its support was drawn for the most part from the settler smallholders and the poorer urban whites who formed between them the European 'lower class' which in colonial sub-Saharan Africa was unique to the Portuguese territories. The nearest historical equivalent to *os Ficos* would have been the *pieds noirs* of Algeria (although they would never attain the degree of support or political impact of their French counterparts). FICO's first public rally in Lourenço Marques in mid-May attracted some 5000 supporters; a week later, however, it could only bring 1000 on to the streets.[76]

Initially FICO was loud in asserting its 'total adhesion to the principles of the Junta of National Salvation' but its pronouncements did little to disguise its essential nature as a settler independence party.[77] As events moved towards a settlement with Frelimo, FICO made less and less effort to present itself as a progressive political party responding to changing circumstances and became increasingly associated with a disorganized though destructive campaign of white terrorism and sabotage. Although the settler reactionaries of FICO may have looked to South Africa and Rhodesia for models of white supremacy, their prospects of successfully installing a minority regime were scant. Just as disenfranchised as the native Africans by the peculiar egalitarianism of repression under the old regime, the 'poor whites' of FICO had none of the political and administrative experience which underlay the unilateral declaration of independence in Rhodesia.

With the abandonment of plans for a referendum, the whites had no prospect of power through electoral contest – the Spinolist option. In the absence of any tradition of local devolution and the political skills that develop with it, they were also denied the possibility of hijacking existing structures of government – the Rhodesian option. The one alternative left to them was the 'Algerian option', and this would prove no more successful in Lourenço Marques in 1974 than it had in Algiers in 1962.

The obstacles to the effectiveness of both African and white 'third force' activity were manifold and formidable. The creation of efficient political movements from a virtual standing start was all but impossible. The variety of interests which had to be corralled into the embryonic parties if they were to have sufficient weight and breadth of support to be sustainable was just too great. As the extent of the Portuguese collapse became evident and as the local media fell into the hands of forces sympathetic to Frelimo, newer and less ideologically certain movements were left foundering. Finally, the ever-present doubt over Lisbon's intentions and the continually shifting configuration of power in the metropole were quite incompatible with the development of pluralist activity.

These metropolitan uncertainties, the on-off commitment to a referendum and wrangles over the legitimacy of potential inter-locutors remained unresolved until the balance of forces moved decisively from Spínola and his supporters. Yet despite the suspicions of Frelimo and its champions in Portugal, the actual Spinolist contribution to the creation and nurturing of a political third force seems to have been only tentative and ultimately ineffectual. For Spínola to have been more successful in this would have required an authority and control which was totally unachievable in the cross-currents of power which defined the post-revolutionary environment.

The Negotiations and the Lusaka Accord

Although informal contacts had been maintained between the Lisbon government and Frelimo after the Lusaka talks at the beginning of June, the prospects of settlement could not move forward in any concrete way until the promulgation of Law 7/74. Meetings, often held semi-secretly in restaurants and cafes, continued between Aquino de Bragança and Vítor Crespo in Lisbon while Almeida Santos travelled secretly to Amsterdam in July to speak to another of Frelimo's leading figures, Óscar Monteiro.[78] For the Portuguese these encounters were an essential life-support system for a dialogue made comatose by presidential intractability. For Frelimo they were primarily an aid to an assessment of where power lay and how it was shifting in the uncharted confusion of Lisbon politics during the early northern summer of 1974.[79] But they could achieve little in advancing the process of settlement as long as Lisbon still insisted on some form of referendum.[80]

Present at many of these informal meetings was a figure who quickly became central to the process of negotiation. Major Ernesto Melo Antunes, a career officer from a traditional military background, had been the principal author of the MFA Programme and key participant in the planning of the 25 April coup. Later prominent in the MFA Coordinating Committee, in July 1974 he had been appointed as minister without portfolio in the second provisional government formed by Palma Carlos's leftist successor, Colonel Vasco Gonçalves. Following the adoption of Law 7/74 just two weeks after his entry to the cabinet, Melo Antunes quickly assumed a special responsibility in accelerating the decolonization process. Beyond the considerable personal abilities that the cerebral Melo Antunes brought to his new responsibilities lay his prestige in the MFA. His appearance on the decolonization scene ended the situation in which civilian politicians had been required to negotiate under presidential constraints with the MFA hovering in the political background. Melo Antunes now represented the MFA position on decolonization *within* the provisional government and thus deflected the Spinolist pressures on Soares and Almeida Santos. '(A)s political power lay essentially with the MFA', he later recalled, 'and as the task of decolonization transcended the normal tasks of a minister for foreign affairs, it was intended that someone from the MFA should take on as a priority the question of decolonization.'[81] His new responsibility was to place him, along with General Costa Gomes, at the centre of Spínola's demonology.

Recognizing that the fall of the Palma Carlos government and the adoption of Law 7/74 represented a significant move on the part of Lisbon, Frelimo proposed another round of talks, this time to take place in Dar es Salaam between 30 July and 2 August. Lisbon was now represented by Melo Antunes who went to Dar along with a representative of the Mozambique MFA. It was this meeting which, according to Aquino de Bragança, 'put a stone over colonialism' in Mozambique.[82] The significance of these talks was implicitly confirmed by Spínola himself four years later in his account of his period in office, *País sem Rumo* (*Nation without Direction*). In his anxiety to distance himself from what he considered to be the treason of decolonization, he claimed that Melo Antunes had gone to Dar secretly and had unilaterally 'established the *terms of surrender* of Mozambique to Frelimo . . . which represented our total abdication to the enemy' (original emphasis).[83] In a furious response, Melo Antunes dismissed this as a 'monstrous slur'. The meeting, he insisted, had been fully agreed to not only by Spínola but by all the key players in Lisbon at the time including Costa Gomes, Vasco Gonçalves, Soares and Almeida Santos. During these 'very difficult talks', as he described them, Melo Antunes agreed a framework for a transfer of power which more or less met the terms laid down by Frelimo at the Lusaka meeting in June: independence without prior referendum; the transfer of power to Frelimo after a period of transitional government; and the recognition of Frelimo as the sole legitimate representative of the Mozambican people.[84]

The secrecy surrounding the talks, far from covering unauthorized activities by Melo Antunes, was imposed at Spínola's own insistence. After his acquiescence to Law 7/74 he had abandoned his opposition to a direct transfer of power to Frelimo. For a number of reasons, however, he was unwilling to acknowledge the change of policy too publicly or too quickly. For one thing, he felt everything possible should be done to avoid disturbing the relative equanimity with which Rhodesia and South Africa had responded to events in Mozambique thus far. Similarly, Portugal's western allies, already wary over the confused course of events in Lisbon, should not be further agitated by the sudden revelation of a transfer of power to pro-Soviet forces in Mozambique. Finally, he insisted that it was essential to avoid panic among the already tense European settler community and their right-wing supporters in the metropole. For these reasons Lisbon's effective capitulation to Frelimo's terms should, he demanded, take the form of a 'secret protocol'.[85]

This was the basis of the negotiating mandate Melo Antunes took to Dar, and on returning to Lisbon, by his own account, he immediately went by helicopter to the presidential residence at Buçaco to provide Spínola with a full briefing. Spínola apparently did not react unfavourably. A report on the talks prepared by Melo Antunes was then considered by the newly created National Decolonization Commission and the composition of a delegation for another, more formal round of talks was agreed. A few days later Almeida Santos gave some heavy hints of significant movement in the negotiating process in a press interview. Although insisting on 'complete confidentiality' about the details of negotiations, he could 'say that we are not asleep' and that 'we have laid the foundations of a new structure. The circumstance of Frelimo as practically the only movement representative of the mass of Africans facilitates things. We know, with no hesitation, with whom to negotiate and cooperate.'[86] To Melo Antunes, Spínola's denial of knowledge and involvement in these developments was 'entirely false'. 'By this', he protested, 'one can judge the political, intellectual and moral honesty of the author of *País sem Rumo*.'[87]

The formal follow-up talks, also held in Dar es Salaam, took place between 14 and 17 August, less than two weeks after Melo Antunes's preliminary negotiations. The composition of the Portuguese delegation included, as well as Melo Antunes, the familiar figures of Mário Soares and Almeida Santos. The content of the secret protocol now emerged into the public domain. A number of specific matters, however, remained to be agreed. These included the details of a cease-fire and the composition of the transitional government and its relationship to the Portuguese high commissioner who was to oversee the transfer of power. There were also issues surrounding the longer-term settlement which were to elude rapid resolution and were left to taint post-independence relations between the two countries. Among these were guarantees for the property rights and security of Portuguese citizens who wished to remain in Mozambique after independence, and the division of financial obligations between Portugal and the new state.[88] But whatever the short-comings in the drafting of the settlement, it was clear that by the time of this substantive meeting in Dar, Lisbon was speaking with a more or less united voice.[89]

In truth, there was now neither the opportunity nor the will to sustain divisions in Portugal. As Almeida Santos later acknowledged, regardless of the precise terms of the settlement negotiated by Melo Antunes, the *fundamental* nature of the agreement was pre-determined by the realities on the ground in Mozambique and by international pressure.[90] On the day that Melo Antunes returned from his preliminary meeting in Dar, Spínola himself had agreed with Kurt Waldheim in Lisbon 'to enter into negotiations with Frelimo to accelerate the process of independence'.[91] Lisbon was, moreover, engaged in simultaneous talks over Guiné-Bissau and it was inconceivable that the outcome there would involve anything other than the largely unconditional transfer of power to the PAIGC. Frelimo was obviously aware of the progress in these parallel negotiations and ready to capitalize upon their outcome.[92] It was not 'the treason of the left in the Portuguese military' denounced by Spínola which determined the transfer of power to Frelimo but a complex of issues – domestic and diplomatic, political and military – which he himself had come to acknowledge, however reluctantly and however much he might deny it later.[93]

On 4 September Frelimo and a Portuguese delegation met in Lusaka to seal the agreement. The proposed terms were circulated to the Portuguese delegation by Melo Antunes prior to departure at Lisbon airport. The so-called 'typed sheet' affair was reported to

Spínola by 'his man' in the party, Major Casanova Ferreira, and was later used in *País sem Rumo* to suggest a political fix on the part of the MFA left.[94] According to Melo Antunes, the sheet was merely a briefing for members of the negotiating team who had taken no previous part in the process.[95] Certainly, Almeida Santos seemed happy to accept a *modus operandi* in which the MFA worked out the basics of the agreement and then passed things over to the civilians for refinement as the terms of the final agreement were now, after Lisbon had abandoned its insistence on a referendum, largely prescribed.[96]

Inevitably, there was a tension between the efficient settlement of such large issues and Frelimo's insistence on a rapid agreement and transition to independence. Ever aware of the volatility of the situation in Lisbon, Frelimo was anxious to get an agreement signed before any potentially complicating change in the political landscape could take place. For Frelimo, paradoxically, caution dictated haste. The Lusaka Accord, which was concluded on 7 September, was therefore a short agreement which perforce left much to be resolved during the transition period.[97] But this period itself, at Frelimo's insistence, was to be as short as possible. The presence of Portuguese troops in the territory while the political climate in Lisbon remained subject to sudden and dramatic change was a constant danger in Frelimo's assessment.

The Portuguese preference was for a relatively protracted period of transition during which outstanding financial questions (the so-called *contenciosos*) could be resolved, the economy prepared for independence, and training programmes established for the Frelimo cadres taking over the public service. A longer period of transition might also prevent a destabilizing out-rush of nervous whites.[98] Once again, however, Frelimo was conscious of the precedent of Guiné-Bissau and anxious to exploit it. Having undertaken to recognize Guiné's independence within a matter of weeks of the final agreement, it was difficult for the Portuguese to deploy convincing arguments for an extended transition in Mozambique, regardless of the dissimilarities between the two territories.[99] The independence date finally agreed, 25 June 1975, was later than Frelimo had wished but it was too soon, in the Portuguese view, to permit the effective completion of the necessary detailed arrangements for the transfer of power and subsequent relations.[100]

A further point of contention between Frelimo and the Portuguese negotiators was the composition of the transitional government. Portugal sought an equal distribution of portfolios while Frelimo insisted that the proportions must represent the political reality of Mozambican control.[101] Frelimo's arguments prevailed on this issue as virtually all others and the transitional government was composed of six Frelimo-nominated ministers and three appointed by Lisbon.[102] There would, in addition, be a Frelimo prime minister. Joaquim Chissano, one of Frelimo's most able senior cadres, was nominated for this. The Portuguese would, though, appoint the high commissioner who would have powers analogous to those of a head of state and who would be commander of the joint Frelimo–Portuguese armed forces in the transition. The high commissioner could issue decrees but had no authority over the transitional government itself. With Frelimo's approval the MFA's Vítor Crespo was appointed.[103]

On the question of the war, which in theory if not in reality was still continuing, the Accord provided for an immediate cease-fire from midnight on 7 September. A joint military commission with equal Portuguese and Frelimo membership was established to oversee it. All prisoners of war were to be released and Portuguese forces were to be progressively concentrated in urban areas.[104] This arrangement, while really designed to facilitate their repatriation, served in the meantime to give some sense of security to the largely town-based European population. Settler confidence was also encouraged by the fact that under the terms of the Accord Portuguese police would remain on duty throughout the transition period.[105]

The other, longer-term components of the Accord included a commitment to the creation of a new central bank to replace the Banco Nacional Ultramarino, which although part of the private Champalimaud monopoly had been the issuing bank in Mozambique. The new Mozambique state was to accept those existing financial obligations entered into by the colonial regime which were in the interests of the territory and its development. It was in these areas that the major *contenciosos* would lie and the Lusaka Accord itself did little to provide the basis for their resolution.

White Resistance and the Transitional Government

Within hours of the conclusion of the agreement in Lusaka on 7 September Lourenço Marques was in turmoil. The final agreement triggered desperate actions from the remnants of the 'third forces', both black and white. A crude coalition was born among settler extremists and the disempowered leaderships of the anti-Frelimo

African movements. FICO's Gomes dos Santos along with other prominent white rightists, Velez Grilo and Gonçalo Mesquitela who had been prominent in the UN/ANP (the 'party' of the old regime), came together somewhat uncomfortably with Simeão, Simango, Kavandame and Gumane to form the Free Mozambique movement (Moçambique Livre).[106] Also involved on the fringes of the movement was a fascist organization of ex-servicemen already engaged in anti-Frelimo terrorism, the colourfully named Dragons of Death (Dragões da Morte).

In a series of vaguely coordinated escapades several hundred Free Mozambique supporters in Lourenço Marques managed to release a number of DGS agents imprisoned after the April coup and succeeded momentarily in taking over the airport. They were, however, foiled in an attempt to march on a large Frelimo rally in the Machava football stadium. Eventually the movement's forces were concentrated in the occupation of the despised 'frelimista' Rádio Clube de Moçambique which they renamed Radio Liberty (Rádio Liberdade).

In the months following the Free Mozambique affair there was much speculation on its possible place as part of a broader conspiracy. One view held that the *attentado* had taken place prematurely, having originally been planned for later in the month. The plan, it was suggested, was for anti-independence uprisings to take place in both Mozambique and Angola to coincide with Spínola's attempt to restore his authority in Lisbon when he called, de Gaulle-like, for a public demonstration of support at the end of September. The most persistent advocate of this theory was the MFA radical, Admiral Rosa Coutinho, who at the time of the events in Lourenço Marques was president of the governing junta in Angola.

According to Rosa Coutinho, the abortive 'march of the silent majority' planned for 28 September in Lisbon, on which Spínola gambled his future in office, had colonial rather than metropolitan roots. The undertaking, he claimed, 'was to begin in Mozambique, spread to Angola and end in Portugal with the dissolution of the MFA and the removal of the powers of its Coordinating Committee'.[107] The brain and resources behind the Mozambican part of the conspiracy were, he suspected, supplied by Jorge Jardim.[108] The precipitate move by the Mozambican conspirators, Rosa Coutinho argued, caused a premature and ragged implementation of the plan not only at the wrong time but in the wrong place in that the original scheme was for an initial move in the white reactionary stronghold of Beira (which had also been Jardim's home) rather than in Lourenço Marques.[109] Following the events in Mozambique, the Angolan part of the plan, set for 20–21 September, was anticipated and easily smothered by Rosa Coutinho himself. As a result, Rosa Coutinho concluded, 'when on 28 September the counter-revolution should have culminated in Lisbon, it had already lost its colonial bases. And therefore it failed.'[110]

The entire revolutionary process in Portugal and Africa during 1974 and 1975 was punctuated with conspiracy theories, few of which have ever been decisively authenticated or refuted. Immediately following the events in Lourenço Marques, Melo Antunes called for an investigation of possible links with metropolitan 'fascist groups' but he himself stopped short of suggesting a conspiracy.[111] Vítor Crespo, however, insists that a coordinated plan *did* exist and that Spínola was implicated in it. Crespo's conviction is based on the behaviour of Spínola during the crucial early phase of the Rádio Clube occupation.[112] Despite the existence of sufficient Portuguese forces to nip the rising in the bud, Spínola refused to order them into action even in the face of direct appeals from Samora Machel in Lusaka.[113] Instead, as he later wrote, 'refusing to censure the attitude of this handful of Portuguese' who had acted 'in defence of the honour and dignity of the homeland', Spínola sent two of his trusted military loyalists, Lt. Col. Dias de Lima and Commandant Duarte Costa to speak to the rebels.[114] The crisis was finally resolved after three days by the intervention of pro-MFA paratroops who were flown to Lourenço Marques from the northern base of Nampula on the direct orders of General Costa Gomes.

In light of his, to say the least, equivocal behaviour during the crisis and the terms of his later recollections, it is hardly surprising that a web of conspiracy was woven around Spínola. There is, however, no more than this circumstantial evidence to support the theory. Certainly, the chronicler of Angolan decolonization, Pedro Pezarat Correia, who as a leading figure in the Angolan MFA was no Spinolist and who was involved in suppressing the Luanda component of the supposed plan, was doubtful of any larger conspiracy.[115] The nearest approximation to a witness of complicity was Uria Simango who claimed in 1975 that his fellow-rebels Velez Grilo and Gomes dos Santos had assured him of Spínola's support for the action. Even putting on one side the possibilities of wishful thinking or deliberate deceit on the part of these two, Simango's position at the time of his testimony as a prisoner of Frelimo anxious to exculpate himself from responsibility hardly reinforces his testimony.[116] It is certainly likely that Spínola would have wished to exploit the Lourenço Marques crisis in his own political interests. This would, of course, explain his reluctance to act against potential supporters among the former 'third forcers' involved in the events. The rebels, for their part, were clearly anxious to claim the vestiges of legitimacy which the support, however tacit, of the president of the Republic would have conferred on them. But while such a scenario involves a high degree of mutual interest, it is some distance from a premeditated plan. One of the principal factors in ending the rebellion was Spínola's presidential ratification of the Lusaka Accord on 9 September.[117] Although he would later justify this as a mere acknowledgement of a *fait accompli*, he nevertheless *had* accepted the settlement, an unlikely action from a leader of a revolutionary conspiracy.[118]

Those involved in the affair were probably driven by a mixture of the purely visceral and the semi-calculating. The anger at the 'betrayal' of Lusaka pushed them to test, *vide* Algiers, the loyalties of the metropolitan forces on the ground.[119] In the light of the Lusaka Accord's commitment to joint Portuguese–Frelimo security arrangements, it was logical for the rebels to move before the balance of forces in the capital changed. And, initially at any rate, the Portuguese army in Lourenço Marques did appear to wobble, forcing Costa Gomes to bring in the more reliable units from the north. Although the army accepted the deaths of some 100 Africans in the troubles with apparent equanimity, the first signs of a violent African backlash brought a re-assertion of reality when the rebels realized that the military would not exercise itself any more energetically to defend insurgent whites either. All hope of military support then evaporated. The whites in the conspiracy now managed to escape with little difficulty to the more congenial climate of South Africa. This was not, however, an option for the Africans in Moçambique Livre, many of whom, Uria Simango and Joana Simeão among them, now found themselves in the hands of Frelimo.

Although the Rádio Clube rebellion itself crumbled into mildly farcical disarray, it had a considerable effect for the worse on the general climate in the territory. African anger at the largely unpunished racial attacks they had suffered in the course of the crisis led to a series of assaults on white premises which carried on for several weeks.[120] This in turn added to white insecurity which was unallayed by Lisbon's attempts to play down the dangers of the situation.[121] Nor did the disintegration of the Rádio Clube occupation mark the end of racial disturbance and social instability. A further round of rioting and killings took place in Lourenço

Marques on 21 October after a brawl between a group of Portuguese commandos awaiting repatriation and some pro-Frelimo youths. What in a less charged atmosphere would have amounted to no more than a testosterone-driven scuffle, detonated a spasm of violence. Looting and killing, for the most part the work of *mabandidos* (African youth gangs) spread to the suburban *bairros* (squatter settlements) of the city.[122] The disturbances were suppressed only after the intervention of a 2000-strong mixed force of Portuguese and Frelimo troops. This time, in contrast to the disturbances surrounding the Rádio Clube affair, the majority of the victims were white.[123] For the remainder of 1974 tension was high throughout the country, maintained by rumour and outbreaks of low-level terrorism on the part of the Dragons of Death.

It was in this climate of uncertainty that the transitional government took office on 21 September. Vítor Crespo, originally intending to arrive on 7 September immediately after the conclusion of the Lusaka Accord, was forced by the Moçambique Livre crisis to divert his aircraft to Luanda and arrived in Lourenço Marques via Beira only on the 12th. Four days later Joaquim Chissano flew from Dar es Salaam with a staff of eighty.[124] The two men quickly established a good working relationship and despite the obvious tensions of the times managed to navigate the period of transition with considerable success. In their government's first month some 12,000 Portuguese troops were withdrawn from garrisons in the interior to await disembarkation in port cities. By the end of November five of the territory's eight provinces had African governors and both Lourenço Marques and Beira had African mayors.[125]

No amount of goodwill among the leaders of the transitional government could make any significant impact on Mozambique's desperate economic situation, however. The chronic balance of payments difficulties which pre-dated 25 April and the more acute problems derived from post-revolutionary labour unrest were now compounded by the flight of European expertise and capital. Despite an improvement in the security situation during the early part of 1975, this haemorrhage of human resources was unrelenting. Nor was Portugal either willing or able to maintain the economic safety net in place prior to April 1974. The metropole's own post-revolutionary economic crisis, as Almeida Santos made clear to the UN General Assembly in December 1974, made it impossible to underwrite those of its former colonies.[126] During the transition period regular negotiations took place between Frelimo and

Portuguese officials over the *contenciosos*, particularly with regard to the liquidation of the Banco Nacional Ultramarino and the associated establishment of a new national bank as well as on future responsibilities for the Cabora Bassa project.[127] These talks proved difficult, however, and many conflicts remained unresolved to pollute post-independence relations. This was part of the inevitable price of an independence agreement reached in circumstances where speed and concision were more important than detail and precision.

On 23 June 1975 Samora Machel arrived in Lourenço Marques and two days later became president of the People's Republic of Mozambique. Mozambique's independence came at the high point of revolutionary radicalism in Portugal during the *verão quente* ('hot summer') of 1975. The ceremony, which was attended by prime minister Vasco Gonçalves and the increasingly powerful Otelo Saraiva de Carvalho, was accompanied by warm commitments on the part of the two countries to future revolutionary solidarity.[128] The course of the Portuguese revolution still had some way to run, however, and its ultimate destination would be rather different from that envisaged by the leadership of June 1975. The post-independence relationship between Mozambique and Portugal was to prove the most difficult of all those between the ex-colonies and metropole.

Notes

1 In January 1974, for example, a white mob attacked the officers' mess in Beira after the killing, presumably by Frelimo, of a European woman near Villa Pery in Manica province close to the Rhodesian border.

2 In *País sem Rumo: Contributo para a História de uma Revolução* (Lisbon: Scire 1978), Spínola claims that at the time of the Lisbon coup Frelimo was staggering under a burden of 'insuperable difficulties', demoralized, war-weary and faced with hostility from local populations. p.290fn.

3 See, for example, Barry Munslow, *Mozambique: The Revolution and its Origins* (London: Longman 1983), pp.125–9.

4 *Público Magazine*, 20 February 1994.

5 *O Jornal*, 19–26 April 1984.

6 Vítor Crespo, 'Descolonização de Moçambique', *Seminário: 25 de Abril 10 Anos Depois* (Lisbon: Associação 25 de Abril 1984), p.320.

7 Interview with Vítor Crespo, Lisbon, 2 March 1995.

8 Allen Isaacman and Barbara Isaacman, *Mozambique: From Colonialism to Revolution, 1900–1982* (Boulder CO: Westview 1983), p.106.

9 Statement of executive committee of Frelimo, Algiers, 27 April 1974, reprinted in *A Revolução das Flores: do 25 de Abril ao Governo Provisório* (Lisbon: Aster 1975?), pp.275–8.

10 Aquino de Bragança, 'Independence without decolonization: Mozambique 1974–1975', Prosser Gifford and William Roger Louis, eds, *Decolonization and African Independence: The Transfers of Power 1960–1980* (New Haven CT: Yale University Press 1987), p.436.

11 Crespo, 'Descolonização de Moçambique', pp.320–1; *República*, 22 May 1974.

12 Thomas H. Henriksen, *Mozambique: A History* (London: Rex Collings 1978), p.220.

13 Crespo, 'Descolonização de Moçambique', p.320.

14 Spínola's claims also formed part of his larger campaign of denigration against General Costa Gomes on whom, he claimed, he relied for intelligence on Mozambique and who had systematically misled him. Spínola, *País sem Rumo*, p.296 and pp.289–90.

15 *Expresso*, 18 May 1974.

16 Quoted by Davidson in his introduction to Bragança, 'Independence without decolonization', p.429.

17 Spínola's insistence that this was done without his knowledge or approval was dismissed by Melo Antunes who was emphatic that Costa Gomes had acted 'with the full support of General Spínola'. Spínola, *País sem Rumo*, p.294; Interview with Melo Antunes, *Expresso Revista*, 17 February 1979.

18 *Diário de Notícias*, 31 July 1974.

19 Telegram from governor-general of Mozambique to minister for interterritorial coordination, 23 July 1974, reprinted in Spínola, *País sem Rumo*, Appendix XVIII, p.438.

20 Interview with Vítor Crespo, Lisbon, 2 March 1995.

21 Spínola, *País sem Rumo*, p.302. Spínola was outraged that retaliation for the humiliation was restricted to limited and largely symbolic air-strikes.

22 Pedro Pezarat Correia, 'Portugal na hora de descolonização', António Reis, ed., *Portugal Contemporâneo*, vol. VI (1974–1992) (Lisbon: Alfa 1992), p.138.

23 Crespo, 'Descolonização de Moçambique', p.321. Interview with Vítor Crespo, Lisbon 2 March 1995.

24 Henriksen, *Mozambique*, p.222.

25 Munslow, *Mozambique*, p.128. Vítor Crespo described the Democrats of Mozambique as 'more frelimist than Frelimo'. Interview, Lisbon, 2 March 1995.

26 Grupo de pesquisa sobre a descolonização portuguesa, *A Desolonização Portuguesa: Aproximação a um Estado* (Lisbon: Instituto Amaro da Costa 1982), vol.2, pp.38 0.

27 Crespo, 'Descolonização de Moçambique', p.321.

28 Bragança, 'Independence without decolonization', p.440.

29 *Expresso*, 18 May 1974.

30 *Ibid.*, 15 June 1974.

31 *Tempo*, 12 May 1974, reprinted in Almeida Santos, *15 Meses no Governo ao Serviço da Descolonização* (Lisbon: Representações Literária 1975), pp.58–66.

32 *República*, 17 May 1974.

33 Spínola's subsequent assertion that neither he nor the JSN's Diogo Neto, who was part of the Costa Gomes delegation to Mozambique, knew of this initiative was disingenuous and was merely part of his relentless assault on Costa Gomes's integrity. *País sem Rumo*, pp.292–3. It is difficult see how a high-level mission to Mozambique at this time would have *done other* than attempt to establish contact with Frelimo and the mission to Dar received widespread press coverage.

34 *Diário de Notícias*, 7 May 1974.

35 *República*, 21 May 1974.

36 Press Conference in Lourenço Marques, 21 May 1974, *15 Meses no Governo*, p.84.

37 *República*, 21 May 1974.

38 Lester Sobel, *The Portuguese Revolution* (New York: Facts on File 1976), p.68.

39 Aquino de Bragança was to become the rector of Eduardo Mondlane

University (formerly the University of Lourenço Marques) in Maputo after independence. He died with Samora Machel in the 1986 plane crash.

40 Interview with Vítor Crespo, Lisbon, 2 March 1995. Later, after the final agreement in September, the Frelimo prime minister in the transitional government, Joaquim Chissano, claimed that the Lusaka meeting would not have taken place without the help of 'Frelimo's friends' in Portugal. Interview in *Expresso*, 28 September 1974.

41 *Ibid.*, 17 February 1979.

42 Press Release, Lisbon, 4 June 1974, *15 Meses no Governo*, p.94.

43 Bragança, 'Independence without decolonization', p.437.

44 *Descolonização Portuguesa*, vol.2, p.38.

45 Coremo statement of 6 May, reprinted in *Revolução das Flores: do 25 de Abril . . .*, p.278.

46 Bragança, 'Independence without decolonization', pp.437–8.

47 Soares interview in Maria João Avillez, *Do Fundo da Revolução* (Lisbon: Público 1994), p.273.

48 Aquino de Bragança remembered Otelo as even less guarded than Soares suggests. At one point, according to Bragança, he intervened with the comment, 'I don't know much about politics, but I assure you that I find myself much closer to Frelimo than to my General on this issue. Neither I, nor my colleagues in the MFA, made the revolution to defend a plebiscite, or the other ideas which our General advocates in *Portugal and the Future.*' 'Independence without decolonization', p.438.

49 Interview in Hugo Gil Fereira and Michael W. Marshall, *Portugal's Revolution Ten Years On* (Cambridge: CUP 1986), p.116.

50 Aquino de Bragança interview, *Expresso*, 10 May 1975.

51 Melo Antunes interview, *Do Fundo da Revolução*, p.19.

52 Spínola, *País sem Rumo*, pp.290–1.

53 When his name was raised in connection with the appointment, the Democrats of Mozambique declared that they would not cooperate with any administration led by Soares de Melo. *Expresso*, 25 May 1974.

54 *Ibid.*, 27 July 1974.

55 Confusion surrounds the circumstances of Soares de Melo's departure. Press reports at the end of July suggest he resigned on 25 July and was called to Lisbon two days later when he may have been appealed to, unsuccessfully, to stay in office. *Expresso*, 27 July 1974. In contrast, Carlos Camilo, prominent in the Mozambique MFA at this time, later wrote of his 'abrupt dismissal'. 'Mocambique: os acontecimentos de 7 de setembro e 21 de outubro de 1974', *Seminário: 25 de Abril 10 Anos Depois*, p.342. It may have been that Soares de Melo sought and failed to receive certain guarantees of support during his visit to Lisbon and considered himself dismissed when these were not forthcoming.

56 Two decades later Almeida Santos considered that Frelimo would have had everything to gain by submitting its programme for independence to a vote. It would assuredly have won and, henceforward, its popular legitimacy would have been beyond question. Interview, Lisbon, 3 March 1995.

57 Henriksen refers to the emergence of two hundred political and pressure groups. *Mozambique*, p.221. Pezarat Correia suggests about fifty. 'Portugal na hora de descolonização', pp.135–6.

58 Coremo's leader, Paulo Gumane, had announced at the beginning of May that 'a federation is out of the question for us'. Coremo might, however, consider an arrangement 'similar to the English [*sic*] Commonwealth which obviously is a quite different thing from a federation'. *A Revolução das Flores: do 25 de Abril . . .*, p.278.

59 Pezarat Correia, 'Portugal na hora de descolonização', p.136.

60 This was Jardim's own assessment. Interview in *Expresso*, 17 August 1974.

61 Munslow, *Mozambique*, p.128.

62 *Expresso*, 11 May 1974.

63 Statement reprinted in *A Revolução das Flores: do 25 de Abril*..., p.266.

64 *Diário de Notícias*, 28 April 1974.

65 Spínola, *País sem Rumo*, p.291.

66 *O País*, 21 May 1976.

67 Interview with António de Almeida Santos, Lisbon, 3 March 1995.

68 *Expresso*, 8 June 1974. In August 1974, at the height of the mercenary scare, Almeida Santos argued that Jardim 'has his own conception of the future of Mozambique. He loves risk and political adventure, but I do not doubt that in his own way he loves Mozambique as well.' Interview with *Diário Popular*, 12 August 1974, reprinted in *15 Meses no Governo*, p.144. Interview with António de Almeida Santos, Lisbon, 3 March 1995.

69 *República*, 14 May 1974; *Expresso*, 18 May 1974.

70 *Expresso*, 15 June 1974.

71 *Ibid.*, 6 July 1974.

72 *Revolução das Flores: do 25 de Abril*..., pp.268–9.

73 *Expresso*, 6 July 1974.

74 Henriksen, *Mozambique*, p.223.

75 There appears to have been no definite basis for the acronym FICO. Contemporary accounts render it variously as: Frente para a Continuação Ocidental (Front for Western Continuity); Frente Independente de Convergência Ocidental (Independent Front for Western Unity); Frente para a Continuação de Civilazação Ocidental (Front for the Continuation of Western Civilization) and also, less threateningly, as Ficar Convivendo ('staying together'). Clearly the overall impact of the acronym was more important than its composition.

76 Henriksen, *Mozambique*, p.221.

77 *Diário de Notícias*, 14 May 1974.

78 Interview with Vítor Crespo, Lisbon, 2 March 1995; Melo Antunes interview, *Expresso Revista*, 17 February 1979.

79 Aquino de Bragança interview, *Expresso*, 10 May 1975.

80 Interview with António de Almeida Santos, Lisbon, 3 March 1995.

81 Melo Antunes interview, *Do Fundo da Revolução*, p.17.

82 *Expresso*, 10 May 1975.

83 Spínola, *País sem Rumo*, p.301.

84 Melo Antunes interview, *Expresso Revista*, 17 February 1979.

85 Bragança, 'Independence without decolonization', pp.441–2; Melo Antunes interview, *Expresso Revista*, 17 February 1979.

86 Interview in *Diário Popular*, reprinted in *15 Meses no Governo*, p.143.

87 *Expresso Revista*, 17 February 1979.

88 For Melo Antunes it was the broad brush fundamentals of the agreement which mattered: '(w)hat was at issue was whether or not Portugal would recognise in a clear and unequivocal way the right of Mozambique... to... independence. If this was the political objective of the revolution, we could not get ourselves bogged down in questions which I considered secondary.' Interview, *Do Fundo da Revolução*, p.18.

89 Crespo, 'Descolonização de Moçambique', p.327.

90 Interview with António de Almeida Santos, Lisbon, 3 March 1995.

91 *A Capital*, 5 August 1974.

92 *Descolonização Portuguesa*, vol.2, p.38.

93 Spínola, *País sem Rumo*, p.303.

94 *Ibid.*, p.305.

95 Interview with Melo Antunes, *Expresso*, 17 February 1979.

96 Interview with António de Almeida Santos, Lisbon, 3 March 1995. Melo Antunes suggests that Almeida Santos had not always expressed such a relaxed view; at one point he claimed to have been 'mentally and politically conditioned' on Mozambique by Melo Antunes's early negotiations. Melo Antunes interview, *Do Fundo da Revolução*, p.17.

97 Translation of the Lusaka Accord in *Africa Contemporary Record 1974–75* (London: Rex Collings 1975), pp.C42–4.

98 Crespo, 'Descolonização de Moçambique', p.330; Interview with Vítor Crespo, Lisbon, 2 March 1995.

99 Interview with António de Almeida Santos, Lisbon, 3 March 1995.

100 Manuela de S. Rama and Carlos Planier, *Melo Antunes: Tempo de Ser Firme* (Lisbon: Liber 1976), p.28.

101 *Expresso*, 21 September 1974.

102 Frelimo appointed the ministers of internal administration; information; justice; economic coordination; labour; and education. The Portuguese nominations were: health; public works; and communications. *República*, 20 September 1974.

103 Melo Antunes had himself been mentioned as a possible high commissioner but his duties as a minister took precedence. *Expresso*, 21 September 1974. Spínola later claimed that Frelimo had indicated that it would accept only Melo Antunes or Crespo and that he (Spínola) had ruled out Melo Antunes. *País sem Rumo*, p.308fn.

104 Crespo, 'Descolonização de Moçambique', p.333.

105 Portuguese police remained in post in Mozambique for some six months after independence.

106 In the typical confusion of nomenclature of the time Free Mozambique was also known as the Mozambique Liberation Movement (MML: Movimento para a Libertação de Moçambique).

107 Rosa Coutinho, 'Notas sobre a descolonização de Angola', *Seminário: 25 de Abril 10 Anos Depois*, p.361.

108 Interview in Gil Fereira and Marshall, *Portugal's Revolution Ten Years On*, pp.169–70.

109 Simultaneous disturbances did in fact take place in Beira and other towns. Munslow, *Mozambique*, p.128.

110 Rosa Coutinho, 'Notas sobre a descolonização de Angola', p.361.

111 *Expresso*, 21 September 1974.

112 Interview with Vítor Crespo, Lisbon, 2 March 1995.

113 *Expresso*, 10 May 1975.

114 Spínola, *País sem Rumo*, pp.307–8.

115 Interview with Pedro Pezarat Correia, Lisbon, 2 March 1995.

116 *Expresso*, 10 May 1975. Joana Simeão, also a prisoner of Frelimo after the collapse of the Rádio Clube rebellion, admitted to having contacts with Spínola and to have had his help in moving in and out of Mozambique. *Diário de Notícias*, 23 April 1975.

117 Camilo, 'Moçambique: os acontecimentos de 7 de setembro e 21 de outubro de 1974', p.342.

118 Spínola, *Ao Serviço de Portugal*, p.21; *País sem Rumo*, p.306.

119 Carlos Camilo judged the actions of the rebels to be based on a calculation of either support or neutrality on the part of the army and paramilitary forces. 'Moçambique: os acontecimentos de 7 de setembro e 21 de outubro de 1974', p.342.

120 *Ibid.* Frelimo was active in calming the situation in the African *bairros* around the city.

121 At a press conference on 13 September Soares was at pains to emphasize the loyalty of the army and to point up the fact that the majority of whites remained neutral during the disturbances. *Democratização e Descolonização: Des Mezes no Governo Provisório* (Lisbon: Dom Qixote 1975), p.105. Vítor Crespo took up the theme in an interview some days later. His observation that *only* 10,000 whites of the 100,000 in Lourenço Marques had demonstrated against the Lusaka Accord was not wholly reassuring. *Expresso*, 21 September 1974.

122 Camilo, 'Moçambique: os acontecimentos de 7 de setembro e 21 de outubro de 1974', pp.342–3.

123 Of the forty-nine fatalities thirty-three were Europeans. *Descolonização Portuguesa*, vol.2, pp.124–5.

124 *República*, 17 September 1975.

125 *Africa Contemporary Record 1974–75*, p.B395.

126 UN Document A/PV.2305, 3 December 1974.

127 *Expresso*, 7 June 1975.

128 Frelimo was selective in its invitations to the independence celebrations. Not only Rhodesia and South Africa, but France, West Germany and the United States as military suppliers to the colonial regime were excluded. Henriksen, *Mozambique*, p.225.

CHAPTER SIX

Angola

The Impact of 25 April

Of the three major territories of Portuguese Africa Angola received the first news of the April coup with the greatest equanimity. In Guiné the events of 25 April were immediately recognized by nationalists and the beleaguered Portuguese military alike as having moved the liberation war to its endgame. While the situation in Mozambique was not quite so critical for the colonial state, there was a clear apprehension there, particularly on the part of the settler population, that the basic foundations of Portuguese imperialism were now cracking. In Angola, however, the relative stability of the military situation gave a normality to day-to-day life in most of the territory which distracted attention from the likely extent of the transformation in train.

At the time of the coup Portuguese military strength in the territory stood at about 60,000, about 40 per cent of which consisted of locally recruited Africans. Yet in all of 1973 – as the PAIGC in Guiné intensified their war with the deployment of anti-aircraft missiles and as Frelimo accelerated its southward thrust into the settler heartlands of central Mozambique – the colonial military in Angola suffered just eighty-one deaths, of which only fifteen had been the result of direct engagements with the guerrillas.[1] In this climate of relative security Angola's settler population remained reasonably confident of its future.

The necessary changes at the upper echelons of the colonial administration took place calmly and with relative smoothness. The incumbent governor-general, General Augusto Santos e Castro, publicly announced his own suspension on 27 April and was replaced in the interim by Colonel Soares Carneiro, an officer in whom the MFA had greater confidence. A yet more openly pro-MFA officer, General Joaquim Franco Pinheiro, was placed in command of the armed forces in the territory.

The liberation movements, divided between and within themselves, were taken by surprise by the Lisbon coup and were slow to formulate positions in response to it. Agostinho Neto, who was on a speaking tour of Europe and North America during April 1974, was reluctant to make any pronouncement on the MPLA's stance until the new Junta of National Salvation in Lisbon clarified its own position on Africa. In interviews in London with the Portuguese press Neto merely fired some warning shots across Spinolist bows by warning that the MPLA would reject a change of regime in Lisbon which 'was no more than a simple demagogic manoeuvre with the sole objective of perpetuating colonial domination in a slightly different form'.[2] Beyond this he said little of the MPLA's plans and declined an invitation to Lisbon for early talks. When he did agree to meet Mário Soares, his old comrade of the anti-Salazar resistance, in Brussels in early May nothing of substance emerged from their talks. A further meeting, with Spínola's aide Nunes Barata (who had already met with Léopold Senghor over Guiné), was also held in early May in Geneva. Here Neto claimed a primary role for the MPLA in any negotiations but, according to the report passed on to Spínola, he appeared reluctant to take any concrete position without consulting his executive in Brazzaville.[3] Given the extent of the MPLA's internal problems at this time Neto's caution was understandable.

While the MPLA was slow to take any firm position, the FNLA appeared unwilling even to signal its interest in the new political landscape. Maintaining its reputation for organizational inefficiency and ineptitude, the movement declined to make any statement whatsoever or nominate any spokesperson.[4] Holden Roberto, although leader of the numerically largest of Angola's liberation movements, apparently had no point of view on developments in Lisbon.

Characteristically, it was UNITA, at this time by far the weakest of the movements, which sought to press as much advantage as possible from events. Demonstrating the opportunism which had served him so effectively in the past and which would maintain his prominence in the Angolan tragedy for the next two decades, Jonas Savimbi set about maximizing returns from UNITA's limited investment in the liberation war. By the middle of June he had renewed UNITA's cease-fire with the Portuguese through the mediation of a missionary priest. By doing this UNITA became the only liberation movement to agree a formal cessation of hostilities before Lisbon had made any definitive statement on independence.[5] The movement's Maoist rhetoric was quietly abandoned as it began advertising itself as the only 'Angolan-based' of the three movements and the one most sympathetic to the concerns of the white population.[6]

Militarily, the situation remained little-changed after 25 April. The FNLA, emboldened by the recent arrival of Chinese military instructors in its bases in Zaire, sought to increase the pressure on the Portuguese in the north, while Daniel Chipenda maintained operations, nominally on behalf of the MPLA but increasingly on his own account, in the sparsely populated eastern areas on the Zambian border. The impact of these efforts was not, however, great. By 18 May General Franco Pinheiro felt confident enough to announce the end of Portuguese operations.[7] But the political process had not advanced, and Lisbon's attentions being focused on the currently more pressing problems of Guiné and Mozambique, Angola's relative stability could not be taken for granted. By mid-May, industrial troubles were spreading throughout the port cities as they had in Mozambique and, ominously, racial tensions were beginning to emerge. Lisbon could not drift on the cross-currents between Angola's divided nationalist movement indefinitely. However attractive the prospect of deferring the issue of Angola until other troubles had been eased, the manifest economic, political and – in the realm of luso-tropical theology – *mythic* importance of the territory demanded that initiatives be taken.

The Spinolist Endeavour in Angola

In an interview in 1984 the MFA luminary Vasco Lourenço recalled an encounter with Spínola immediately after his address to the nation on the promulgation of Law 7/74 at the end of July 1974: '(t)o our great surprise we found him very agitated, as if he had just taken a beating. We congratulated him on his speech and he replied: "I know that this is what you wanted. But now Angola is for me." '[8] As Spínola himself later put it, he saw Angola as 'destined to occupy one of the most prominent positions in a Luso-Afro-Brazilian Community'.[9] Angola held a central place in the Spinolist scheme of things and, superficially at least, the particular circumstances of the colony offered some encouragement to federalist ambitions.

The extent of the territory's wealth, both realized and potential, gave pause to even the most enthusiastic of Lisbon's European-orientated economic modernizers. Moreover, this wealth had brought Angola into much closer alignment than the other African colonies with the global economy through the activities of multinationals like Gulf Oil. International economic forces might therefore be expected to resist too dramatic a discontinuity in any Angolan settlement. Additionally, Angola had a particularly large white settler community. Over 300,000 strong, this was the largest in sub-Saharan Africa outside of South Africa. Its presence suggested a momentum of social and cultural links which would influence any constitutional change in the direction of a continuing relationship. Finally, the evident inability of the nationalist guerrillas to mount an effective war supported the view that Angola's future could be engineered to produce a status quite different from that of the other territories. As Richard Robinson put it, for Spínola and his supporters 'the loss of Guiné was regrettable, the loss of Mozambique a tragedy which should and could have been avoided, but the abandonment of Angola was unthinkable'.[10]

Initially, Spínola appeared to have some success in his attempts to prevent Angola's departure from the 'Portuguese space'. General Silvino Silvério Marques, whose appointment he had sought to the governor-generalship of Mozambique before it was vetoed by General Costa Gomes, was successfully installed in Angola. The circumstances of Silvério Marques's appointment have remained controversial. Well to the right of Spínola himself on the *ultramar*, Silvério Marques had already occupied the post of governor-general of Angola under Salazar in the mid-1960s. According to Pedro Pezarat Correia, a dominant figure in the MFA in Angola at this time, Spínola made it clear to Almeida Santos as the latter left for Angola to take soundings on the issue at the end of May that Silvério Marques was to be appointed.[11] Consequently, when the minister held his consultations in Angola – which did not involve the local MFA – he constantly raised Silvério Marques's name.[12] Spínola claimed that he had merely 'suggested' Silvério Marques and Almeida Santos later insisted that 'whites, blacks, everyone' brought up his name in the soundings.[13] But it is difficult to see how the name of a Salazarist general would leap unprompted to the minds of those offering views on the construction of a post-revolutionary administration for Angola. Still just weeks from the coup, however, and as yet unlegitimized by the democratic process, Almeida Santos along with the other civilian ministers remained warily respectful of presidential prerogative and its military underpinnings.

At the swearing-in ceremony for the new governor-general Spínola reiterated the basic mechanism of his chosen process for the *ultramar*: cease-fires with the guerrillas followed by a referendum. Any 'recognition of the rights of peoples to independence', which was the price demanded by all the main liberation movement for formal cease-fires, was redundant, according to Spínola, because this recognition was implicit in the exercise of 'self-determination' by referendum.[14] The argument was central to Spínola's ambitions because the assertion of 'third force' positions in the period prior to any referendum would, hopefully, guarantee an outcome other than independence. To make a prior commitment to independence would undermine this process. To Spínola and his supporters Angola among all the African territories offered the greatest prospect of success for this scheme.

By the end of May a number of significant third force groupings had already emerged in Angola and, to this extent, the Spinolist project seemed to be on course. One of the largest of these movements at the outset was the white-dominated Angolan Christian Democratic Party (PCDA: Partido Cristão Democrático Angolano) led by António Ferronha. Despite its reassuring name, the PCDA became increasingly associated with settler extremism. More overtly racist from the beginning was the frequently violent Angolan Resistance Front (FRA: Frente de Resistência Angolana) which drew its support mainly from white ex-servicemen and which was similar in its outlook to FICO in Mozambique. The Angolan United Front (FUR: Frente Unida Angolana) led by Fernando Falcão had relatively liberal and autonomist aspirations, though it was still largely European in membership. These were only the most prominent among about thirty groupings which came into being after 25 April to stake a political claim to the new Angola. There was, though, a notable absence in this burgeoning third force of any significant African parties comparable to Gumo or the PCN in Mozambique. The three guerrilla movements in their different ideological and ethnic facets appeared adequately to represent the various aspirations of the African intelligentsia as well as the broader masses.

While the early development of third force groupings may have seemed favourable to Spínola's federalist ambitions for Angola, all was not going well at the level of the territory's administration. Having succeeded in installing Silvério Marques as governor-general, Spínola tried to expand his foothold by having him appointed as military commander as well. Here he was again blocked by Costa Gomes who insisted that this would be a slight to the current commander, General Franco Pinhero, who was known to have the confidence of the local MFA.[15]

The governor-general's relations with this quarter were already bad. From his arrival on 11 June Silvério Marques had the greatest difficulty in working with the movement. Initial contacts, according to Pezarat Correia, were 'polite, formal and cool', but they were to deteriorate rapidly.[16] The focus of conflict became MFA representation on the administration's Council of Defence which was responsible under the chairmanship of the governor-general for territorial security. Despite his orders to the contrary, Silvério Marques found 'a dozen boys from the MFA' at his first meeting with the council.[17] The dispute soon involved the military commander who supported the MFA on the issue and communicated this to General Costa Gomes as chief of the general staff.

In the febrile atmosphere of the time and place events now began to slip out of control. The schism between governor and military would have been dangerous in any circumstances but, critically, it coincided with a rapidly deteriorating public order situation in Luanda. Mounting inter-racial tensions exploded on 11 July after the killing by an African of a white taxi driver. The resulting anti-black violence cost about 200 lives in the African *muçeques* around the capital. Simultaneously both African troops in the colonial army and white activists were demanding the means to defend their respective communities from each other.[18] On 17 July an assembly of the MFA in Luanda issued what was in effect an ultimatum demanding the replacement of Silvério Marques within seventy-two hours.[19] General Franco Pinheiro, considering the situation 'extremely grave', communicated the demand to Spínola. Costa Gomes meanwhile warned Spínola that the MFA were perfectly capable of simply putting Silvério Marques on a plane and sending him back to Lisbon, and that it would be preferable to act on the ultimatum.[20] The approach adopted by the JSN was not to replace Silvério Marques with another governor-general but to reorganize the administration of the territory under a 'governing junta'. The president of this junta would be the naval representative on the JSN, former frigate captain and marine hydrographer Admiral António Alva Rosa Coutinho, who would also take over command of the military in the territory. The political colour of the Portuguese administration in Angola now moved to the other end of the spectrum. The former Salazarist was now effectively replaced by a pro-MPLA Marxist and the consequences for Spínola's project in Angola were considerable.

The appointment of Rosa Coutinho, fully approved by Spínola himself, raises questions about the degree of political control exerted over African policy by the competing factions in Portugal's fragmented post-coup leadership. Rosa Coutinho himself has expressed bewilderment at his appointment. In 1975 he suggested that Spínola had assumed that he would fail in his task of holding things together in Angola and would thus open the way for he himself to take personal control.[21] Almeida Santos, on the other hand, suggested more recently that his nomination was an indication of the increasing power of the MFA left at this time.[22] Self-serving hindsight, however, haunts the study of the Portuguese revolution. Most probably the appointment had less to do with the calculations of one or other faction than with the generalized post-revolutionary confusion in which decisions with far-reaching consequences had to be taken with minimal reflection. Spínola's own recollections ring true when he claims that up to his appointment to Angola 'the behaviour of the Admiral . . . had been balanced, and he identified with the Junta of National Salvation in matters of decolonization; there was nothing to raise suspicions that we were dealing with a pro-Communist in thrall to the Soviet Union'.[23] In this, perhaps uniquely, the general was in agreement with Melo Antunes who later recalled that Rosa Coutinho was at this time an unknown quantity: '(t)hings were going on at a frantic pace. He was in the JSN, he had the confidence of naval elements in the MFA . . . '.[24]

Rosa Coutinho's impact was quickly felt in Luanda. On his arrival on 25 July he dismissed in its entirety the 43-member 'government' which had been appointed by Silvério Marques.[25] His MPLA sympathies were made plain by his permitting the movement access to the military radio network to build its support base.[26] The origins of Rosa Coutinho's partisanship may have been personal as well as ideological. During the war he had been captured and mistreated by the UPA (the earlier incarnation of the FNLA) and as a result nursed a deep antipathy for Roberto and all his works.[27]

There was, though, a generalized undercurrent of sympathy for the MPLA in Lisbon's revolutionary politics at this time. Neto and other MPLA leaders had, as we have seen, been close to the metropolitan opposition during their student days. Neto's association with the Portuguese leftist intelligentsia was strengthened by his white Portuguese wife and his considerable reputation as a Portuguese-language poet. With its large *mestiço* membership and significant level of white left-wing support in Angola itself, the MPLA could draw on a prestige of a different order from the ideologically promiscuous ethnic nationalism of the FNLA and UNITA. Even the MPLA's internal divisions, while deeply debilitating to the movement, seemed to be based on political conflicts comprehensible to the non-Angolan left. Rosa Coutinho was not, therefore, alone in his sympathies for the MPLA. These were expressed in various times and in various ways by other key figures such as Almeida Santos, Melo Antunes and Mário Soares. But it was Rosa Coutinho who was in a position to give immediate aid to the movement and who was by temperament less concerned than others about the appearance of impartiality.

One figure in Lisbon immune to sentiments of sympathy to the MPLA was, of course, President Spínola. The culture of the metropolitan leftist intelligentsia was alien to him. He had been a loyal servant of the regime that the young Mário Soares and Agostinho Neto had resisted as students and he was untouched by the radical sympathies of the new generation of officers prominent in the MFA. His reservations at the actions of Rosa Coutinho mounted during his final months in the presidency. Reports from his personal intelligence sources spoke of 'the vertiginous disintegration of the armed forces and the pro-Communist policies pursued by the admiral'.[28] His apprehensions must have appeared well-founded when Rosa Coutinho, on his first visit to Lisbon after his appointment, proposed a Portuguese–MPLA–UNITA alliance to expel the FNLA from Angola on the basis that Roberto was merely the voice of Zaire. Unsurprisingly Spínola rejected the suggestion out of hand. For him, no relationship could be contemplated with an organization which 'takes its orders from Moscow'.[29] Such a dramatic alignment would also, of course, have destroyed federalist ambitions by legitimizing the MPLA's goal of total independence.

In contrast to the impact it had on Guiné and Mozambique, the advent of Law 7/74 at the end of July did nothing to resolve the political uncertainty in Angola. Its immediate effect, on the contrary, was to intensify white suspicions of the MPLA's political intentions and evoke memories of the FNLA's propensity for racial violence.[30] In mid-August 1974, some two weeks after the publication of Law 7/74, the JSN on Spínola's initiative produced a programme for Angola which proposed a protracted period of 'decolonization' of about three years. Formal cease-fires with each of the liberation movements were to be sought as a priority (though on the ground military activity had dwindled almost to nothing over the previous months). A provisional government would then be formed which would include representatives of all three liberation movements as well as ethnic and other sectional interests. During a two-year period this provisional government was to arrange elections, on the basis of universal suffrage, to a constituent assembly which would formulate a constitution defining future relations with Portugal. A legislative assembly would then be elected on the basis of this new constitution. In earnest of its good faith, Portugal would accept United Nations monitoring of all electoral procedures.[31] The plan might have been written on the blueprint of *Portugal and the Future*.

The key weakness of the scheme was identical to that which had earlier confounded Spínola's attempts to impose his agenda on both Guiné and Mozambique. It cut directly across the fundamental precondition laid down by the MPLA and FNLA (and the PAIGC and Frelimo before them) for agreeing to cease-fires: a commitment to the principal of unconditional independence. In the event, the JSN initiative was a double failure. It was rejected by both the FNLA and the MPLA (UNITA announcing that it would participate only with the other two movements), and it re-ignited white violence.[32] While the nationalists saw it as an attempt to twist away from the commitment to independence laid out in Law 7/74, the settlers saw it as the first step towards fulfilling it. By the autumn of 1974, therefore, the problem of Angola was intensifying almost step by step with the easing of those of Guiné and Mozambique.

The Sal Island Meeting

In mid-September, with agreements reached on Guiné and Mozambique, Spínola was nursing a battery of grievances over his loss of initiative on the *ultramar*. He now took a number of steps with minimal consultation with the MFA, the provisional government or even the JSN. The first and most dramatic of these was to arrange a personal summit with President Mobutu of Zaire.

The circumstances and significance of this meeting, which was held on Sal Island in Cabo Verde on 14 September, were at the time far from transparent and have remained the subject of often overheated speculation. Even the origin of the initial invitation has been the subject of dispute. Spínola has claimed that he merely 'accepted a proposal from the President of Zaire for a meeting', but it is much more likely that the initiative was his own.[33] Members of his personal staff had cultivated contacts in Kinshasa over the northern summer of 1974. The main figure in this was his trusted aide, Colonel

Alexandre Dias de Lima, who, it will be recalled, was sent to talk on Spínola's behalf with the Rádio Clube plotters in Lourenço Marques.[34] His entourage at the Sal talks consisted entirely of military loyalists from within his personal staff and Almeida Santos who as well as being the responsible minister was one of the civilian members of the provisional government most trusted by Spínola.[35] Even these favoured lieutenants were excluded from the actual talks, however, which took place between Spínola and Mobutu attended only by a Zairean interpreter.[36]

Following the meeting the mystery surrounding its purpose was deepened by the wholly uninformative official communiqué which followed it.[37] In the over-charged atmosphere of the 'revolutionary process' in Lisbon, the secrecy surrounding the talks and their outcome provided fertile ground for speculation and rumour. The most elaborate reconstruction of the encounter had Mobutu urging Spínola's open support for the FNLA. According to this supposed Zairean plan, Angola would be governed by an interim administration dependant on Mobutu and Spínola, and Cabinda would be handed to the pro-Zaire faction of FLEC. Spínola would then work towards the creation of an Angolan-Zairean-Cabindan federation ruled by Mobutu and Roberto. Spínola was supposed to have agreed to this if in return Mobutu would support Portugal's African diplomacy – in particular attempts to regain Mozambique and Guiné-Bissau. Zaire was also to accept Portuguese control of all economic concessions from Angola for a period of twenty years.[38]

Other speculative accounts had Spínola and Mobutu agreeing to recognize Chipenda as the only legitimate leader of the MPLA with the consequent marginalization of Neto and his pro-Moscow faction.[39] According to the historian of Angola, John Marcum, the Zairean president calculated that Spínola was ready to accept a Mobutu–Roberto–Savimbi–Chipenda alliance for Angola. To this end a plan was reportedly discussed whereby a twelve-strong provisional government would be established consisting of two nominees of each of the liberation movements – with Chipenda and Mário de Andrade representing the 'MPLA' – and six others representing ethnic groups and white settlers.[40] Rosa Coutinho, who despite (or perhaps because of) his key position had been kept entirely in the dark about the Sal talks, later added his weight to this theory. In a television interview in April 1975, he spoke of a plan 'to install Holden in first place with Chipenda and Savimbi at his side, and to eliminate Neto'.[41]

None of this can be more than speculation founded on greater or lesser degrees of sensitivity to the political disposition of the time. The Sal talks were unique in the decolonization process in having been conducted in conditions of genuine and durable secrecy. Spínola's own 'account' of the meeting merely refers to his success in extracting an undertaking of non-interference from Mobutu.[42] Significantly, perhaps, one of the most cautious in his assessment of events is Pedro Pezarat Correia. Although holding no brief for Spínola, he has nevertheless been dismissive of the 'fantastic revelations lacking credibility' which surrounded the Sal talks.[43] It is entirely possible that Spínola on this occasion was speaking the prosaic truth and that nothing of dramatic substance was contemplated or agreed with Mobutu at Sal. Following his flight into exile after the abortive coup of March 1975, Spínola showed no reluctance to express the extent of his disaffection with the revolution or to hold back any significant revelation which would underline his anti-leftist position. That no such revelations emerged about the Sal encounter perhaps suggests that there were none to be made.

It is possible that the key to the Sal meeting is to be found not in Angola in 1974 but earlier and in Guiné. In this perspective Mobutu might be cast as the Senghor of the process: a powerful, conservative African neighbour, well-connected with the west and open to pragmatic and self-interested discourse. Unable to pursue the possibilities of this discourse with Senghor in 1972 following Caetano's prohibition, Spínola was now unconstrained by political superiors and able to formulate his own policies (however remote the possibility of their implementation). Mobutu, with his close connections to both the United States and China, was an obvious ally against the encroachments of the Soviet Union *via* Neto's MPLA. This process of 'internationalization' might, in Spínola's view, be the most effective obstacle to the transfer of power to pro-Soviet Marxists which had already taken place in both Guiné and Mozambique. The Sal talks may therefore have had more to do with high diplomacy than low conspiracy. It was suggested at the time that Spínola might have had similar intentions for Mozambique through the involvement of Presidents Kaunda of Zambia and Banda of Malawi but that he had been outmanoeuvred in this by the radicals in the MFA, notably by Melo Antunes. He would therefore have been all the more determined to keep ahead of any such 'sabotage' over Angola.[44]

On 22 September, a week after the Sal talks and a week before his fall, Spínola announced that he was taking full personal responsibility for the problem of Angola. The announcement was precipitated by a rancorous meeting between Spínola and Rosa Coutinho in Lisbon. Recriminations flew between the two with Rosa Coutinho complaining of being kept in ignorance of the Sal talks and Spínola denouncing him in turn for his pro-MPLA bias.[45] In reality, of course, there was not a great deal that Spínola could do to change in any fundamental way the direction of Lisbon's policy. That policy was the JSN's own programme which had been published only a few weeks previously and which already bore obvious signs of Spínola's own hand. His aim, though, was to emphasize his authority in the process and steer it in his desired direction. In what he later described as his 'last political act in relation to decolonization' he summoned to Lisbon a group of so-called *forças vivas* (interested parties) from Angola who might be expected to participate in the provisional government proposed by the JSN plan. His initiative was controversial and, like the Sal meeting, somewhat secretive, at least to begin with.[46] In the face of the suspicions of the MFA Coordinating Committee and elements in the provisional government, on 27 September twenty-three 'leaders of thought' from Angola duly assembled at the ministry of territorial coordination in Lisbon. They were, for the most part, members of 'third force' groups which had emerged in Angola since 25 April, many of which had connections with Zaire. No representatives of any of the liberation movements or of white liberal groups were present.[47]

In his keynote address to his meeting with the *forças vivas* Spínola was at pains to insist that he was committed to a democratic, majoritarian future for Angola; there could be no question of a white minority regime. But, while the liberation movements must be included in the democratic process, they must learn to distinguish 'the line separating liberation from usurpation'. The sequence laid out in the JSN plan, he argued, could lead to a true independence – and one, as we have observed, remarkably close to the prescriptions of *Portugal and the Future*. '(T)here will soon be born in the South Atlantic', he predicted, 'a new Portuguese-speaking state which will constitute, with Brazil and Portugal, the enclosing triangle of a sea which carved out our histories and which will perpetuate the links which will in the future unite once more our three brother countries.'[48] His grandiloquence though could not disguise, in fact seemed to underline, the irrelevance of his words to the realities of the time. In effect it was the final verse of the federalists' swan song. Three days later Spínola resigned following the failure of his appeal to the 'silent majority' against his leftist enemies. He was succeeded in the presidency of both the Republic and the JSN by General Costa Gomes who now assumed the posts he had declined five months earlier on 25 April. The momentum towards a rapid transfer of power in Angola was now unobstructed.

The Road to Alvor

In Angola the immediate consequence of Spínola's departure was a dangerous increase in settler insecurity. Whether as part of a broader Portuguese–African conspiracy or not, on 2–3 October the white extremist FRA led by the mercurial ex-soldier, Pompílio da Cruz, attempted to succeed where Moçambique Livre had failed a week previously. Alerted to the danger by the prior events in Lourenço Marques, the MFA which was better established in Angola than in Mozambique moved against the rebels and some Portuguese officers who had been compromised in the conspiracy.[49] The 'Rhodesian temptation' in Angola, as Rosa Coutinho described it, was effectively ended at this point, though the white extremists' capacity for violent mischief continued to make itself felt for several more months.[50] Having hesitated while Spínola appeared to offer the prospect of a federal solution, the forces of white separatism now lost momentum.[51]

In Lisbon meanwhile there was no single decisive shift in policy after the fall of Spínola. At his inauguration as president, however, Costa Gomes warned that, 'we must not let ourselves be bound by rigid and pre-conceived plans' on the Angolan issue.[52] Greater flexibility of approach – in particular towards the fuller inclusion of the Neto-led rump of the MPLA – was aided by the fact that the composition of the JSN changed radically after Spínola's resignation. His key supporters on the junta (Generals Diogo Neto, Jaime Silvério Marques, and Galvão de Melo) all left with him, and talk of *forças vivas* and protracted electoral processes soon faded without ever being explicitly forsworn.

While Lisbon was now committed to having the MPLA in a central position in the negotiating process, the MPLA itself had yet to pull itself together sufficiently to occupy such a position with any degree of conviction. The schisms within the movement which had their origins in the frustrations of military stalemate during the war widened markedly after 25 April when the political spoils of victory suddenly beckoned. Though Spínola may have been willing to exploit the movement's divisions for his own ends, he had not created these divisions and they did not disappear with his fall. By May 1974 the movement had three distinct and mutually hostile wings. There was firstly the Neto faction which represented the main line of continuity in the movement from the early 1960s until 1974. The objections to this group from within the MPLA were as much personal as ideological. There was no real political opposition to Neto's pro-Moscow position but there was considerable dislike of his somewhat imperious and authoritarian style and his perceived detachment from the day-to-day travails of the armed struggle.

This 'presidentialism' was particularly resented by Daniel Chipenda, the military commander of the MPLA's most effective fighting force which operated in the eastern part of the territory and whose faction thus became know as the 'Eastern Revolt' (Revolta do Leste). The split between the two, which dated from 1972, was in some ways an understandable one between international figurehead and commander in the field. There was, however, a racial element in the equation as well. Chipenda, an Ovimbundu, was suspicious of the extensive *mestiço* influence in the Neto leadership.[53] In terms of tangible resources, Chipenda could call on the loyalty of some 1500–2000 guerrillas.

The third faction, about seventy strong but with support from influential elements among the urban intellectual supporters of the movement, was led by Neto's old rival from the earliest days of the MPLA, Mário de Andrade and his clergyman brother Joaquim Pinto de Andrade. This grouping became known as the 'Active Revolt' tendency (Revolta Activa) and, so far as its position was based on more than the long-standing animus between the Andrades and Neto, it derived from a rejection of the latter's supposed 'Stalinism'.[54] The Active Revolt faction became a serious challenge to Neto's leadership only in May 1974, after the Lisbon coup.

These splits in the MPLA were reminiscent of those which had afflicted Frelimo in 1968 and 1969. The timing was obviously much more dangerous for the MPLA, however. In an urgent attempt to resolve the problem, the three factions met in Lusaka in mid-August 1974 under the joint chairmanship of Zambia and Congo-Brazzaville. Eleven days of meetings in a Zambian military base between the 400 delegates proved unable to heal the basic divisions within the movement. A vote on the presidency produced deadlock, with 165 for both Neto and Chipenda and 40 for Pinto de Andrade. The congress then broke up in confusion with the Neto faction walking out and Chipenda claiming in consequence to be the duly elected president of the MPLA.[55]

The Lusaka débâcle was followed by a crisis meeting in Brazzaville a few weeks later. Despite direct pressure from the presidents of Tanzania, Zambia, Zaire and Congo, this encounter was hardly more successful. A complex arrangement was constructed by which Chipenda was prevailed upon to relinquish the 'presidency' and assume along with Pinto de Andrade the role of joint vice-president under Neto. This triumvirate was to preside over an intricately proportioned structure of central committee and politburo.[56] The arrangement disintegrated almost at once, with Chipenda again insisting that he was the movement's legitimate president.

The turn of events in Lusaka and Brazzaville marked the high-point of Chipenda's fortunes in the MPLA. After the leadership wrangle he moved his base to Kinshasa where he was taken up by Mobutu and in consequence moved gradually closer to Roberto and the FNLA. He was formally expelled from the MPLA at the end of November 1974. Yet the strength of his position at the Lusaka and Brazzaville meetings should not be underestimated. The subsequent history of the MPLA and the ideological predisposition of many who have written it has tended to deride his position and to suggest a security of tenure for Agostinho Neto in the MPLA leadership which he did not in reality enjoy.[57] The inescapable fact is that Chipenda, as commander of the MPLA's only effective fighting forces in the later stages of the armed struggle, enjoyed for a time equal support in the movement, an equality evident in the Lusaka vote. He also had the support of Kenneth Kaunda who had never been prominent among Neto admirers. From this perspective the speculation about discussion during the Spínola–Mobutu meeting at Sal Island of Chipenda as an alternative MPLA leader becomes comprehensible. The Sal talks took place just days after the Brazzaville meeting when Chipenda's status was far from that of the marginalized outcast manipulated by neo-colonialists that was later suggested by Neto's supporters abroad.

But however narrowly, Neto did finally emerge as the victor in the faction struggles of May–September 1974. In October, as Chipenda sought new friends in Kinshasa, the 'presidentialist' rump of the MPLA reorganized itself at a conference in Moxico inside Angola. A new central committee and politburo were created, now fully under the control of Neto and his closest supporters, Lúcio Lara, Lopes de Nascimento and José Eduardo dos Santos. The price of this cohesion was a certain narrowing of the movement's ethnic base; the leadership was now almost entirely made up of Mbundus and *mestiços*.[58] But the new-found unity immeasurably increased the movement's political effectiveness and it began a rapid process of recovery and consolidation. Meanwhile its relative position within the triangle of liberation movements continued to benefit from the backing of Rosa Coutinho whose own powers were enhanced at the end of November by the dissolution of the governing junta in Luanda and his appointment as high commissioner. Aware from the time of the Sal talks of the threat of the MPLA's marginalization, Rosa Coutinho sought to forestall any agreement being made before the MPLA was in a position to fight its corner in negotiations.[59] With the movement's star so clearly on the rise under Neto, the Active Revolt faction soon sought a *rapprochement* and at the beginning of 1975 adjustments were made in the leadership to permit the reintegration of the Andrades.[60]

Nowhere, perhaps, was Rosa Coutino's support for the MPLA at this time more important than in the Cabinda enclave. Rather overlooked in the post-25 April ferment, Cabinda nevertheless posed particular problems for the liberation movements and for Lisbon. Since 1963 the local micro-nationalist movement, FLEC, had subsisted with rival and variable support from Brazzaville and Zaire, both of which had covetous eyes on Cabinda's huge oil deposits. By 1974 these were worth some $US450 millions annually to Portugal. Two months after the April coup FLEC, which had been more or less inactive for a number of years, was re-launched.

A new and potentially dangerous element had entered the situation in October 1974 when it emerged that the local Portuguese governor, Brigadier Themudo Barata, was openly sympathetic to the separatists and was facilitating their organizing efforts.[61] The MPLA were particularly aggrieved at this as it constituted the main nationalist counter-weight to FLEC in Cabinda. Among the governor's military staff were a number of younger officers close to the MFA and, in support of the MPLA, they reported their superior to Luanda. With Rosa Coutinho's approval, a joint MPLA–MFA force entered Cabinda, encountering only minimal resistance from FLEC. The separatist forces were dispersed in the direction of Congo-Brazzaville and Brigadier Barata was arrested and returned to Portugal. The joint action with the MPLA was justified by Rosa Coutinho on the grounds that the integration of Cabinda in Angola was the policy of not only the OAU and the UN but of all three Angola liberation movements. It was also argued that a joint force was preferable to leaving the MPLA to act alone.[62] It would, though, have been inconceivable for Rosa Coutinho's administration to have engaged in a similar operation with either the FNLA or UNITA. The effect of the undertaking in legitimizing the MPLA could not have been absent from the 'red Admiral's' calculations.[63]

The first significant move forward in the decolonization process in the post-Spínola period began with the conclusion of formal cease-fire agreements between Portugal and the liberation movements. UNITA had, as we have seen, agreed a cessation of hostilities with the Portuguese as early as June, and there had been a *de facto* cease-fire in operation with the MPLA since Rosa Coutinho's arrival at the end of July. There now began a pre-negotiation process in which these truces with the Portuguese were formalized and separate bilateral agreements were reached between the movements themselves. In the second week of October a Portuguese delegation led by the former Spinolist defence minister Firmino Miguel had talks in Kinshasa with both Mobutu and Roberto. These led to an agreement for a cease-fire with the FNLA to take immediate effect.[64] Two weeks later a formal cease-fire agreement was signed with the MPLA inside Angola close to the Zambian frontier after a day of talks between Neto and the Portuguese naval commander in Angola, Admiral Leonel Cardoso.[65] A few days after this UNITA was given guarantees that it too would still be considered a legitimate interlocutor in formal negotiations after a meeting between Savimbi and Rosa Coutinho, also inside Angola.[66]

Communications between the movements themselves were less fluent. The formalization of cease-fires had the unintended effect initially of worsening inter-movement relations as rival offices were opened in Luanda and their respective supporters began to clash in the streets.[67] Left to itself Lisbon would probably have had a major struggle to achieve any cross-movement cooperation. The process was, however, lubricated by the OAU which pressed the three movements to find a common platform as a preliminary to any substantive negotiations with the Portuguese. Confronted with this unlikely front between Portugal and their African supporters, the movements bowed to the inevitable and concluded their own agreements. On 25 November the relatively easy advance of an FNLA–UNITA agreement was achieved under the chairmanship of Mário Soares in Kinshasa. Rosa Coutinho, once again concerned at the possible marginalization of the MPLA, succeeded in bringing a UNITA delegation to Luso in Angola and managed to broker an agreement between it and the MPLA on 18 December.[68] The most obviously difficult agreement – that between the MPLA and the FNLA – was not concluded until the last moment. Again under pressure from neighbouring governments, the three Angolan movements met in Mombassa in Kenya in the first days of January 1975. The MPLA–FNLA agreement was reached on 4 January and the next day the common platform was announced. Two days later the delegations began to arrive at the Penina Hotel in the Algarve resort of Alvor for what were intended to be the definitive negotiations for the independence of Angola.

The Alvor Agreement

The Alvor talks were held over five days between 10 and 15 January 1975 with the participation only of the three principal liberation movements. A number of other groupings (including the Chipenda faction, FLEC and Fernando Falcão's FUR) sought representation, but to no avail. The principle was the now familiar one of 'revolutionary legitimacy'. This 'prevailing doctrine' was followed at Alvor, according to Melo Antunes who led the Portuguese delegation, because 'there was no retrospective way of legitimizing in a democratic manner the groups we would be talking to . . . the only legitimacy lay with those who had fought with arms for independence'.[69] In addition to Melo Antunes the Portuguese team consisted of Almeida Santos, Soares and Brigadier António da Silva Cardoso of the Luanda administration. Rosa Coutinho, although present at the talks, was not officially part of the Portuguese delegation. Neto, Roberto and Savimbi led the delegations of their respective movements.[70]

The Alvor agreement involved the creation of a transitional government with a Portuguese high commissioner and a three-man presidential collegium which would be drawn from the three movements. The 'president' of the transitional administration would be provided in rotation by each of the members of the collegium and all decisions would be taken by a two-thirds majority. There were to be twelve ministries divided equally among the four parties (that is to say, including Portugal). The transitional government was to organize elections to a constituent assembly before the end of October 1975 from candidates chosen by the three movements and this assembly would produce a new constitution. Crucially, the agreement committed the signatories to the formation of a new national army with each of the movements providing 8000 men and the Portuguese matching this with 24,000 of their own who were to remain in Angola until February 1976. Rosa Coutinho, now deeply compromised by his support for the MPLA, was regarded with such hostility by the FNLA and UNITA that there was no question of his continuing as high commissioner. He was therefore replaced by Brigadier Silva Cardoso who by his acceptability to Roberto and Savimbi inevitably incurred the suspicions of the MPLA.[71]

The calamitous consequences of the failure of the Alvor process have led·to some desperate efforts by the Portuguese players involved to shuffle off responsibility. The main line of argument, which seems to have some justification, has been that the 'Alvor' agreement had been reached before anyone arrived at Alvor. Almeida Santos, for example, has suggested that the terms of the agreement were worked out in Angola itself between the MFA and the three movements and that the function of Alvor was merely 'to tidy up the language'.[72] From the perspective of the MFA in Angola at this time, Pedro Pezarat Correia suggests that the outcome of the talks was based largely on the common platform worked out by the movements in Mombassa.[73] It is certainly the case that the essence of the agreement was pre-determined, whatever the precise location of its drafting. Unconditional independence based on a transitional period of quadripartite administration between Portugal and the three movements was the only *politically* feasible programme to be followed. That it was to prove wholly unviable in application does not mean that any more successful a formula could have been produced at Alvor, merely that what was possible was not sufficient.

The one outcome which *was* determined at Alvor itself and which *might* have affected Angola's slide into chaos was the timetable for implementation. Melo Antunes later acknowledged this and, untypically of the Portuguese political class of the time, accepted some personal responsibility. It was, he said, a 'fundamental error' not to have ensured the possibility of creating an effective unified army from the movements before agreeing a date for independence.[74] But identifying the basic weakness from a distance is one thing, imposing political conditions to avoid it at the time would have been quite another. It is extremely doubtful that the Portuguese at Alvor had the capability to force such conditions any more than they had in the discussions with Frelimo the previous September. Confronted not merely by three liberation movements anxious to see its departure but by two powerful international organizations, the OAU and the UN which were still lingeringly suspicious of its intentions, Portugal's capacity for delay was distinctly limited. In the event, on 31 January 1975 the transitional government was sworn-in and charged with the implementation of a process which would have been difficult to undertake even among like-minded politicians in a stable civil environment. So far from this was the reality of Angola that the project was never in effect initiated.

Civil War

As the supposed transitional period began, the balance of forces between the three movements in Angola was approximately the following. The FNLA was numerically the strongest with about 21,500 fighters divided between bases in northern Angola and training camps in Zaire. The MPLA army (FAPLA: Forças Armadas Populares de Libertação de Angola) was about 8000 strong, the greater part being in eastern Angola but with a considerable body in Cabinda and several hundred in Luanda. UNITA had around 6000 guerrillas, having increased its numbers dramatically since 25 April, but its forces remained ill-equipped and ill-trained. In addition, Chipenda still controlled an army of about 2000, though it was an increasingly demoralized one, located in eastern Angola and in Zaire.[75] Each of the movements was actively recruiting and the MPLA was systematically arming its civilian supporters in the *muçeques* of Luanda. All three groups were moving increasing numbers of their people into the capital in the first weeks of 1975.

In this atmosphere it was not surprising that fighting broke out virtually before the ink on the Alvor agreement had dried. In mid-February the MPLA launched an attack on the headquarters of their former comrade-in-arms, Daniel Chipenda, and expelled his supporters from the capital.[76] The unlooked for effect of this was to propel Chipenda finally into the arms of the FNLA and to bolster the latter's forces in eastern Angola with about 2000 seasoned fighters.[77] The main fighting, however, was between the MPLA and the FNLA. In mid-March the FNLA, which had been relentlessly increasing its military strength in Luanda, embarked on a sustained attempt to dislodge the MPLA from the capital. Roberto had perhaps been encouraged in this move by the receipt of some limited but politically significant clandestine American funding, the first to come directly to the FNLA rather than through Mobutu.[78] The conflict reached its peak in the last week of March when the MPLA suffered heavy losses. But the movement remained entrenched in the capital which was, after all, its main national power base.[79]

The worst of the violence coincided with the appointment of Melo Antunes as minister for foreign affairs, Mário Soares having resigned in the midst of a deepening conflict between his Socialists and the increasingly powerful PCP. The coincidence of crises in Luanda and Lisbon was a significant one. As the situation in Angola deteriorated over the spring and summer of 1975, so did that in Portugal itself, and the capacity of the metropole to intervene in any meaningful way quickly evaporated. Exerting such authority as he could, Melo Antunes, who had flown to Luanda immediately on being sworn-in, attempted to lay down the law to the presidential triumvirate. Anxious to play down the extent of the crisis on his return to Lisbon, he insisted that his visit had been 'routine' and that the problems were ones 'which, naturally, emerge in the process of decolonization'.[80] With, in the MPLA's calculation, 200 dead in the previous week's fighting, the minister's assessment was less than realistic.[81]

Outside the capital spheres of influence, frequently ethnically defined, were being established by each of the movements. In February fighting broke out in the Caxito district as the FNLA sought to expel MPLA elements there. Between November 1974 and January 1975 the FNLA had moved several thousand fighters into the Uige and Zaire provinces of northern Angola. They were followed by several more thousands of pro-FNLA Bakongo refugees who had fled across the Zairean border after the 1961 uprising and who now returned in force. This major population movement displaced some 60,000 Ovimbundu plantation workers from the area who in turn returned to the central plateau to swell support for UNITA.[82]

In addition to the military build-up, the propaganda struggle also intensified. In this the MPLA's loss of Rosa Coutinho at the head of the administration was somewhat compensated for by its control of the ministry of information (which it gained in the distribution of transitional government portfolios). The FNLA, bank-rolled by its foreign backers, was able to buy a television station as well as the main Angolan daily, *A Província de Angola*, in which it reinstated a previously ousted anti-MPLA editor.[83] UNITA, the most meagrely resourced of the movements at this time, attempted to capitalize on what it saw as the political vulnerabilities of the other two: the FNLA's reputation for racial violence and the MPLA's Marxism. UNITA's efforts to portray itself as a moderate non-racial movement worthy of the trust of both white settlers and international community were redoubled when Savimbi declared in mid-April 1975 that his movement now saw itself as 'European-orientated' in international terms.[84]

Throughout April and May fighting intensified in Luanda and in the north. The 'silent invasion' of FNLA forces from Zaire continued amidst MPLA denunciations of Portuguese inactivity.[85] The MPLA in turn accelerated its arming of supporters in Luanda's *muçeques*. By mid-May the death toll in the capital had run into thousands and any prospect of inter-movement *rapprochement* had disappeared. Within the protracted tragedy of Angolan history after 1974, the four months which followed the Alvor agreement can be seen as pivotal. This was the period in which the weaknesses of the 'settlement' were fully exposed and the characters of the parties to it most clearly revealed.

Lisbon's 'Hot Summer' and the Crisis of Control in Angola

By April 1975 the metropole itself was deep in crisis. The legitimacy, indeed the very survival, of the revolution was in question as fragmentation and polarization overtook the various centres of power which had emerged over the previous year. On 11 March there had been an attempted coup by a residue of Spinolists in the armed forces which, although easily defeated, served to heighten already considerable tensions. Violent protest was growing in the conservative north against the increasing power of the PCP in the provisional government and MFA. The same issue had come to dominate politics in Lisbon itself where Soares and the PS were more and more voluble in their denunciations of PCP manoeuvring. Talk of civil war was being taken increasingly seriously. Discipline within the military had largely broken down and the authority of the provisional government over it was extremely limited. In Portugal's *verão quente* of 1975, it was problematic as to which faction in the regime – if any – the military or any part of it would obey. While many within the armed forces – particularly on the MFA left – rationalized and legitimized this collapse of authority in the ideological language current at the time, among its roots was a largely self-interested rejection of continuing African service. The recurring slogan of MFA-backed demonstrations at this time was '*nem mais um soldado para o ultramar e o regresso daqueles que lá estão*' ('not one more soldier for the colonies and the return of those already there'). Metropolitan crisis and military disaffection could provide no basis on which Portugal might impose the terms of Alvor on Angola.

This sharp limitation of the metropole's capacity to act in Angola was compounded on the ground by a lack of control by the movements over their own forces. During his visit in March and again when he went to Luanda in the deteriorating conditions of mid-May, Melo Antunes held what appeared to be reasonably successful meetings with the leaderships of the three movements. Agreements for cease-fires were reached and commitments to the creation of effective joint forces were agreed.[86] According to Melo Antunes, however, communication *between* the movements at leadership level was less important in achieving peace on the streets than communication *within* each of the movements between top and base.[87]

Here again there was perhaps an element of wishful thinking on the minister's part. Even if these problems of interior control had been overcome it is unlikely that the broad course of events would have been much different. The Alvor agreement was unenforceable because for the MPLA and FNLA it was little more than a means of removing the residual Portuguese dimension from what had already become the 'real' Angolan conflict: that between themselves. It was not a failure of internal communication which brought the influx of FNLA fighters from Zaire. Nor can a misunderstanding of orders explain the MPLA's arming of the *muçeques* or its recruitment of thousands of former Katangese separatist 'gendarmes' to its ranks.

Twenty years later Melo Antunes was more realistic when he accepted that each of the movements, 'totally separated ideologically, politically and in their interests . . . looked on the agreement as a base for the conquest of power'.[88] At the time, however, he was required to present an impression that the agreement was fundamentally on course and that it was only necessary to find 'forms most appropriate to the Angolan reality' to reinvigorate the plans laid out at Alvor.[89] And, if this should prove beyond Lisbon's capabilities, there was even virtue to be made of impotence. 'The originality of our decolonization process', he insisted, 'lies precisely in the fact that we are not exporting models. One of the worst forms of colonialism is paternalism. It will be for Angolans to choose the model they wish to follow in the future.'[90] The reality, though, was that the Portuguese were now largely irrelevant to the process by which that 'choice' was being made. Portugal was now, in the words of Pezarat Correia, 'obliged to take on the thankless role in a war situation of exercising *de jure* power without the capacity to exercise it *de facto*'.[91]

The extent to which Lisbon's role in the transitional process had diminished was highlighted in mid-June when a last desperate attempt was made to re-establish dialogue between the movements. It was not Portugal which sought to rescue its own decolonization process now, but Kenya. A five-day meeting between the three groupings was organized by Jomo Kenyatta at Nakuru in the Rift Valley. Portugal was not invited.[92] The main focus of the conference was on the conflict between the FNLA and the MPLA but it was UNITA which was most anxious to see a reversion to the political process. Having managed to stay out of the worst of the fighting in Luanda for several months, it had been attacked by the MPLA in early June and was now, as the smallest of the movements, very much aware of its own vulnerability in a protracted armed conflict. By the terms of the Nakuru agreement which emerged on 21 June, the three movements renounced violence and committed themselves to the electoral process. The creation of a national army – which had been a centre-piece of the Alvor agreement – was again given high priority along with the disarming of civilians and the expulsion of foreign elements within the military forces of the movements.[93]

Despite some initial optimism the Nakuru agreement soon crumbled and the major round of fighting which followed it proved the most significant in the conflict thus far. The 'battle of Luanda' which began on 9 July lasted four days and ended with the expulsion of the FNLA from the capital. Another trip to Luanda by Melo Antunes in the middle of the fighting merely underlined the irrelevance of Lisbon in the unfolding civil war. His unrealized – and probably unrealizable – threat to 'intervene energetically' now sounded merely feeble.[94] Even if the Portuguese had commanded the will and resources to act decisively, 'facts on the ground' severely limited political possibilities as by now only the MPLA was left to talk to in the capital.

The ineffectualness of Portugal's professed 'active neutrality', denounced only a few weeks previously by the MPLA, was now taken by the FNLA as proof of Lisbon's Marxist sympathies. Having re-grouped in its northern strongholds, and emboldened by Roberto's return to Angola after a fourteen-year exile, the FNLA threatened to march on Luanda and to declare war on Portugal if it got in the way.[95] The Portuguese commander in Luanda now sought urgent reinforcements from Lisbon. In the midst of Portugal's crisis summer, however, these amounted only to a company each of paratroops and commandos and an infantry group, along with a promise of more when available.[96] In the meantime, rather grandly, Melo Antunes ordered the defence of Luanda 'at all costs'.[97] Fortunately for Lisbon, the commitment was not put to the test, as the FNLA stayed its hand.

From mid-July 1975 until the eve of independence in the second week of November the course of the 'decolonization process' was at first sight extremely favourable to the MPLA. With the FNLA out, the MPLA 'held' the capital with all the practical and psychological advantages that conferred. Luanda was now for all practical purposes under the joint administration of the outgoing colonial bureaucracy and the MPLA with its politically and ethnically secure base there.

Of potentially greater advantage to the MPLA, however, *should* have been the fact that the Portuguese government during these crucial months ought by all ideological indicators to have been strongly partisan. The government of prime minister Vasco Gonçalves was widely perceived as close to the PCP and dependent on the more radical elements in the MFA for its survival. The Marxist left had reached the zenith of its power in Lisbon by mid-1975 and its natural allies in Africa might have been expected to benefit. Yet despite all this there was no indication that the MPLA was especially favoured by Lisbon at this time. Indeed it appears to have received less practical support than it had the previous year during the pre-Alvor administration of Rosa Coutinho. At the end of July, for example, Portuguese troops killed several MPLA supporters and destroyed the movement's Luanda headquarters in the Villa Alice after an apparent attack on Portuguese troops at a road-block.[98] This was a significantly more robust intervention than any in the months when all three movements were in Luanda and public order had disintegrated.

Lisbon was sufficiently concerned at the Villa Alice incident to send a delegation composed of Carlos Fabião (who since returning from Guiné had become chief of the general staff in succession to Costa Gomes) and Rosa Coutinho. Their positions and reputations were designed to reassure respectively the army and the MPLA. This was no more than crisis management, however, nothing concrete emerged from the visit and it did not betoken any new understanding between the MPLA and the Lisbon government. Similarly, the replacement of high commissioner Silva Cardoso by Admiral Leonel Cardoso who was more acceptable to the MPLA was the result of Silva Cardoso's determination to resign rather than any government attempt to accommodate the Angolans.[99] There was, in short, little sense of any special relationship between the Lisbon regime and the MPLA.

The recollections of the participants throw little light on the terms of Lisbon–MPLA relations at this time. Memories appear to be conditioned by the political climate in which they were called up. In

1979, for example, Melo Antunes claimed to have advocated that 'Portugal should . . . abandon the idea of "active neutrality" and bravely and openly support the MPLA . . . '.[100] Interviewed in 1984, he insisted that his call for the defence of Luanda after the expulsion of the FNLA 'meant in effect the recognition of the *status quo* in Luanda which was under the control of the MPLA'.[101] All this suggests a high degree of partisanship on the part of the Portuguese minister for foreign affairs who was both one of the most influential figures in the Lisbon regime and the key decision-maker on African issues. His proposals, he claimed, came to nothing because of 'political indecision in Lisbon [and] the incapacity of political powers there to define the only correct way to Angolan independence'.[102] Yet his later recollections, in the less radical climate of the early 1990s, are more restrained and focus on difficulties in his relationship with Agostinho Neto.[103] The truth of the situation was probably that most senior figures and not just the professed Marxists within the Lisbon regime in mid-1975 did favour the MPLA and hoped for its success. They were, however, too heavily constrained by both domestic and international political circumstances to give tangible expression to this sympathy. '(O)ur heart was often with the positions most favourable to the MPLA', Melo Antunes recalled, 'but on the other hand we had to act with a view to the larger process.'[104]

Particularly telling in this regard was an exchange between Almeida Santos and the left-wing journalist Artur Portello in May 1975 when the former was still minister for interterritorial coordination. Criticized by Portello for not supporting the MPLA against the FNLA in the fighting then taking place in Luanda, Almeida Santos was clearly stung. 'I too', he replied, ' . . . sympathize with the MPLA, its struggle, its cause. I do not believe this would be doubted by its highest leadership, some of whom have been my friends since the old days in Coimbra.' But the responsibilities of office demanded circumspection: 'I love Angola, sympathize with the MPLA and its ideas, but I love above all peace.'[105]

Internationally, for Lisbon to have more actively supported the pro-Soviet MPLA would immediately have placed it at odds with the OAU, the UN and most of western Europe. Perhaps most importantly, it may well have been the last straw for a United States which was already questioning Portugal's continuation within the western alliance system.[106] And, had these vast systemic constraints not been enough, there were still somewhere around 200,000 white settlers in Angola whose influence on metropolitan politics had to be considered. As with so much else in Africa in 1974 and 1975, Portugal did what it had to do in Angola, and policy preferences – let alone counsels of ideological perfection – played little part in the process.

The interplay between metropolitan instability and Angolan developments was made explicit in early August when a group of prominent figures in the MFA led by Melo Antunes produced the 'Document of the Nine' (*Documento dos Nove*), an open letter to President Costa Gomes expressing grave concern with the direction of the revolution. The document came in the wake of the formation, on 31 July, of the fifth provisional government since the revolution. Under the increasingly pro-Communist prime minister Vasco Gonçalves, this was composed entirely of MFA leftists gathered loosely around the ideological leadership of Otelo Saraiva de Carvalho (by then commander of the Lisbon military region and head of the key military security unit, Copcon), and civilians unattached to the main parties. The Socialists and Social Democrats were now boycotting all government posts. Although most of the 'nine' had played prominent roles in the original revolutionary conspiracy, they now found themselves 'moderates' amidst the revolutionary ferment of the *verão quente*. Among them were the most influential military players in the decolonization process. In addition to Melo Antunes (who had been dropped as minister for foreign affairs in the new government), they included Vítor Crespo, Pezarat Correia and Vasco Lourenço.

The 'nine' mounted a comprehensive attack on the drift of the revolution in mid-1975, on the deviation of sections of the MFA from its original Programme and on the east European model of socialism favoured by elements in the latest provisional government. More particularly in relation to Africa, they argued that the instability of the political situation in the metropole threatened the 'most crucial phase of decolonization' which had now been reached in Angola. It was 'not possible to "decolonize", guaranteeing an effective, peaceful transition to true independence without a firm internal political cohesion and without, above all, continuing to consider "decolonization" until its completion, as the principal national objective'. The nine's prognosis was not optimistic: 'We are now struggling with a problem in Angola that will probably be beyond our capacities, and may create a conflict of national proportions which could, in the short term, have catastrophic and tragic consequences for Portugal and Angola.'[107] The emphasis on the interrelationship between the political prospects of Portugal and Angola was revealing. It spoke of a state of symbiosis between metropole and colony which had been absent from the decolonizing experience of Britain, or even of the Netherlands or Belgium. The closest parallel was that of France and Algeria in the final days of the French Fourth Republic. The implications of this were not lost in Portugal in August 1975.

Although dismissed by the far left in the MFA as *divisionistas*, the nine struck a chord with both President Costa Gomes and a broad strand of public feeling which was committed to a transition to 'socialism' but concerned at the direction of the MFA and provisional governments since the failure of the Spinolist *putsch* the previous March. The Document of the Nine proved crucial in accelerating the fall of the *Gonçalvistas* and the construction of a new Portuguese politics. Under pressure from a wide alliance of military moderates, the president, the non-Communist parties and an increasingly self-confident public opinion, the fifth provisional government fell on 29 August. It was succeeded by an administration led by the moderate leftist Admiral Pinheiro de Azevedo who had been one of the original members of the JSN, and Melo Antunes was re-appointed as minister of foreign affairs.

The political readjustment to which the nine and their manifesto contributed brought the revolution back in alignment with the shift in pre-coup elite opinion to a view of Portugal as a west European democracy. This change in world-view had been one towards modernization not Marxism. For the MPLA – which had anyway received little concrete solidarity from its fellow leftists when they were in power – the end of the so-called 'revolutionary process' in Lisbon and the passing of the 'hot summer' into a more reflective winter ended any hope of advantage in the run-up to independence.

Internationalization

As the Portuguese revolution passed through its pivotal moments in August 1975, the civil war in Angola and the political frame within which it was being fought continued to evolve. On 9 August the FNLA and UNITA formally announced their departure from the provisional government, a largely symbolic gesture as it had barely functioned since its formation after Alvor. More significant than the announcement itself, however, was the fact that it was made jointly by the two movements.

At the beginning of the month a final attempt had been made by Melo Antunes to broker an agreement between the MPLA and UNITA with a view to the establishment of some kind of working relationship. This proved impossible, largely as a result of MPLA intransigence.[108] Now abandoning the fiction of the existence of a transitional government, Lisbon suspended the Alvor agreement on 22 August. Such meagre authority as Portugal could exercise passed into the hands of the new high commissioner, Admiral Leonel Cardoso, who arrived on 5 September. With a rueful honesty uncharacteristic of the generality of Portugal's pronouncements on Angola, he observed that he had left Lisbon 'without the comfort of the presence of any political or military leader . . . to give me some words of farewell, sympathy or encouragement'. He had accepted 'a mission that nobody would want'.[109] The contrast with the pomp and grandness of the swearing-in ceremonies of the Spínola presidency could hardly have been greater – or more telling.

By the beginning of September the MPLA appeared to be making major advances. It had extended its control over twelve of Angola's sixteen provinces and was poised to expand its influence even further before 11 November, the date fixed for independence. The cost of this had been a generalized civil war in which some 8000 had died since the beginning of the year. For Portugal itself, a major consequence was an army of *retornados*, white settler refugees, flooding back to strain an already straitened economy. A significant outflow of Europeans had begun shortly after the Alvor agreement and had gradually increased until, by July, it had become a major population movement. Although many made their way to other African destinations, mainly South Africa and Rhodesia, the majority of the 200,000 or so whites who remained in the territory at the middle of the year sought to return to Portugal. At the beginning of August Lisbon announced an airlift which with the help of a number of foreign governments would repatriate all Europeans before independence.[110]

That Portugal succeeded not only in bringing the *retornados* home but in integrating them (and their Mozambican counterparts) into the national life with so little social and political upheaval is one of the most remarkable – though often unremarked – achievements of the revolution. Their abandonment of Angola, so obviously permanent, confirmed the growing sense that the situation was simply moving out of Portugal's field of responsibility. Keenly aware of the damage the revolutionary process had done to its prestige in Europe, however, and anxious to sustain the image of the revolution as harbinger of an 'exemplary decolonization', Lisbon sought to maintain the outward signs of authority.[111]

Following the suspension of the Alvor agreement at the end of August, Portugal embarked on a major diplomatic offensive aimed both at asserting its own continuing role in the crisis and encouraging a wider international interest. Almeida Santos, although no longer in the government, was despatched to the UN to speak to both the secretary-general and the president of the Security Council while other emissaries were sent to key African capitals and to Brazilia.[112]

In mid-September Leonel Cardoso announced that Portugal would resist making any final independence arrangements with a single movement and that the UN might be called on to mediate.[113] This line of thinking was ill-received by the MPLA which on the strength of its control of the capital sought to have power formally transferred to it alone on 11 November. The movement was further angered by Melo Antunes's ministerial address to the UN General Assembly at the beginning of October. In this he called for an international effort aimed at 'the immediate convening of a conference between the three liberation movements and Portugal . . . in which specific forms or means of transferring . . . powers would be studied'.[114] Such a development would have represented a return to the pre-Alvor *status quo* and rendered the MPLA's victory in the 'battle of Luanda' and its losses throughout the civil war meaningless. The MPLA position was that Portugal had been forced to suspend Alvor as a result of FNLA and UNITA misdeeds and that any renegotiation of the agreement would only serve to legitimize these infractions.[115] To the MPLA, therefore, the UN speech had been 'unrealistic and patronizing'.[116]

On his return from Mozambique after its independence in June, Vítor Crespo had been appointed minister for cooperation, the successor portfolio to that of interterritorial coordination which had been held by Almeida Santos since May 1974. Crespo's appointment was an astute one; direct responsibility for Angola now lay in the hands of a leading figure in the revolution who had won the trust and respect of Frelimo, the MPLA's ideological partner and sister-movement in the CONCP. At the end of October Crespo sought to exploit this prestige by travelling to Luanda in a final attempt to bring the three movements together. The extent to which Portugal's influence on the course of events had diminished was now plain: the MPLA declined to discuss the issue with the ministerial representative of the colonial power on the eve of independence.[117]

While Portugal's residual influence on events evaporated there was no shortage of other international actors disposed to intervene and with varying capacities to do so. Those most immediately concerned were of course Angola's regional neighbours. Like Mozambique, Angola provided major infrastructure services to adjacent countries. The Benguela railway, which ran for 1500 km inland from the port of Lobito, was used by Zaire and Zambia to export around half of their copper which was the main foreign exchange earner of both. Beyond this economic dependence, each country had major concerns over its borders with Angola. Zaire's position, with a 2400 km frontier, has already been considered in relation to its support for the FNLA. That support was based on the fact of the Bakongo ethnic group straddling the border as much as ideological preference for the FNLA's anti-communism. But Zambia too, with its 950 km frontier, had also ethnic accounts to balance on its western border. More even-handed than Zaire during the armed struggle – having favoured both the MPLA and UNITA at different times – Lusaka was nevertheless anxious to achieve a durable settlement. The energy expended by Zambia in attempting to unify the MPLA in August 1974 bore witness to this. A third significant African neighbour was Congo-Brazzaville which, although largely unconcerned by the security of its frontier (which was with Cabinda alone) was certainly anxious to prevent any significant extension of the influence of its other neighbour and rival, Zaire. Nominally Marxist in orientation, the Brazzaville regime supported the MPLA with a view to winning an ideological ally in the region. Relatively poor in resources, Brazzaville had also an eye to a share of Cabinda's mineral wealth.

With such disparate interests Angola's African neighbours could do nothing to impose coherence on the inter-faction struggle in Angola. On the contrary, despite their obvious mutual self-interest in achieving a stable settlement, they continued to support their respective clients as the civil war deepened. These differences were reflected more widely in black Africa. The OAU was itself divided and sought to cover its own weakness in the situation by insisting that the ultimate responsibility for a viable outcome lay with Portugal. Fact-finding missions were dispatched by the organization but produced confused and unconvincing reports. Lofty talk of an OAU peace-keeping force which emerged from its Kampala summit at the beginning of August 1975 was brushed aside by the protagonists in Angola.[118] So far as the OAU had a 'policy' on Angola it was for a tripartite coalition government. Like Portugal the OAU sought refuge in the illusion that the Alvor formula could be resurrected. The Angola crisis proved to be the first of a sequence of sub-Saharan problems in the late 1970s and 1980s in which the inherent weaknesses of the OAU as an inter-governmental organization would be exposed.

There was, however, one regional actor with the physical capacity to influence events and the political motivation to exercise it: South Africa. The Angolan crisis was to become for South Africa, in the view of one veteran observer of the region, the most traumatic event since the Anglo-Boer war.[119] Pretoria's interests in Angola and the nature of its post-colonial regime were numerous and pressing. The course, indeed the outcome, of South Africa's protracted bush war against the South West Africa Peoples Organization (SWAPO) in Namibia was one major concern. While Angola was Portuguese the South African Defence Force (SADF) enjoyed a broad freedom of action in the Angola–Namibia border area and on occasion the active participation of the colonial army in joint operations.[120] A hostile regime in Luanda would not only end this advantage but would be likely to extend base facilities to SWAPO inside Angola.

Beyond these direct security concerns, considerable South African investment – much of it from state funds – had also gone into the Cunene Dam project in the border area. Like the Cabora Bassa project in Mozambique, Cunene was intended to supplement energy and water needs in South African-controlled territory.[121] In addition, considerable private investment had been made by South African companies in recent years in Angola's developing mineral industries, particularly in diamond mining.

The end of Portuguese Angola was not seen by Pretoria as inevitably and wholly threatening to South African interests. A biddable post-colonial regime in Angola might not merely protect these security and economic interests but offer new economic and political opportunities. Diplomatically there was the potential for an important new dimension to Pretoria's current project for *rapprochement* with black Africa. Up to 1975 this had been pursued with some success in relation to Malawi, Zaire and even Zambia. It was in part the reason for South Africa's generally restrained response to the transfer of power to Frelimo in Mozambique and a cordial working relationship with the new regime in Luanda would represent a huge advance for the project. To this end Pretoria had maintained a relatively low public profile on Angola in the immediate aftermath of the Lisbon coup, adopting a position of outward diplomatic correctness similar to that taken towards Mozambique. But it was following the unfolding of events extremely closely.

Initially only an FNLA victory appeared to meet South Africa's requirements. The MPLA was clearly ruled out by virtue of its Marxism while UNITA, with ethnic affinities to the

Ovambo-dominated SWAPO, had long associated itself with the cause of Namibia. Savimbi's post-coup campaign for white support in Angola and western sympathy abroad, however, caused a gradual revision of Pretoria's assessment.[122] By the northern summer of 1975 meetings were being held in Windhoek in Namibia between senior figures in the SADF and with the leaders of the FNLA and UNITA as well as with Daniel Chipenda.[123]

At the beginning of August 1975 South Africa finally committed its forces to the Angolan civil war, but still with a degree of caution. Troops were sent across the border to occupy and secure the Ruacana Falls at the centre of the Cunene project. Fighting had broken out between the FNLA and MPLA in the area and the South African operation was presented as a limited one in line with the reasonable protection of national interests.[124] By the end of the month the SADF force in Angola was about 1000 strong and its presence extended to the southern administrative centre of Pereira d'Eça.[125]

Pretoria's intentions were now coming under increasing scrutiny abroad. These intentions seemed to become clearer at the end of October when two South African-led strike forces were launched northwards. Operation 'Zulu' moved up along the coast while 'Foxbat' shadowed it further to the east.[126] The forces were composed of SADF armoured cars and specialist troops, elements of the FNLA, UNITA and the Chipenda faction. They also included a considerable formation of Portuguese 'settlers' – or 'mercenaries', depending on the political disposition of the observer. In all somewhere between 1500 and 2000 South African regulars were involved in the operation.[127] By the first week of November 1975, on the eve of the independence date, the apparently unstoppable invasion force was within striking distance of Luanda. To nobody's surprise there were no orders this time to Portuguese forces for the defence of the capital 'at all costs'.

The factors underlying South Africa's decision to invade were complex. In one view, Pretoria's intervention seems wholly at odds with its larger objective of achieving a regional *rapprochement*. This apparent contradiction between long-term diplomatic objectives and the pursuit of short-term strategic interests lay in the divided attitudes of the key decision-makers. Prime minister John Vorster and the defence minister P.W. Botha disregarded the advice of the more cautious security chief General Hendrik Van den Bergh.[128]

The realization that South Africa was engaged in an outright invasion of Angola predictably brought a furious response throughout black Africa. In the wake of this the standing of Pretoria's collaborators, both the FNLA and UNITA, dropped dramatically throughout the continent. Yet viewed from another position the decision, though a gamble, might not have been such a reckless one. With Zaire firmly committed to the FNLA–UNITA alliance which had emerged since the battle of Luanda, and with Zambia at least ambivalent in its sympathies, the South African invasion could have been seen as *building* on *rapprochement* rather than undermining it. The invasion, after all, had the clear effect of shifting the balance of power between the movements away from the MPLA which had hitherto been extending its military successes around Luanda. Zaire itself had as early as July 1975 sent regular troops into northern Angola in support of the FNLA and had expanded this commitment in August, just as the South Africans were moving from the south.[129]

Zaire, though, had never represented the sensibilities and sympathies of black Africa as a whole. If Pretoria saw its own actions in the broader context of a regional anti-MPLA alliance it was a fatal miscalculation. News of its involvement forced African leaders who in their own councils may have been at least open-minded about the effects of the South African action into fierce public denunciations. Perhaps most significantly, Nigeria, which by virtue of its oil wealth appeared at the time to be the emerging leader of the sub-Saharan region, immediately abandoned its original sympathies with the FNLA and enriched the MPLA's war chest by about $US20 million.[130]

Outside of Africa Pretoria still had some reason to believe its actions were acceptable. Far from being anathematized by the international community, it had already received the tacit approval of some major actors, most importantly the United States. The extent of collusion between Pretoria and Washington in the latter part of 1975 has never been fully established. But the United States' support for the FNLA in the north was hardly secret by this time. As we have seen, Washington's links with Roberto were long-standing if irregular, going back to the Kennedy administration in the early 1960s. The United States had also maintained a special relationship with Zaire which had been in receipt of economic and military aid since the 'pro-western' Mobutu had seized power in 1964. Roberto and the FNLA had benefited from the 'trickle down' from this American *largesse*. As the situation inside Angola deteriorated during 1975, American assistance to the FNLA soon went far beyond the limited political funds provided immediately after the Alvor agreement.

In July President Ford agreed to a plan by his secretary of state,

Henry Kissinger, for the provision of $US32 million in funding and a further $US16 million in arms for the FNLA which were to be delivered through Zaire. The plan went ahead despite the reservations of influential elements in the American intelligence community.[131] The intervention was also apparently opposed by the American consul-general in Luanda who considered the MPLA, its Marxism notwithstanding, to be the only one of the contending movements capable of forming a competent administration.[132] According to Nathaniel Davis, who had recently become assistant secretary of state for African affairs, the decision was taken in the crisis atmosphere following the expulsion of the FNLA from Luanda.[133] It was no more than common sense that an operation of this type, already clandestine, should involve cooperation with other like-minded players – in this case South Africa. It is only the extent of this cooperation which remains unclear. John Marcum has argued that the US relied to a considerable degree on South African intelligence assessment of the situation in Angola and at 'the very least the US connived at the South African intervention and sought to cooperate with it'.[134] Elsewhere he noted the South African prime minister's refusal to discount suggestions that Washington had actually 'solicited' the invasion.[135]

Nor was implicit support for South Africa forthcoming only from America. France too, ploughing its own foreign policy furrow as always in Africa, sought to safeguard its economic interests in the region by supporting the FNLA–UNITA alliance.[136] Gerald Ford himself recorded France's aid for 'forces sympathetic to the west' and recalled that Paris had 'agreed to work in conjunction with us'.[137] It is clear then that some triangle of tacit collusion existed between Pretoria, Washington and Paris, though the nebulousness of the relationship created great latitude for mutual misperceptions.

One element of the arrangement which had always been quite apparent, however, was its fundamental dependency on American policy. When in December 1975 the extent of American involvement was publicly exposed after a press leak, the entire foreign effort on behalf of FNLA–UNITA began to disintegrate.[138] The American legislature, its post-Vietnam suspicions of executive clandestinity fully engaged and keenly aware of the possible consequences of association with the South African invasion, brought the operation to a halt. In December 1975 the Senate ended all further funding and was supported by the House of Representatives the following month. The so-called Clark amendment put and end to significant American involvement in Angola until its repeal during the Reagan administration a decade later. With the American withdrawal France too backed away from its more limited involvement. Now without even tenuous western support, South Africa prepared to cut its mounting losses and withdraw from Angola. In the meantime the entire character of the Angolan conflict and its international significance had been transformed.

It was not primarily concern over the regional politics of south-central Africa that brought Angola to the attention of Henry Kissinger and the FNLA its $US50 million in American aid. The essence of Kissinger's world-view as secretary of state (and indeed of the academic theories of international relations he had espoused in his previous incarnation as university professor) was a 'realism' which placed the international system rather than the polities and ideologies which composed it at the centre of analysis. His concern, as he freely admitted, was not with Angola or even Africa as such but with their role in a 'globalist' central balance.[139] It was a mindset which had been little altered by recent American experience in south-east Asia. The Vietnam débâcle should, as Gerald Bender observed, have 'warned against grafting a global construct onto local conflicts fired by historical, ethnic, political and economic realities'.[140] Kissinger had not, evidently, heeded the warning.

There were, of course, considerable American economic interests in play in Angola with both Gulf and Texaco heavily involved in exploration and exploitation of the territory's oil resources. But these interests were not significantly threatened by the MPLA. Indeed, in the pragmatic way of these things, relations between the Marxist liberation movement and the American multinationals were rather good.[141] Kissinger's concerns lay elsewhere. The executive manager, if not the architect of *détente*, he regarded what he perceived as Soviet incursions in the region as a breach of the superpower rules then in force. Vietnam had already cast doubts on the continuing viability of *détente* as a means of organizing superpower relations. Quiet approaches by Kissinger aimed at re-aligning Moscow with the *détente* process during the first rounds of fighting in Angola had apparently been rebuffed and Soviet aid to the MPLA increased.[142] Now, in Marcum's words, 'Angola was to be the post-Vietnam testing ground of American will and power in the face of the global expansion of a bullish rival whose recently realised military outreach was seen to be leading it towards dangerous adventures'.[143] Not only did Kissinger's approach ignore Angolan realities, but, less explicably in one claiming an olympian awareness of global dynamics, it also misperceived the nature of the Soviet 'threat'.

The real object of Moscow's rivalry in Angola was less Washington than Beijing.[144] Chinese influence in southern Africa had been growing steadily since the mid-1960s. Initially this had been most evident in the eastern part of the region, notably in the construction of the Zambia–Tanzania railway, but it gradually extended to Zaire and eventually Angola. Beijing's favour in the form of weapons and instructors was bestowed mainly on Roberto but it extended in more modest form to Savimbi as well – particularly during his 'Maoist' phase. Chinese interests in Africa were primarily political rather than economic and were therefore expressed in support for avowedly anti-Soviet movements. While Frelimo, as the single viable liberation movement in Mozambique, escaped Chinese hostility, the MPLA shared the stage in Angola with rival movements more than happy to act as Beijing's proxies against a perceived Soviet client. In 1973 Roberto visited Beijing and secured the provision of 100 military advisers and 450 tons of weapons.[145] Although the original purpose of this aid – the pursuit of the anti-colonial war – was superseded by events, it was still provided and weapons and trainers began to arrive in Kinshasa in June 1974. They were now employed on a new project which was congenial to both donor and recipient: the war against the pro-Soviet MPLA.

The Soviet response to this was to reverse the reductions in its aid to the MPLA imposed when the movement appeared to be imploding into factions in 1972 and 1973. A US government estimate put Soviet military aid to the MPLA between March 1975 and the end of the year at between $US100 million and $US200 million. This included some 170 advisers as well as armoured vehicles, aircraft and what was to prove one of its most devastating weapons on the ground, the 122 mm rocket.[146] Of much greater significance both militarily and politically, however, was Soviet influence over an asset not available to either the United States or China. From the beginning of November 1975 the war in Angola and the diplomatic context within which it was fought changed decisively with the appearance of the first combat units of the Cuban army.

The origins of the Cuban intervention, its timing and the extent of foreknowledge of it remain disputed. According to the Colombian novelist Gabriel García Márquez who published an account of the operation in the *New Left Review* in 1977, the decision to intervene was not taken by Fidel Castro until 5 November, less than a week before the date fixed for independence.[147] A limited Cuban presence had, however, been evident from September as supplies and military equipment for the MPLA flowed in through

Congo-Brazzaville.[148] Castro had apparently informed Otelo Saraiva de Carvalho of his intention to intervene with combat forces during a visit to Havana by the latter just before the first troops were dispatched, though the information was not communicated by Otelo to the Lisbon government.[149] But even without Otelo's intelligence it is difficult to see how the government could have been unaware of Cuban intentions. Talks he had held with Julius Nyrere and Samora Machel prior to the arrival of the Cubans convinced Vítor Crespo that both Tanzania and Mozambique knew at least that some major foreign intervention was in preparation.[150] The first contingent of 650 men arrived by air in Luanda on 8 November when the airport was still under Portuguese military control. According to García Márquez, prior permission for the landing had been given by the high commissioner, Leonel Cardoso.[151] The important question is perhaps not whether Lisbon *knew* of the coming intervention but whether its complaisance was due to partisanship or impotence.

The extent to which Cuba intervened in Angola as a Soviet proxy is no more easy to judge than the extent of US collusion with the South African invasion. Cuban interest in the anti-Portuguese struggle seems to have begun after a meeting between Amílcar Cabral and Fidel Castro at the Havana tricontinental conference in 1966. The PAIGC were the first to benefit from this interest with the establishment of Cuban-staffed training camps in Guinea-Conakry and even Cuban participation in attacks inside Guiné-Bissau.[152] Around the same time Che Guevara had been in Congo-Brazzaville where he came into contact with the MPLA and this led to Cuban support for Neto as well. In Mozambique Frelimo received relatively little military aid from Cuba during the armed struggle, but in common with the other territories, it sent a steady flow of its younger cadres for education and training in Cuba.[153] Cuba's participation in the Angolan war, therefore, came as the culmination of a considerable history of African involvement. The Cuban 'Operation Carlotta' (named in honour of the leader of a slave uprising which took place in November 1843 on the anniversary of the Angolan intervention) may reasonably be thought to have begun on Havana's own initiative in response to a direct plea by the MPLA.[154] What can be said with some confidence, however, is that Cuba would not have intervened *against* Soviet wishes, and given the nature of the Cuban–Soviet relationship, the fact that opposition was not expressed must itself be taken as collusion. It is inconceivable that Soviet acquiescence was not sought before concrete commitments were undertaken by Havana.

The intervention proved crucial to the outcome of the war. On their arrival the first Cubans had apparently judged the situation so grave that they thought their best hope would be to hold the Cabinda enclave.[155] But the seemingly irresistible South African advance northwards, which in less than three weeks had swept through the main southern population centres of Sá da Bandeira, Moçamedes and Nova Lisboa, had been halted. The MPLA had destroyed the bridges over the Queve river 200 km south of Luanda which were essential for the passage of the South African armoured column. With the arrival of the Cubans the invading force was pushed back inexorably towards the Namibian border. Finally, in March 1976, pressed militarily by the Cubans and abandoned politically by the United States, South Africa withdrew from its nine-month war in Angola. Meanwhile, to the north of Luanda, the Zairean–FNLA thrust was also met by Cuban forces. Despite extensive covert American support and the dubious assistance of white mercenaries, Roberto's challenge to the MPLA soon disintegrated, along with the FNLA itself.[156] China, sensing the FNLA cause lost and fearing the consequences for its broader African policy of continuing to be associated with it, had quietly withdrawn its support in the middle of November.[157] By February 1976 the 'second war of liberation', as the MPLA was to describe it, had ended, at least for the present.

Independence

In the meantime, Angola had been 'decolonized'. On 11 November Portugal formally transferred sovereignty to 'the Angolan people'. This formulation was proposed by a panel of constitutional experts commissioned by Vítor Crespo to find a way out of the crisis for Lisbon as the independence date fixed at Alvor approached.[158] The two other options presented – recognition of the Luanda regime (that is to say the MPLA) and recognition of a government of national unity – were respectively politically unacceptable and simply meaningless.

The 'responsible' course of action for a metropole determined to control the decolonization process would, of course, have been to postpone the date of independence until the situation had been stabilized. This was neither feasible nor remotely attractive. Lisbon wanted out and was determined to get out regardless of the short-term damage to its prestige. Although the suspension of the Alvor agreement had not brought any reconsideration of the timing of independence, it *was* used by Lisbon to justify a change in the timetable for the withdrawal of its forces. These were now to be out of Angola by independence instead of the previously agreed date of February 1976.[159] Accordingly, the Portuguese flag was lowered with minimum ceremony on 10 November and the Portugal's 500-year occupation of Africa ended as the last remnants of the colonial army rushed to their waiting ships. There was no Portuguese presence at the following day's ceremony which proclaimed the People's Republic of Angola under the presidency of Agostinho Neto.[160] Rosa Coutinho, characteristically, sent his revolutionary greetings and regretted that his position in the Lisbon regime prevented his accepting Neto's personal invitation.[161]

Even as the MPLA proclaimed its republic in Luanda, the FNLA–UNITA alliance was declaring national independence under the 'Democratic Republic of Angola' in Savimbi's stronghold of Nova Lisboa (which henceforward reverted to its pre-1925 name, Huambo). Roberto meanwhile remained in his base at Ambriz, 120 km north of Luanda, and there was some confusion as to where the seat of the Democratic Republic's government was actually located. The MPLA regime was immediately recognized by its fellow lusophone African states, by other African radicals such as Algeria and Guinea-Conakry, by Brazil and by the Soviet bloc. Portugal, however, in conformity with its post-Alvor 'even-handedness' between the three movements and fully aware of the sharpening global dimension to the situation, withheld its recognition. The political climate in Lisbon had changed dramatically during the autumn of 1975. Portugal was now moving rapidly away from the fragmented and unstable radicalism of the 'hot summer' and, although the MPLA had derived no particular benefit from this radicalism, it was now victim of Lisbon's 'morning after' determination to make amends to its western allies for its ideological binge.

Beyond these jurisprudential and diplomatic considerations, Portugal's reticence at this time also had a sound practical base. As independence was declared the MPLA controlled only a coastal enclave around Luanda, a narrow corridor inland to Malanje and one or two isolated centres in the interior. The Cuban intervention was still winding up and the military tide had still to turn. Portugal would not, in the event, recognize the MPLA regime until the following February when the totality of the Cuban-aided MPLA victory had become apparent and to have withheld recognition further would have constituted an act of obvious diplomatic hostility.

To the MPLA, however, Portugal's 'neutrality', of which it had complained consistently since the Alvor agreement, was merely pusillanimous. Lisbon's stance in the immediate aftermath of independence was to be a significant complicating factor in the building of post-independence relations with Luanda and contributed, in the view of Melo Antunes, to Angola's continued reliance on the Soviet Union.[162] Unable to exercise any significant influence on its 'own' decolonization process in Angola over most of its final year, Portugal seemed determined to assert itself in the post-independence period – however counter-productive that assertion might eventually prove.

Notes

1 Kenneth L. Adelman, 'Report from Angola', *Foreign Affairs* 53(3) 1975, p.563.

2 *Expresso*, 4 May 1974.

3 António de Spínola, *País sem Rumo: Contributo para a História de uma Revolução* (Lisbon: Scire 1978), p.312.

4 Pedro Pezarat Correia, *Descolonização de Angola: A Jóia da Corona do Império Português* (Lisbon: Inquérito 1991), p.100.

5 Keith Somerville, *Angola: Politics, Economics and Society* (London: Pinter 1986), p.41.

6 Franz-Wilhelm Heimer, *The Decolonization Conflict in Angola: An Essay in Political Sociology* (Geneva: Institut Universitaire de Hautes Etudes Internationales 1979), p.45.

7 Pezarat Correia, *Descolonização de Angola*, p.74.

8 José Friere Antunes, *O Factor Africano* (Lisbon: Bertrand 1990), p.100.

9 Spínola, *País sem Rumo*, p.311.

10 R.A.H. Robinson, *Contemporary Portugal: A History* (London: George Allen and Unwin 1979), p.212.

11 Pezarat Correia later claimed Spínola had 'put the name of Silvério Marques in the briefcase' of Almeida Santos. Interview with author, Lisbon, 2 March 1995.

12 *O Jornal*, 19–26 April 1976.

13 Spínola, *País sem Rumo*, p.313; Interview with António de Almeida Santos, Lisbon, 3 March 1995. Rosa Coutinho undermined the claim that a consensus had emerged in favour of Silvério Marques when he recalled Almeida Santos as complaining that 'there are forty potential governors and the appointment of any one would upset the supporters of the others'. Rosa Coutinho, 'Notas sobre a descolonização de Angola', *Seminário: 25 de Abril 10 Anos Depois* (Lisbon: Associação 25 de Abril 1984) p.360.

14 António de Spínola, *Ao Serviço de Portugal* (Lisbon: Ática 1976), p.87.

15 Spínola, *País sem Rumo*, p.313.

16 Pezarat Correia, *Descolonização de Angola*, pp.78–9.

17 Recollections of Silvério Marques in *O País*, 21 May 1976.

18 *Africa Contemporary Record 1974–1975* (London: Rex Collings 1975), p.B531.

19 Pezarat Correia, *Descolonização de Angola*, p.82.

20 In his message to Spínola, General Franco Pinheiro observed that: 'the MFA in Angola does not see the governor-general as integrated in the spirit of the Movement and attributes to his attitudes much of the deplorable politico-military panorama in Angola'. Quoted in Spínola, *País sem Rumo*, p.315.

21 *Sunday Times* Insight Team, *Portugal: The Year of the Captains* (London: Deutsch 1975), p.157. Ten years later Rosa Coutinho suggested, half jokingly, that 'perhaps, purely and simply, it was to get rid of me'. 'Notas sobre a descolonização de Angola', p.361.

22 Interview with António de Almeida Santos, Lisbon, 3 March 1995.

23 Spínola, *País sem Rumo*, p.317.

24 Melo Antunes interview, in Maria João Avillez, *Do Fundo da Revolução* (Lisbon: Público, 1994) p.33.

25 *O Jornal*, 19 March 1976.

26 Adelman, 'Report from Angola', p.561; Spínola, *País sem Rumo*, p.319fn.

27 Insight, *The Year of the Captains*, p.158.

28 Spínola, *País sem Rumo*, p.318.

29 Rosa Coutinho, 'Notas sobre a descolonização de Angola', p.362.

30 *Expresso*, 3 August 1974.

31 Translation of JSN text in *Africa Contemporary Record 1974–1975*, p.C40.

32 John Marcum, *The Angolan Revolution*, vol.2: *Exile Politics and Guerrilla Warfare, 1962–76* (Cambridge MA: MIT Press 1978), p.244.

33 Spínola, *País sem Rumo*, p.321.

34 *Diário de Notícias*, 17 September 1974.

35 As well as Almeida Santos and Dias de Lima, the Portuguese side consisted of defence minister Lt. Col. Firmino Miguel, Lt. Col. Almeida Bruno, and Colonel Robin de Andrade – all Spínola acolytes from his days as governor-general of Guiné. Pezarat Correia, *Descolonização de Angola*, p.87.

36 Before the talks began Almeida Santos had been sent by Spínola to investigate the pro-PAIGC demonstration which had confronted them on their arrival. Spínola, *País sem Rumo*, p.322fn.

37 This communiqué stated merely that the 'presidents of the Republic of Zaire and of Portugal met on the island of Sal for an exchange of views. Among other things discussed were problems related to the decolonization process underway in the Portuguese African territories.' *Diário de Notícias*, 16 September 1974.

38 Robinson, *Contemporary Portugal*, p.213.

39 Charles K. Ebinger, 'External intervention in internal war: the politics and diplomacy of the Angolan civil war', *Orbis* 20(3) 1976, pp.686–7.

40 Marcum, *Exile Politics and Guerrilla Warfare*, p.251.

41 Quoted in Kenneth Maxwell, 'Portugal and Africa: the last empire', P. Gifford and W.R. Louis, eds, *The Transfer of Power in Africa: Decolonization 1940–1960* (New Haven CT: Yale University Press 1982) p.364.

42 Spínola, *País sem Rumo*, p.322.

43 Pezarat Correia, *Descolonização de Angola*, p.87.

44 *Expresso*, 21 September 1974.

45 Insight, *Year of the Captains*, pp.158–9; Spínola, *País sem Rumo*, p.319.

46 *Diário de Notícias*, 24 September 1974.

47 Pezarat Correia, *Descolonização de Angola*, p.89. Some dispute surrounds the selection of the participants. Pezarat Correia suggests the meeting was organized for Spínola by Almeida Santos. The latter, however, has subsequently denied any role other than provision of a venue in his ministry. Interview with António de Almeida Santos, Lisbon, 3 March 1995.

48 Spínola, *Ao Serviço de Portugal*, pp.204–7.

49 Pezarat Correia, *Descolonização de Angola*, pp.108–9.

50 Rosa Coutinho, 'Notas sobre a descolonização de Angola', p.361. Further disorder was provoked in particular by the PCDA. Now unconstrained by Spínola, Rosa Coutinho was able to act with some firmness against the various plotters. Heimer, *The Decolonization Conflict in Angola*, pp.45–6.

51 Marcum, *Exile Politics and Guerrilla Warfare*, p.244.

52 *Africa Contemporary Record, 1974–1975*, p.B534.

53 Ebinger, 'External intervention in internal war', p.686.

54 Marcum, *Exile Politics and Guerrilla Warfare*, p.248.

55 Maxwell, 'Portugal and Africa', p.365.

56 The Central Committee was to be composed of sixteen from the Neto camp, thirteen from Chipenda's Eastern Revolt and ten from the Andrades' Active Revolt. The Politburo would consist of three members of each faction.

57 Rosa Coutinho, for example, claimed in May 1975 that Chipenda had originally been infiltrated into the MPLA by PIDE. *Diário de Notícias*, 15 May 1975. There is no corroboration for this accusation though it is characteristic of the Admiral's increasingly close identification with the MPLA at that time.

58 Marcum, *Exile Politics and Guerrilla Warfare*, p.251.

59 Heimer, *The Decolonization Conflict in Angola*, p.50.

60 *Expresso*, 8 March 1975.

61 The actual strength and support of FLEC in Cabinda at this time has been the subject of wildly differing calculations. Joseph C. Miller suggests 'no more than a few dozen men under arms', 'The politics of decolonization in Portuguese Africa', *African Affairs* 74(295), April 1975, p.145. Kenneth Adelman, in contrast, claims an 'army of a thousand soldiers', 'Report from Angola', p.565. The evident failure of FLEC to make any significant impact on either the Portuguese or the MPLA suggests that Miller's assessment may be closer to reality.

62 Pezarat Correia, *Descolonização de Angola*, pp.112–13. Pezarat Correia himself led the Luanda MFA delegation which arrested the governor.

63 The arrest of Barata was regarded by Spínola as proof of Rosa Coutinho's 'plan to hand Angola over to a single group – the MPLA.' *País sem Rumo*, p.319 and fn.

64 Firmino Miguel stood down as defence minister after the fall of Spínola. His range of contacts in Zaire was, however, too valuable to permit his complete removal from the decolonization process.

65 Pezarat Correia, *Descolonização de Angola*, p.103.

66 Rosa Coutinho later pointed to what he saw as the significant fact that the cease-fire with the FNLA was the only one agreed outside of Angolan territory. 'Notas sobre a Descolonização de Angola', p.361.

67 The FNLA opened its Luanda office on 6 November, followed by the MPLA on the 8th and UNITA on the 9th. The week between 5 and 11 November was marked by sporadic violence between the movements.

68 Rosa Coutinho, 'Notas sobre a descolonização de Angola', p.363.

69 Melo Antunes interview, *Do Fundo da Revolução*, p.27.

70 The FNLA delegation, 106 strong, was the first to arrive at Alvor, significantly perhaps, in an Air Zaire plane provided by President Mobutu. *Diário de Notícias*, 8 January 1975.

71 The misgivings of the MPLA over Silva Cardoso's appointment were evidently shared by the MFA in Luanda which suspected him of weakness under pressure and attempted, too late, to prevent his nomination. Pezarat Correia, *Descolonização de Angola*, p.130.

72 Interview with António de Almeida Santos, Lisbon, 3 March 1995.

73 Interview with Pedro Pezarat Correia, Lisbon, 2 March 1995. This view is borne out by Heimer who writes of the 'Mombassa options' being 'ratified' at Alvor, *The Decolonization Conflict in Angola*, p.57.

74 Melo Antunes interview, *Do Fundo da Revolução*, p.27.

75 Calculations of the respective strengths of the movements vary widely. In truth there are no reliable figures available. The numbers given here are based on the differing assessments of Marcum, *Exile Politics and Guerrilla Warfare*, pp.256–7; Adelman, 'Report from Angola', pp.570–1; and Tony Hodges, 'How the MPLA won in Angola', in Colin Legum and Tony Hodges, *The War over Southern Africa* (London: Rex Collings 1976), p.50.

76 *Diário de Notícias*, 14 February 1975.

77 Marcum, *Exile Politics and Guerrilla Warfare*, p.258.

78 The joint CIA–National Security Council '40 Committee' had approved the transfer of 300,000 dollars directly to the FNLA for non-military purposes a week after the Alvor agreement. Walter Isaacson, *Kissinger: A Biography* (London: Faber & Faber 1992), p.676.

79 *Expresso*, 28 March 1975.

80 Manuela de S. Rama and Carlos Planier, *Melo Antunes: Tempo de ser Firme* (Lisbon: Liber 1976), p.47.

81 *Diário de Notícias*, 2 April 1975.

82 Maxwell, 'Portugal and Africa', p.368.

83 Hodges, 'How the MPLA won in Angola', p.50.

84 *Diário de Notícias*, 16 April 1975. Two months previously another senior figure in the movement, Jorge Valentim, had described UNITA's ideology as 'a scientific socialism impregnated by Angolan realities'. *Expresso*, 15 February 1975.

85 *Diário de Notícias*, 9 May 1975.

86 A key element of the Alvor agreement had, of course, been the formation of a national army from the ranks of the three guerrilla movements. Only very limited progress had been made towards the creation of these *forças integradas* (integrated forces), however. Heimer, *The Decolonization Conflict in Angola*, p.66.

87 *Diário de Notícias*, 29 March 1975; 16 May 1975.

88 Melo Antunes interview, *Do Fundo da Revolução*, p.27.

89 *Diário de Notícias*, 14 May 1975.

90 *Ibid.*, 16 May 1975.

91 Pezarat Correia, *Descolonização de Angola*, p.149.

92 Portugal's participation at Nakuru was apparently vetoed by Roberto who considered the MFA to be sympathetic to the MPLA. Hodges, 'How the MPLA won in Angola', p.52.

93 The full terms of the Nakuru agreement are reprinted in Legum and Hodges, *The War over Southern Africa*, pp.69–75.

94 *Diário de Notícias*, 14 July 1975.

95 *Ibid.*, 22 July 1975.

96 Pezarat Correia, *Descolonização de Angola*, p.144. Even this relatively small reinforcement was the subject of demonstrations aimed at preventing its embarkation from Lisbon. Grupo de pesquisa sobre a descoloniz Zação portuguesa, *A Descolonização Portuguesa: Aproximação aun Estado* (Lisbon: Instituto Amaro da Costa 1982), vol.2, p.242.

97 Interview with Melo Antunes by Dinis de Abreu, 15 April 1984, in Fernando Pires, *Palavras no Tempo* (Lisbon: *Diário de Notícias* 1990), p.277.

98 The white extremist FRA leader, Pompílio da Cruz, later claimed that his movement was responsible for the original provocation as part of a successful conspiracy to sow dissension between the MPLA and the MFA. Pompílio da Cruz, *Angola: os Vivos e os Mortos* (Lisbon: Intervenção 1976), pp.220–1. Both Pezarat Correia and Rosa Coutinho have been prepared to believe this, though it is possible that da Cruz was merely re-writing events to exaggerate the capabilities of his movement.

99 The FNLA and UNITA affected to believe that Silva Cardoso had been forced out after criticisms of him by the MPLA at the Nakuru meeting, and attempted to prevent his replacement. In fact the outgoing high commissioner, never comfortable in the post, had simply had enough. *Diário de Notícias*, 6 August; author's interview with Pedro Pezarat Correia, Lisbon, 2 March 1995.

100 *Expresso Revista*, 17 February 1979.

101 Melo Antunes interview, *Palavras no Tempo*, p.277.

102 *Expresso Revista*, 17 February 1979.

103 Melo Antunes interview, *Do Fundo da Revolução*, p.20.

104 Interview in *Do Fundo da Revolução*, p.33.

105 Almeida Santos, *15 Meses no Governo ao Serviço da Descolonização* (Lisbon: Representações Literária 1975), pp.353 and 355.

106 On American concern at events in Portugal at this time see, for example, Kenneth Maxwell, 'The thorns of the Portuguese revolution', *Foreign Affairs* January 1976, pp.265–8 and Ingmar Oldberg, 'The Portuguese revolution in US foreign policy', *Cooperation and Conflict* XVIII (1982), pp.181–5.

107 'Documento dos Nove', reprinted in Rama and Planier, *Melo Antunes: Tempo de ser Firme*, pp.225–33.

108 Pezarat Correia, *Descolonização de Angola*, p.145.

109 *Diário de Notícias*, 6 September 1975.

110 The operation was a multinational one with aircraft and facilities being provided by the United States, Britain, France, West and East Germany and the Soviet Union. The main point of departure was the city of Nova Lisboa, Luanda being insufficiently secure in August and September 1975. *Descolonização Portuguesa*, vol.2, pp.283–5.

111 The self-congratulatory term *descolonização exemplar* was common within the MFA and provisional governments during 1974 and early 1975.

112 Pezarat Correia, *Descolonização de Angola*, pp.148–9.

113 *Diário de Notícias*, 19 September 1975.

114 UN Document A/PV.2382, 9 October 1975.

115 *Expresso*, 25 October 1975.

116 *Diário de Notícias*, 23 October 1975.

117 Interview with Vítor Crespo, Lisbon, 2 March 1995.

118 Marcum, *Exile Politics and Guerrilla Warfare*, p.262.

119 Colin Legum, 'Foreign intervention in Angola', Legum and Hodges, *The War over Southern Africa*, p.35.

120 Robin Hallett, 'The South African intervention in Angola 1975–76', *African Affairs* 77(308) 1978, p.350.

121 As with Cabora Bassa in Mozambique, the Portuguese interest in the Cunene project involved ideas for white settlement on *colonato* lines.

122 Miller, 'Politics of decolonization', p.146. The change of mind was not a rapid one. Hallett reports a meeting between UNITA and South African representatives in Europe, possibly Paris, as late as March 1975 at which Pretoria declined to provide Savimbi with any material help. 'The South African intervention in Angola', p.358.

123 Rosa Coutinho, 'Notas sobre a descolonização de Angola', p.364; Maxwell, 'The last empire', p.380.

124 SADF units had infiltrated Angola the previous month but the overt August intervention was, properly speaking, the beginning of the South African invasion. See Legum, 'Foreign intervention in Angola', p.36.

125 Michael Wolfers and Jane Bergerol, *Angola in the Frontline* (London: Zed 1983), p.12.

126 Hallett, 'The South African intervention in Angola', p.369.

127 Hodges 'How the MPLA won in Angola', p.56.

128 Hallett, 'The South African intervention in Angola', p.366.

129 Nathaniel Davis, 'The Angola decision of 1975: a personal memoir', *Foreign Affairs* 57(1) 1978, p.121.

130 John A. Marcum, 'Lessons of Angola', *Foreign Affairs* 54(3) 1976, p.419.

131 Isaacson, *Kissinger*, p.677. Nathaniel Davis's opposition to the American operation led to his removal from the State Department in September 1975. Legum makes the point that these internal divisions among American decision-makers undermine the Marxist analysis 'which assumes a monolithic US imperialist commitment to defend its monopoly of financial interests'. 'Foreign intervention in Angola', p.26.

132 Inge Tvedten, 'US policy towards Angola since 1975', *Journal of Modern African Studies* 30(1) 1992, p.34.

133 Davis, 'The Angola decision of 1975', p.117.

134 Marcum, 'Lessons of Angola', p.422.

135 Marcum, *Exile Politics and Guerrilla Warfare*, p.271.

136 Hallett, 'The South African intervention in Angola', p.363.

137 Gerald Ford, *A Time to Heal* (London: W.H. Allen 1979), p.345.

138 American involvement was revealed in a series of articles by Seymour Hersh in the *New York Times* in mid-December 1975.

139 The academic Richard Falk recalled Kissinger admitting almost complacently that 'I am not much interested in, nor do I know anything about, the Southern portion of the world from the Pyrenees on down'. Quoted in Maxwell, 'The thorns of the Portuguese revolution', p.266.

140 Gerald Bender, 'Angola, the Cubans and American anxieties', *Foreign Policy* 31 Summer 1978, p.5.

141 Isaacson, *Kissinger*, p.683.

142 Legum, 'Foreign intervention in Angola', p.26.

143 Marcum, 'Lessons of Angola', p.407. Melo Antunes, visiting the United Sates as foreign minister at this time, recalled that Kissinger and Ford 'were obsessed with the degree of Neto's dependency on the USSR'. Melo Antunes interview, *Do Fundo da Revolução*, p.31.

144 See, for example, Ebinger, 'External intervention in internal war', p.687; Davis, 'The Angola decision of 1975', p.120; Marcum, 'Lessons of Angola', p.415.

145 Adelman, 'Report from Angola', p.568.

146 Christopher Stevens, 'The Soviet Union and Angola', *African Affairs* 75(299) April 1976, p.144.

147 Gabriel García Márquez, 'The Cuban mission to Angola', *New Left Review* Nos.101–2 February–April 1977, p.128. García Márquez's account, although revealing in its detail, is steeped in the revolutionary romanticism which characterized contemporary left-wing attitudes to the conflict.

148 Hallett, 'The South African intervention in Angola', p.365.

149 Interview with Vítor Crespo, Lisbon, 2 March 1995. Crespo believed that the knowledge of impending Cuban support lay behind the MPLA's disinclination to negotiate with him when he made his crisis trip to Luanda as minister for cooperation at the end of October.

150 Interview with Vítor Crespo, Lisbon, 2 March 1995. García Márquez suggests that the United States was unaware of what was happening until the Cubans had actually arrived. García Márquez, 'The Cuban mission to Angola', p.129. The operation had supposedly been secret in Cuba itself, but, as García Márquez put it, 'as usually happens in Cuba with such delicate military matters, the operation was a secret jealously guarded by eight million people'.

151 *Ibid.*

152 Maxwell, 'Portugal in Africa', p.352.

153 Basil Davidson, 'Portuguese speaking Africa', Michael Crowder, ed., *The Cambridge History of Africa*, vol. 8: *From c.1940 to c.1975* (Cambridge: CUP 1984), p.786. Davidson insists that the liberation movements consistently refused to allow Cubans or other foreigners to participate directly in the fighting. In 1969, however, Lisbon scored a considerable propaganda victory when a Cuban officer, Captain Pedro Peralta, was captured during an engagement with the PAIGC inside Guiné-Bissau. He was only released several months after the April revolution. Mário Soares, *Democratização e Descolonização: Dez Meses no Governo Provisório* (Lisbon: Dom Quixote 1975), p.108.

154 Inge Tvedten, 'US policy towards Angola', p.35. According to García Márquez, '(c)ontrary to numerous assertions, it was a sovereign and independent act by Cuba; the Soviet Union was informed not before, but after the decision had been made'. 'The Cuban mission to Angola', p.128.

155 *Ibid.*

156 A revealing account by a well-placed insider of American clandestine actions in northern Angola at this time is given in John Stockwell's *In Search of Enemies: the CIA in Angola* (New York: Norton 1978).

157 Hallett, 'The South African intervention in Angola', p.379.
158 Pezarat Correia, *Descolonização de Angola*, p.170.
159 *Diário de Notícias*, 29 September 1975.
160 Costa Gomes later claimed, unconvincingly, that Vítor Crespo had been nominated to attend the independence ceremony on behalf of Portugal but had been prevented from doing so by the sudden withdrawal of Portuguese Airline flights to Luanda. *Sobre Portugal: Diálogos com Alexandre Manuel* (Lisbon: A Regra do Jogo 1979), p.45.
161 In his message Rosa Coutinho assured Neto that his 'heart, in common with those of all progressive Portuguese is with the Angola people' and saw inevitable victory for the MPLA 'despite the dark clouds of imperialism gathering now'. *Diário de Notícias*, 11 November 1975.
162 Melo Antunes interview, *Do Fundo da Revolução*, p.31.

CHAPTER SEVEN

Conclusions and Consequences

The Dimensions of Collapse: The Caetano Regime and the Pressure of Modernization

Much of the exploration of decolonization as a phenomenon of the post-1945 international system has been conducted around two contending 'general theories'. The narrative of victorious colonial nationalism has been pitched against that of metropolitan calculation and policy choice. Within this reductive framework the general assumption has been that, however problematic the cases of, say, France or the Netherlands, the Portuguese example appeared unambiguous. A clear victory for the political and military forces of radical African nationalism had, it seemed, brought imperial collapse. Moreover, in the Portuguese case, colonial nationalism appeared to precipitate not just African independence but metropolitan revolution as well. In reality, though, the end of Portuguese imperialism in Africa, no less than that of the other European colonial empires, can be comprehended only in terms of *both* insurgent nationalism in Africa *and* the logical conclusion of long-term change in the metropole. In the Portuguese case these African and European forces, partly independent of each other but at critical junctures highly interdependent, were always complementary. A further factor, present to some extent in the politics of all decolonization after the Second World War, was particularly significant in the case of lusophone Africa. African nationalism, Portuguese policies and their reactions to each other were shaped to a greater extent perhaps than the other imperial relationships by continuing change in the broader international system.

The decade of the 1960s in Portugal was, as we have seen, one of rapid economic and social modernization. That this process was in part the result of economic policies forced on a reluctant Salazar by the economic requirements of the colonial wars is significant and ironic, but it is of only limited importance in explaining the general phenomenon. Underlying the immediate contingencies of war economics was a more fundamental shift brought about by an economic elite which was gradually outgrowing the policy *milieu* created for it by its political sponsors three decade earlier. The great oligopolies like CUF and Champalimaud which had thrived on the rigid protectionism of the *Estado Novo* were moving inexorably towards a new view of their corporate futures: one firmly focused on western Europe rather than Africa. Fears of displacement in lusophone Africa by stronger, more developed capitalisms (whether American, French, British or South African) if formal colonial protectionism was withdrawn, no longer paralysed Portuguese entrepreneurs into frozen support for the regime. The issue now was not the feasibility of shifting from colonialism to neo-colonialism in Africa, but the prospect of economic relationships with new partners preferably with – but if necessary without – strong residual African links.

Where this economic elite wished to tread, however, the Salazar regime seemed unwilling to follow. Cause and effect here are, of course, difficult to disentangle. The extent to which the push from Africa generated by the nationalist wars enhanced the pull exerted by European opportunities to produce the impetus for this new thinking at the heart of Portuguese capitalism is problematic. It is, though, inconceivable that Portugal could in any circumstances have remained untouched by the forces which were coming to bear on the economies of 'underdeveloped' southern Europe as a whole at his time. The play of these forces, after all, was perhaps at its most striking in Portugal's neighbour, Spain. Equally encumbered by an ultra-conservative political regime, but free of any significant 'push' from colonial conflicts, Spain's economic elite was beating its own path towards Europe in the 1960s.

Salazar's replacement at the end of the decade by the supposed 'liberal' Caetano could almost have been scripted by the modernizers. Having squeezed such benefits as were to be wrung from 'ultra-colonialism' and having endured only a short period of frustration in the last phase of Salazarism, they now had their own man in power. Portugal's political and economic elites *should* now have been brought back into alignment with each other. Yet Caetano was to prove a considerable disappointment to his friends. His premiership was constrained by two factors, one structural the other psychological. Caetano inherited not just Salazar's office but his entire regime. This included an unreconstructed integrationist in the presidency in the person of the aged Admiral Thomáz, and a military establishment which, while including reformists like Spínola and Costa Gomes, was also populated by powerful Salazarists like Kaúlza de Arriaga. But this alone did not cut off all routes to fundamental reform on the *ultramar*. The powers of the premier, as might be expected of a post created by and for Salazar, were considerable; careful manipulation of factions within the regime could well have cleared a road to significant change. Here, though, Caetano's character came into play. Indecisive, vacillating, on occasion simply timid, he proved unable to confront the redoubts of Salazarism in the regime and lead the movement for political modernization from the front. It was this, and perhaps only this, which distinguished Caetano from the junta of senior officers which replaced him in power on 25 April.

The Junta of National Salvation initially sought to perform a role familiar to 'political' military establishments across a range of authoritarian regimes by delivering a 'corrective' coup which would permit a timely readjustment within elite politics. But the coup itself had been conceived, prepared and executed by other officers who saw as it as 'programmatic' in nature rather than merely corrective.[1] The JSN was in power ultimately under licence from the Armed Forces Movement. It was from within the process of reclamation of revolutionary control by the MFA that a decolonization 'policy' emerged.

There was, though, a further ingredient in the Portuguese coup in addition to those typical of the generality of military interventions. The military did not act in April 1974 as a political *deus ex machina* from a position of olympian judgement on the shortcomings of the regime and the damage it was inflicting on the nation. Spínola, the senior officers in the JSN and the captains of the MFA were driven by other, more immediately personal concerns. The military was a player rather than a referee. The spectre of Goa haunted the consciousness of the Portuguese military throughout the period of the African wars. The humiliation of defeat in the field by a non-European power had been immensely aggravated in the armed forces by Salazar's attempt to offer up the military as scapegoat for national dishonour. The apprehension of a similar political 'betrayal' was to find new expression in the late 1960s and early 1970s, particularly in Guiné-Bissau.

Africa, Spínola and 25 April

If the origins of the coup of 25 April 1974 had any geographical base it was Guiné. Guiné confronted the Portuguese army with its fiercest military challenge. The PAIGC, alone in Portuguese Africa, threatened not just a protracted guerrilla campaign but outright military defeat for Lisbon. Guiné, with its lack of obvious economic resources and negligible European population, raised the most fundamental questions about the reasons for the wars. Guiné, with its besieged garrisons and absence of 'civil' diversion for its colonial army, produced the most heightened sense of self-identity among the Portuguese forces in Africa. And, it was Guiné too which was entrusted to the vice-regal control of General António de Spínola with his huge capacity to attract loyalty and his unconventional ideas about both colonial administration on the ground and imperial policy as a whole.

By the separate accounts of the principal actors it was Guiné which drove a wedge between Caetano and Spínola. Up until this breach the two had appeared largely at one on the colonial issue, both favouring a graduated extension of autonomy to the territories in opposition to the integrationists of the right. Caetano and Spínola might have been considered something of a 'dream ticket' for the management of colonial policy, a prospect evidently not lost on Caetano when he sought to have Spínola as his colonial minister in 1973. The breach had already opened up between the two men, however. Caetano's apparent adherence to an imperial domino theory led him to see withdrawal from Guiné – offered by the embryonic Senghor–Spínola plan of 1972 – as the inevitable first step towards expulsion from Mozambique and Angola. Although Caetano himself appears not to have withdrawn his patronage from Spínola in any significant way, Guiné had drawn the first, barely discernible battle lines for April 1974.

It may be one of the enduring ironies of the last years of Portuguese imperialism that Caetano's insistence on the indivisibility of the empire, his apparent conviction that it must stand or fall as one, became self-fulfilling. The dogma that there was in essence a single challenge to the empire rather than three largely separate guerrilla wars had the unsought effect of consolidating a common identity among major movements in the three territories. This, of course, had its organizational expression in the CONCP and an ideological one in the gradual adjustment of the political programmes of the PAIGC, Frelimo and the MPLA into very similar species of Marxism. By refusing to disaggregate the 'special case' of Guiné from the broader African problem in 1972 Caetano may be said to have precipitated the crisis of the metropole which made imperial collapse so rapid and so total two years later. The dominos were indeed in place to fall one on the next, but they had been positioned by Caetano himself.

After the 25 April coup the federal vision, to which Caetano probably remained faithful in his inner political being, lost all feasibility as each transfer of power added impetus to demands for the next. There was in reality no alternative to Portugal's acceptance of Guiné's widely recognized *de facto* independence, but when it came Frelimo in Mozambique inevitably redoubled its determination to be part of what it identified as an emerging process. Law 7/74 with its concession of the general right of independence actually confirmed the 'indivisibility' of the empire – though in the context of dissolution rather than perpetuation. With the Lusaka agreement on Mozambique the federalist retreat had accelerated to a point where Angola, despite Spínola's determination, would inevitably follow the others to independence. Finally, Cabo Verde and São Tomé & Príncipe, where some serious practical arguments could be deployed against total independence, eventually passed into the on-rush almost unremarked. This is not to say that the independence of Mozambique or Angola could have been long-delayed, merely that the process might have taken place in a political and diplomatic environment better suited to a more stable outcome.

Was there a 'lost opportunity' then for a different transformation in Luso-African relations, more efficient and less destructive in its consequences? An attractive scenario for the 'liberal' wing of the Caetano regime might have involved a recognition of Guiné's right to independence (excluding Cabo Verde) in 1972. Having thus eased military discontent and laid the ghost of Goa, the release of resources would have permitted both a morale boosting military demobilization and a redoubling of the anti-guerrilla effort in Mozambique and Angola. A Caetano–Spínola alliance might then have negotiated a graduated decolonization for the two larger territories, perhaps with some symbolic post-independence 'special relationship' tacked on. Such a process, of course, would have depended on either the full inclusion or the total marginalization of the MPLA and Frelimo. This may have been feasible in Angola but much less so in Mozambique, given the respective states of the liberation movements and their performance in 1972. Much would have depended on the positions of African neighbours, the OAU and the UN.

Intriguing as such speculation might be, by 1972 it had become clear that such boldness could not be expected of the government of Marcello Caetano, prisoner as it was to its own fears and indecision. In refusing to allow Spínola the initiative on Guiné in 1972 Caetano had sought to placate the integrationist right in the regime without alienating the 'autonomist' reformers. With none of Salazar's adeptness at manipulating factions and none of his natural authority, he failed on both sides. Rightists around Kaúlza de Arriaga began actively to conspire against his government while not only Spínola but whole tranches of the military lost all faith in the reforming potential of the regime. The veto on the Spínola–Senghor initiative, with its whisper of Goa, offended significant sections of the military high command, and in its implicit rebuke of Spínola it sowed resentment among some of the most able of the regime's junior and middle-ranking officers whose loyalty to the general was absolute. In this context the appearance of *Portugal and the Future* and the consequences of its publication became wholly comprehensible.

The later revelation that on the very eve of the April revolution the regime was engaged in secret negotiations with the PAIGC is startling only at first sight. In its secretiveness, its political inconsistency and its failure to inform let alone involve key sources of support, it was in many respects typical of Caetano's entire approach to Africa. And it was one thing to sit down with the PAIGC under pressure from Britain; it would have been quite another for the talks to have produced even a framework for settlement – let alone for Caetano to have gathered sufficient personal and political resources to have sold any such agreement to the right-wing within his own regime.

The conflicts over Guiné and *Portugal and the Future* generated only one strand of military opposition to the regime. The other came from the professional interest group which eventually grew from the 'Captains' Movement' into the Armed Forces Movement. Several officers had a foot in each camp, of course, and Africa was central to the two concerns. Africa kept Goa and the prospect of further humiliation high in the military consciousness. Africa, in its greed for trained manpower, threatened to drain the prestige and prerogatives of the professional officer class as privileges were perforce extended to their conscript counterparts. And, underlying these military issues, Africa seemed no longer to be the dominant preoccupation of the nation's high capitalists. This development would not have been lost on an officer corp which traditionally maintained vigorous business interests in parallel with its military duties.

The Portuguese Military and the Decolonization Process

With its commitment to a programme of complete decolonization following 25 April, the MFA attracted the general, often enthusiastic, approval of liberal and left-wing opinion both nationally and internationally. Some moral caution is necessary here, however. In considering the politics of the period leading up to the Portuguese revolution it is difficult to discern the presence of any obvious *ethical* position against colonialism on the part of the military. Fear of humiliation on the battlefield, resentment at assaults on professional standing, and plain disinclination to undergo discomfort and danger in pursuit of increasingly meaningless ends lay behind the objectives of the MFA in regard to the *ultramar*, not outrage at the immorality of colonialism. There were no Vietnam-style 'moratoriums' against the war and while there was evasion of conscription, the motives appeared to be economic and personal rather than ethical. During the wars few military voices were raised against the indiscriminate bombardment of villages, the use of napalm and defoliants, summary executions, incursions into neighbouring countries and the forced movement of populations. These were, in fact, tactics fully embraced by officers who would later become icons of the international left. No one stood trial for the Wiriyamu massacre or any of the countless other outrages perpetrated by the colonial forces. The inescapable conclusion is that the Portuguese military was generally happy to prosecute the African wars by all means available as long as its own casualties were low and the prospect of defeat remote.

In the warm glow of revolutionary romanticism which descended on the Portuguese revolution during 1974 and 1975, the notion of 'revolutionary contagion' between African Marxist and Portuguese soldier was used to explain the radical political consciousness which emerged in the MFA. It was an idea which served both sides of the supposed relationship. For the colonial army it offered a view of withdrawal from Africa not as a defeat but rather as participation in a revolutionary project. For the liberation movements the idea that their political vision had won over the enemy was the ultimate testament to the superiority of their ideological position. Again though, more prosaic motivations underlay the thinking of the military at all ranks. The soldiers wanted to go home from uncomfortable and increasingly dangerous wars. They did not, by and large, want to go home to spread a revolutionary message. While there were undoubtedly many committed radicals within the MFA leadership both in the metropole and in the colonies, strong ideological motivation was not widespread throughout the officer corps or in the non-commissioned ranks.

But 25 April brought opportunities for the adjustment of image and self-image throughout the armed forces and these required the adoption of at least a degree of revolutionary rhetoric. With the revolution the Portuguese military was transformed from demon of the international left (a status which was largely deserved) and admitted to its pantheon (a status largely undeserved). Understandably, many in the armed forces took up this new image of revolutionary vanguard with enthusiasm without it necessarily impinging very deeply on their actual beliefs and attitudes. Simply, the coincidence of heroic status and self-preservation was irresistible. That said, in the climate of the 'revolutionary process' even rhetoric had considerable political impact. Whatever the basis of military radicalism and its implantation at the level of the individual, its mere proclamation contributed to the general impetus towards the transfer of power to the Marxist movements at crucial junctures in 1974 and 1975. This was particularly the case during the Spínola presidency when the federalist project was still fighting its corner. To this extent at least there was a meaningful cross-fertilization between African nationalist and Portuguese soldier, though it was not one nurtured by years of bush war as the revolutionary romantics suggested.

The April coup, coming as the culmination of a complex of long-term forces in the metropole and Africa, was the catalyst of decolonization, not its cause. But the ensuing 'revolutionary process' dramatically compressed the timescale of imperial disengagement. This compression was in large part the achievement of the African liberation movements. Whatever their varied military success during the war, the nationalist movements proved adept in seizing and deploying the political initiative after the Lisbon coup. Had the movements accepted Spínola's early cease-fire proposals and allowed the initiative to remain with the JSN there would have been no MFA pressure, either locally or in Lisbon, for a rapid and direct transfer of power. Peace would have been maintained between the military factions in Lisbon and the newly 'pacified' *ultramar* would have been left on one side for long-term settlement (probably involving some species of Spinolist federalism) at a later date.

The major confrontations which exposed the split in Lisbon – the

Manutenção Militar meeting in June and even the resignation of Palma Carlos in July – might thus have been avoided. But by rejecting out of hand Spínola's delaying tactics the liberation movements widened this cleavage between MFA and Spinolist JSN which had been patched over on 25 April. By means of both menace and fraternization on the ground, and intransigence at the negotiating table, the PAIGC and Frelimo threatened the entire revolutionary project in Portugal. Without peace in Africa the new Portuguese regime had no way forward. As much as Lisbon's negotiators might regret the pace imposed on them by the liberation movements, they had neither the political will nor the means to oppose this when the price of such opposition could well have been the very future of the revolution.[2]

Continuation of the wars was unthinkable, despite early sabre rattling from Spínola and even Costa Gomes. Whatever the details of the MFA programme, the African wars lay between every line. At the first news of the coup the military situation throughout Africa was essentially lost for Portugal. From questioning the purpose of the wars, the soldiers in Africa turned to questioning the purpose of the coup if it was not to end the wars. In the absence of any viable 'third forces' in the colonies – itself a testament to the previous regime's short-sightedness – the initiative inevitably lay with the guerrillas. With it came control of the Portuguese revolution itself.

The International Background

The power of the liberation movements in the relationship between colony and metropole at this time was enhanced by the diplomatic context in which it was played out. For a variety of reasons Portuguese Africa had been subject to a particularly high level of international attention. In large part, of course, this came from the 'anachronistic' nature of Portuguese imperialism. Up to the 1970s Lisbon pursued imperial policies – and presented philosophical justifications for them – which were already dated in the 1930s. The cold war (and its astute exploitation by Salazar) insulated Portugal from much of the diplomatic consequences of its 'eccentricity', but always conditionally. Portugal's international support (or at least the lack of irresistible international condemnation) was constantly vulnerable to the contradiction at the centre of western policy during the period: the nurturing of strategic anti-communist 'friendships' *versus* the public celebration of colonial 'freedom'.

The liberation movements for their part could exploit this western discomfort (frequently by going beyond governments to appeal directly to 'progressive opinion' in particular countries) and could at the same time rely on at least the declaratory support of their Third World colleagues in the UN General Assembly, the Non-Aligned Movement and, most immediately, the OAU. But the PAIGC, Frelimo and the MPLA remained dependent on the Soviet bloc for material support and, to an extent, for ideological models as well. It is of some significance then that the phase of their greatest effectiveness, both military and diplomatic, coincided with the maturing of superpower *détente*. This was a period when the ideological orientation of an anti-colonial movement was, however temporarily, less significant than before in shaping the policies of the superpowers towards that movement and determining their relationships. It was, in short, a period when 'colonial freedom' tended to take precedence over the maintenance of 'anti-communist friendships'.

In 1974, taken by surprise by the Portuguese coup and confused as to its likely consequences for Africa, western states found themselves without positions on the issue. Many of them at this time had governments of the centre-left and all of them were affected by the spirit of *détente*. As a result, the stance of most west European states, and of the United States itself, was one of vague support for Lisbon's 'policy' (whatever that might be at any particular time) and general sympathy for African nationalist aspirations. The Angolan crisis was in the future and its extent hardly predicted even in Portugal. Foreign governments leaned naturally towards any development which would prevent the continuation or resumption of the wars. Secure in the support of the Soviet bloc, the liberation movements were quick to grasp this essentially favourable reaction in the west and to exploit it through their various informal governmental and non-governmental contacts in Europe. Their capacity to find and utilize foreign support was enhanced by the fact that the guerrillas were more consistent and predictable in their political positions than the Portuguese state. The liberation movements, in other words, presented themselves as more reliable diplomatic interlocutors than their supposed imperial masters.[3]

The Aftermath: External and Internal Factors in Post-Independence Politics

The ideological trajectory followed by all five of the former colonies has been remarkably similar and in many ways paradigmatic of the general movement in 'radical' Third World politics in the last quarter of the twentieth century. The lusophones were in the vanguard of 'Afro-Marxism' in the 1970s, indeed they were in many ways its founders. Similarly, they were the first to demonstrate the limits of command economy and centralized planning when the weaknesses of their pseudo-omniscient states became exposed at the end of the decade. International alignments which at least in the case of the two largest territories placed them firmly in the Soviet bloc were subject to drastic reassessment as the economic benefits of the arrangement failed to accrue at the same pace as its diplomatic disadvantages.

Eventually, by the early 1990s, all five states had been transformed in various ways and at various paces into multi-party regimes, in principle where not finally in practice. Their economies had become, with considerable pain and dislocation, market-orientated, hungry for western investment and with state sectors in headlong, IMF-driven retreat. Remarkably, this great ideological transition and the policy turnabouts which came with it were overseen by the same liberation movements which had fought the wars and negotiated the transfers of power. None of the regimes had been overthrown in revolutionary upheaval. Despite generalized economic misfortune, political instability and, in the case of Angola and Mozambique, virtual destruction by protracted civil war, the political classes forged in the nationalist struggles remained in power into the 1990s.

In the 1980s the new states both contributed to, and became victims of, the shift from *détente* back to cold war. The emergence of five new, avowedly Marxist states in the mid-1970s from the debris of the Portuguese empire had an important effect on superpower calculations. The careful management of relations – which in the previous ten years had maintained stability in the central balance through the Vietnam war, the Soviet invasion of Czechoslovakia and two major conflicts in the Middle East – was already under pressure by 1975, particularly from events in south-east Asia. But that pressure was now significantly increased by the emergence of the lusophone Afro-Marxists, all occupying strategically important locations in the Atlantic and Indian Oceans. The involvement of the United States and Cuba in the war for Angola before and after the Portuguese withdrawal was only the most obvious indication of how the end of Portuguese Africa was affecting the character of superpower relations. Other factors which emerged in the next few years from Nicaragua to Afghanistan were to prove crucial, but they were ultimately part of a general process of which lusophone Africa had been an early part. By 1980 Angola and Mozambique, having contributed to the emergence of the new cold war, were now becoming major victims of it.

Throughout the 1980s the pursuit of advantage between the superpowers took precedence over judgements as to the local appropriateness of regional diplomacy. The phase of American 'constructive engagement' with South Africa began, and US policy in the region gradually became enmeshed with that of Pretoria, at least in regard to Angola. Washington and Pretoria had of course already found common cause in Angola in 1975 but then the 'alliance' had been short-lived and secretive. After the replacement of the Vorster administration in 1978 by the more hard-line one of P.W. Botha, South Africa's own approach had changed. The policy of regional *rapprochement* pursued in the mid-1970s, which had eased the transition in Mozambique and placed limits on the extent of intervention in Angola, was now abandoned. The resulting fusion between American global and South African regional interests was disastrous for both Angola and Mozambique. In Angola, Washington and Pretoria were at one in their support of UNITA's war against the MPLA. In Mozambique little was done initially to discourage South African destabilization and when international public revulsion at the nature of this eventually became vocal, it seemed there was little even the civilian leadership in Pretoria could do to control it.

Alongside these international factors, of course, there must be placed the internal circumstances of the territories. Civil wars cannot be engendered from nothing; some fundamental divisions and discontents must exist to be exploited. In Angola, although the FNLA more or less disintegrated after the MPLA victory in early 1976, UNITA remained to provide the tool for later foreign interventions. In Mozambique the opening for foreign mischief was narrower. But Frelimo's collectivization policies in the countryside and the high-handedness with which they were implemented combined with the state's abject failure to guarantee any security from rebel depredations to provide anti-government forces with at least a degree of passivity from local populations.

Could these endogenous factors and the imported destruction which they facilitated have been avoided by a different approach to the transfers of power in 1974 and 1975? Right-wing opinion in Portugal (and indeed elsewhere) during the 1980s commonly laid the blame for the conflict and instability in Angola and Mozambique and the violent factionalism of Guiné-Bissau at the door of the decolonization process and the soldiers and politicians who oversaw it. The arguments deployed tended to be those originally heard in the aftermath of 25 April and they had become no more convincing over time. Unsurprisingly, some of their most vocal proponents were to be found among the supporters of General Spínola.[4] But the Spinolist plan for the creation and patronage of third force groupings which would supposedly have prevented post-colonial disintegration was never feasible after April 1974. While theoretical and jurisprudential debates on the nature of consultation and participation may at times seem to have dominated the decolonization process in Portugal, the pace and the outcome of that process were, as we have seen, ultimately dictated by the armed nationalists in Africa itself. The liberation movements held the only asset of any importance in the political discourse of 1974: the will and the capacity to resume the armed struggle if their demands were not met in their entirety.

It is hard to escape the conclusion that, once having marginalized the Spinolists, the Lisbon regime was not only willing but deeply grateful to embrace the concept of 'revolutionary legitimacy' in its dealings with the *ultramar*. At a stroke it provided a philosophically defensible and ideologically acceptable escape from a sharp political hook. But its attractions as a political and diplomatic escape route aside, it is difficult to conceive of a practical alternative. The cleavages which were so readily exploited by external forces in post-colonial Angola and Mozambique were not created by the decolonization process itself and, realistically, could not have been avoided by it.

In Angola the Alvor agreement which was aimed at preventing the conditions for later civil war clearly failed, but given the degree of external intervention before its negotiation and during its attempted implementation – as well as the absolute refusal of the rival movements to consider a longer transition – there is little evidence that any other approach could have been more successful. In post-independence Mozambique the war against Frelimo was fought for the most part by forces which had not been present during the independence negotiations. Those among them not involved with the colonial state's police and army appear to have been Frelimo dissidents and deserters who had parted company with the movement only after it had been installed in power. They did not represent any long-standing opposition force which might have been accommodated *before* the transfer of power. The nascent Mozambican 'third force' of 1974 in whatever form – Gumo, Frecomo or Coremo – vanished even more quickly and completely than the FNLA in Angola. Even in Guiné-Bissau the tensions and instabilities which emerged after independence did so from *within* the PAIGC rather than between it and earlier rivals like FLING which might have had a legitimate and negotiable claim to a share of power prior to the Portuguese withdrawal. As flawed as the decolonization negotiations and the subsequent agreements undoubtedly were, by and large they were the only possible ones amidst the Portuguese, African and indeed global realities of 1974 and 1975.

Picking up the Threads: Portugal and Lusophone Africa since Independence

On 25 November 1975 the 'revolutionary process' in Portugal, already decelerating after the fall of Vasco Gonçalves in August, finally shuddered to a halt. A confused and ill-coordinated rebellion by left-wing paratroops at the Tancos air base near Lisbon precipitated an alliance between the moderate leftists of the MFA around Melo Antunes and a strengthening faction within the military which was concerned to reimpose discipline and 'normality' in the armed forces.[5] The influence of the military radicals and of their *de facto* leader, Otelo Saraiva de Carvalho, now evaporated. The government of Admiral Pinheiro de Azevedo, who had succeeded Vasco Gonçalves in August, set about preparations for national assembly elections to be held the following April. Out of these came Portugal's first post-revolutionary constitutional government led by Mário Soares at the head of a minority Socialist administration. The presidential elections which followed brought a new head of state, António Ramalho Eanes, after General Costa Gomes had declined to seek a new term. A leading military 'normalizer', Eanes had played no prominent part in the 25 April revolution but had been appointed chief of the general staff in the aftermath of the November 1975 rebellion.

The implications for post-colonial relations with Africa of this victory for the 'moderates' in Portugal were complex. The Soares–Eanes administration in many ways represented the final victory of the modernizing tendency present in the Caetano regime. Soares was unambiguous in his pursuit of a clear west European identity for post-revolutionary Portugal – indeed the PS election campaign had been fought on the slogan 'Europe is with us' (*a Europa está connosco*). Once in power Soares began the process which would result less then a year later in Portugal's formal application for admission to the European Community.

This shift in Portugal's political economy was reflected in its trade relations with Africa which declined rapidly in the late 1970s and 1980s. Exports to the lusophone Africans dropped to a bed-rock of about 6 per cent of the national total by the early 1980s.[6] Imports from Africa became insignificant. In part, of course, this was a consequence of the economic chaos that overtook Angola and Mozambique after independence. Export production collapsed (with the important exception of Angolan oil) and imports were sharply reduced in consequence. But it was also a part of the more general trend which underlay the entire process of disengagement from Africa: the re-direction of Portugal's economic activity towards Europe and the parallel 'regionalization' of African trade. By 1977 Portugal had been displaced by South Africa as Mozambique's leading trading partner.[7] Portugal's share of Guiné's imports, which had not undergone the same economic collapse as the two larger lusophones, fell from 92 per cent in 1974 to 20 per cent in 1981.[8]

In the aftermath of the events of 25 November the MFA moderates associated with Melo Antunes's *Documento dos Nove*, having thrown their influence against the military radicals, now found their positions undermined by the civilian politicians whose interests they had defended. To the extent that these hitherto influential military personalities had thought out their foreign policy preferences for the new Portugal, they favoured a so-called 'Third Worldist' (*terceiro mundista*) orientation rather than a determinedly west European one. They would have cast Lisbon in the role of 'bridge' between global north and south, and placed re-defined relationships with lusophone Africa in a central position in Portugal's foreign policy. The world-view from which this stance derived bore some striking similarities to that of the Spinolists. These affinities reflected the common origins of the two positions in Portuguese military tradition and myth, though they diverged sharply in preferred policy outcomes.

Despite the general orientation of Portugal's foreign policy towards Europe, the military *milieu* from which the Third Worldist line of thought emerged did have some outlet in policy. In diluted and contingent form it was expressed in aspects of Eanes's 'presidential' diplomacy.[9] The constitutional arrangements put in place in Portugal in 1976 were built on a degree of 'constructive bipolarity' of power between prime minister and president.[10] General Eanes, who remained in office until January 1986, took full advantage of the personal policy initiatives at his disposal. This was particularly evident in relations with Africa where, like all army officers of his generation, Eanes had spent many of his formative years. In exercising his presidential prerogative he drew directly on the experience and contacts of fellow officers who had been more active in both the revolution and its political aftermath. Prominent among these were Ernesto Melo Antunes, Vítor Crespo and Vítor Alves, who became important presidential advisers.

During his decade in office Eanes pursued what amounted to a policy of *rapprochement* with lusophone Africa. In this way Portugal made at least an effort to manage the diplomacy of post-colonial adjustment which would otherwise have been neglected by the civilian politicians. The only other regularized contacts in these immediate post-independence years were those between the Portuguese Communist Party and the pro-Soviet 'vanguard parties' emerging at this time from the pupae of the liberation movements.[11] Eanes's policy involved the conclusion of various cooperation agreements, bolstered by frequent visits to Africa. His efforts were frequently a source of friction with his prime ministers. Both Mário Soares up until his departure from office in mid-1978, and later Francisco da Sá Carneiro of the PSD who was prime minister during 1980, resented the president's powers and the direction in which he exercised them.[12] There is no question, though, that Eanes performed a considerable service in maintaining at least a degree of cooperation and civility in Luso-African relations in these most difficult post-colonial years.[13]

The end of the Eanes presidency in 1986 can in some respects be said to have completed Portugal's post-colonial adjustment. Eanes's departure concluded a largely successful process of re-engagement with the former African colonies. His successor as president was Mário Soares who, on taking office, declared Portugal's transition to democracy within the west European mainstream to be complete. Appropriately, 1986 was also the year of Portugal's admission to the European Community.

Although the consolidation of Portugal's European identity in the mid-1980s underlined the secondary nature of the African relationships, it did not mark their end. France, Belgium and the Netherlands already provided models for the co-existence of 'post-colonialism' and full participation in the process of European integration. In some respects admission to the European Community offered Portugal opportunities for the *enhancement* rather than diminution of its African relationships by giving the lusophones access to new sources of multilateral development funds through Lisbon. The passage of time, the sheer extent of the disaster facing Mozambique and Angola, and the abandonment of previous ideological certitudes had by the later 1980s dissolved much of the sensitivity of post-colonial relationships in Africa. The result was a second phase of the post-imperial relationship, less fraught than that of the first decade, but significant in both objectives and achievement nevertheless.

Guiné-Bissau: Political and Economic Rapprochement

The most comfortable of Portugal's relationships in the post-colonial period was with Guiné-Bissau. The factors which permitted Portugal a relatively easy retreat from the territory actually facilitated the establishment of cordial post-colonial relations. The absence of a 'settler problem', the limited level of economic *contenciosos* between the two countries and the transfer of power to one unchallenged liberation movement made for a comparatively uncomplicated bilateral relationship. Cordiality was only momentarily strained in November 1980 after an intra-PAIGC *putsch* which displaced President Luís Cabral. The coup had been made by the prime minister, the legendary guerrilla leader, João Bernardo ('Nino') Vieira, and was driven by the long-standing tensions in the PAIGC leadership between Cabo Verdean and *mestiço* elements on the one side and indigenous Guineans on the other. It ended for the foreseeable future any prospect of the unification of Guiné and Cabo Verde so enthusiastically proposed at the time of independence.

Post-independence politics in Guiné-Bissau have proved distinctly fissiparous, with divisions between not just Cabo Verdean and Guinean but between indigenous Guinean ethnic groups as well. The Balanta, who had been at the same time the most effective guerrilla fighters and the least politically disciplined cadres of the PAIGC during the armed struggle, perceived themselves discriminated against in the regimes of both Luís Cabral and Nino Vieira, and were the real or imagined architects of a series of plots and conspiracies.[14]

Only occasionally have internal politics impinged on the relationship with Lisbon since 1980. A sharp but temporary cooling of relations occurred in 1981 when Vieira executed a number of alleged coup plotters against Portuguese protests. In general, though, he was anxious to maintain good relations with Portugal after his seizure of power and despite his dictatorial style and behaviour the relationship has been a remarkably good one – remarkable that is in the context of the special ferocity of the liberation war in Guiné. Under both Luís Cabral and Nino Vieira Guiné has been the most 'luso-minded' of the ex-colonies. With Cabo Verde it has been an enthusiastic advocate of formalized relations between the five African lusophones and the former metropole.[15] In 1978, for example, Guiné, along with Cabo Verde and São Tomé & Príncipe, actually lobbied for Portugal's election to a non-permanent seat on the UN Security Council in opposition to their fellow member of the Non-Aligned Movement, Malta.[16]

Guiné was also an early enthusiast for the continuation of post-CONCP links among the five former colonies themselves. There was some opposition to this idea, particularly from Mozambique and Angola which regarded such a movement as a link with the colonial past and considered the existence of a lusophone bloc in the OAU undesirable.[17] But Cabral's original plan took hold and was embraced by a newly converted Mozambique in the early 1980s when the grim necessity of all possible diplomatic support in the face of South African destabilization had become obvious. Summits of '*os Cinco*', as the five states came to be known, were held more or less annually into the 1990s.

Much of Guiné's enthusiasm for such projects can be explained by its geographical location amidst large francophone neighbours with whom relations have frequently been difficult.[18] In 1984 Vieira, evidently influenced by the example of his franc-zone neighbours but anxious to free himself of their economic influence, suggested the creation of an African 'escudo-zone'. Portugal for its part appears to have gained from its special relationship with Guiné by taking on an 'agency' role in the delivery and operation of third party aid projects. American-funded schemes as well as UN, World Bank and IMF projects for Guiné have been 'franchised' to Portuguese companies to Portugal's obvious economic benefit.[19]

Guiné's relations with Portugal in particular and the west in general were helped by the relative distance at which it held the Soviet Union after independence. The rapacity of the Soviet fishing fleet off the Guiné coast caused a distinct cooling of relations soon after independence and Guiné took its professed non-aligned status sufficiently seriously to decline Moscow's requests for base facilities. But other factors too affected Bissau's international orientation. The mid-1980s saw Guiné, in common with the other lusophones, making its peace with the international monetary system and undertaking 'structural adjustment' commitments in return for IMF assistance. Guiné's principal economic difficulty lay in an apparently irreversible decline in food production. In part this was an environmental problem linked to the Sahel drought but it was also the consequence of failures in economic planning. In the early 1980s the country was importing about 90 per cent of its food. By the end of the decade, however, the government was being congratulated by the IMF on its commitment to readjustment and on its evident success.

The early 1990s saw Guiné engaged in another fundamental revision of its original revolutionary project – one which was also being undertaken by its lusophone counterparts elsewhere on the continent. In May 1991 the constitution was amended to permit the development of multi-party democracy. Progress to this end in a country deeply riven by unresolved ethnic tensions and subject to a decade of rule by the authoritarian Vieira was inevitably slow. Nevertheless, elections held in mid-1994 returned a PAIGC majority (though one sufficiently modest to allay most suspicions of foul play) to the national parliament. In simultaneous presidential elections Vieira held on to his post, but with a tiny majority against a strong challenge from a Balanta ethnic opponent.[20]

Considerable political and ethnic tensions persist in Guiné-Bissau. The resentment of the Balanta at what they see as their marginalization from the political process is unlikely to be lessened by the mere existence of pluralist structures, and the Balanta's powerful base in the armed forces makes them a formidable element in any political calculation. There are as well several prominent PAIGC exiles, many based in Portugal, who have not abandoned their political ambitions.[21] The future of Guiné-Bissau is unlikely to be a stable one and Portugal's unexpectedly successful post-colonial relationship with its most troublesome colony could yet be tested.

Angola: From Alvor to Bicesse

Beyond the bilateral relationship itself, Guiné also served Portugal's post-colonial adjustment with Africa in the role of mediator. This was particularly useful in the case of Angola. Relations between Portugal and the MPLA regime had been difficult since independence. Lisbon's refusal to transfer power formally to the MPLA and its subsequent witholding of recognition from the Neto regime until February 1976, had caused considerable resentment in Luanda. This increased after a bomb attack on the Angolan consulate in Porto in May 1976 when diplomatic relations were broken off by Angola. These were renewed a few months later, but the situation remained difficult.

At the root of the problem lay MPLA suspicions of Portuguese 'tolerance' of opposition activity, whether in the form of the FNLA office in Lisbon or the shadowy operations of *retornado* factions. Inevitably the influx of alienated refugees, the greater part from Angola but many thousands from Mozambique as well, caused considerable disquiet both in Lisbon and Africa. In reality, though, early fears that the *retornado* issue would have a dangerously distorting effect on both domestic politics and African relations proved largely unfounded. While the political sympathies of the *retornados* were generally with the right, the beneficiaries were, by and large, the established conservative parties, particularly the PSD and CDS.[22] Of much greater threat to the new regimes in Angola and Mozambique were those settlers who had gone in their hundreds of thousands to South Africa rather than back to Portugal in 1974 and 1975. Whatever Lisbon's tolerance of *pied noir* plotting, it was nothing as compared to Pretoria's evident encouragement of it. Perception, though, was of great importance and in Angola suspicions remained of widespread mischief on the part of the former metropole.

Relations were eventually rescued at a meeting between Eanes and Neto in Bissau in June 1978 which had been prepared by Melo Antunes and facilitated by Luís Cabral. In the wake of this Portugal stretched its own constitutional limits to restrict the activities of anti-MPLA elements in the country. The Guiné summit was one of the more revealing examples of Eanes's distinct 'presidential' African policy.

A similar though less public instance had occurred in May the previous year following a failed coup attempt against the Neto regime by its interior minister, Nito Alves. The origins and objectives of the coup were complex; it was partly a reaction against perceived *mestiço* domination of the regime and partly an ultra-leftist spasm against the revolutionary short-comings of Neto and his supporters.[23] The events provided an opportunity for Portugal to assure Neto of its support, at least against radicals like Alves. This presidential approach to Luanda was made in the face of opposition from Mário

Soares whose relations with the MPLA had declined dramatically since independence. Neto had, with some justice, accused Soares and his PS-led government of obstructing international recognition of the MPLA regime and encouraging support for UNITA.[24] It was a sad conclusion to a once close personal relationship forged in the anti-Salazar opposition of the 1950s.[25]

Eanes was the only western head of state to attend Agostinho Neto's funeral in September 1979, where he took the opportunity to reaffirm friendly relations with the new Angolan president, the former Neto loyalist Eduardo dos Santos. Despite occasional spats in the early and mid-1980s, usually related to opposition activity in Portugal and to Angolan nationalizations of Portuguese assets, the relationship remained generally undisturbed.

Portuguese involvement in the diplomacy surrounding the Angolan civil war at this time was minimal. The internationalized nature of the conflict as a cold war cockpit had become evident by the mid-1980s. In one sense, the primary equation in the issue was not that between the MPLA government and UNITA but one between Namibian independence and Cuban withdrawal from Angola. In July 1985 the US Congress voted to repeal the Clark amendment (which at the beginning of 1976 had put an end to the Ford–Kissinger intervention). The Reagan administration had been pressing for repeal virtually since taking office, and military supplies immediately began flowing to UNITA through Zaire.[26] In the meantime South African air and ground incursions into Angola, supposedly against SWAPO guerrillas but in effect in support of UNITA, had become routine. On the other side, Cuban force numbers had been growing steadily in the 1980s until by 1988 they stood at about 50,000.

The year 1988 was to prove crucial in the resolution of the international dimension to the conflict. Election year in the United States combined with the high water mark of *glasnost* in the Soviet Union to force a breakthrough. Against the background of one of the most destructive and protracted battles of the war around Cuito-Cuanavale in the south-east, an agreement was reached by which Pretoria undertook to decolonize Namibia by 1990 while Cuba agreed to a total withdrawal of its forces by 1991.[27]

The Namibia–Cuban agreement, while serving the broader purposes of superpower relations, did not point to any easy resolution of the MPLA–UNITA conflict which continued in its quotidian horror. But the international setting of the war was unquestionably important and by 1990 this had changed fundamentally. The Soviet Union was moving towards disintegration and losing any interest in global manoeuvring as it did so. It was clear too that revolution had finally arrived in South Africa and change there would be fundamental and irreversible.

This gradual 'de-internationalization' of the war in Angola offered Portugal, under the PSD prime minister Aníbal Cavaco Silva, the opportunity for a major mediatory role. In April 1990 secret talks were held between MPLA and UNITA delegations in Evora in south-central Portugal. Negotiations continued until May 1991 under Portuguese chairmanship with American, Soviet and UN representatives present as observers. Finally, on 31 May 1991, a week after the withdrawal of the last Cuban from Angola, an agreement was signed by the MPLA and UNITA at Bicesse near the Lisbon coastal resort of Estoril.

The agreement, with its plans for the creation of a unified national army from the forces of the antagonists and its timetable for national elections, inevitably brought to mind the Alvor accord whose failure had led, tortuously and tragically, to Bicesse itself.[28] The situation in 1991 was, however, different in many important ways from that of 1975. For one thing, there were only two indigenous players, the FNLA having passed from the national scene. For another, neither superpower was advancing the interests of its clients with anything like the enthusiasm of 1975. And, crucially, after sixteen years of war there were few illusions on anyone's part about the likelihood of a decisive victory on the battlefield.

Yet the Alvor analogy was to prove depressingly apposite. The Bicesse process did move further than that of 1975 in that generally free and fair elections were held in September 1992. But these were rendered largely meaningless when UNITA – or at least the increasingly megalomaniac Savimbi – refused to accept the narrow victory they registered for dos Santos and the MPLA. As in 1975, the process of demobilization of forces and their re-formulation into a unified army had hardly begun and a reversion to civil war was relatively easily engineered.[29] In a further echo of the earlier failure, the military resources available to the supposed guarantor of the process were inadequate both in number and commitment to impose acceptance on the parties. While the Portuguese army had slipped quietly away at the earliest opportunity in 1975, the few hundred troops of the United Nations Angola Verification Mission (UNAVEM II) were wholly powerless in the face of rival national forces some 150,000 strong.[30]

The new phase of the war surpassed any of the previous seventeen years in its ferocity and destructiveness. Now largely disregarded by the forces which had previously stoked the fires, Angola fell victim to the generalized collapse in the authority and resources of the UN which was already evident at the time in Somalia and Bosnia. With the breakdown of Bicesse, Portugal stepped back to join the United States and Russia as observer rather than mediator and left the MPLA and UNITA to stumble on their own in search of a new political dialogue. Having presided over two failed agreements in a seventeen-year period it was unlikely that Portugal would attempt to confront again what the UN representative in Angola had described as 'a human tragedy without precedent'.

Mozambique: The Elusive Relationship

Relations between Portugal and Mozambique were initially even more difficult than those with Angola and took considerably longer to improve. The difficulties with Maputo (as Lourenço Marques was renamed) were quite different from those with Luanda and reflected basic dissimilarities in the conditions of the two territories at independence. Firstly, the economic prospects of Mozambique were infinitely worse than those of Angola and its *contenciosos* with Portugal were consequently more threatening to the overall relationship. Secondly, the civil war in Angola had brought a violent, traumatic but virtually total exit of white settlers. While the behaviour of some of these *retornados* back in Lisbon may have caused difficulties in relations, they were no longer a diplomatically complicating presence in Angola itself. In contrast, the relatively more peaceful transfer of power in Mozambique, though triggering an outflow of settlers, had left many thousands in the country after independence. The often harsh and unjustifiable treatment of these remaining Portuguese became a major point of friction in relations between Lisbon and Maputo.

Both financial and human issues were affected by a series of nationalizations undertaken by the Frelimo regime in the first two years of independence. In July 1975 the main social services were taken under government control, creating resentment among white professionals and outraging parents shocked by the 'communist takeover' of the education system. Then in February 1976 land and buildings were nationalized in clear breach, according to the Soares government, of the Lusaka Accord. Lisbon's concern was further deepened at this time by the fate of about 200 Portuguese citizens held in Mozambican jails without trial. Despite some subsequent easing of the situation and the release of a number of the prisoners, relations remained tense and then deteriorated sharply in January 1978 when Frelimo, in a sudden intensification of the *contencioso* dispute, nationalized all Portuguese banks. Attempts by a high-level Portuguese delegation to resolve this issue in March 1979 ended dramatically when, during its visit, a Portuguese citizen was executed for alleged rebel activity.

Frelimo's refusal to cooperate in improving relations with Portugal at this time is difficult to comprehend. The economy was showing few signs of improvement, despite (or more correctly because of) a far-reaching east European-inspired development programme adopted in early 1977. By 1978 the guerrilla war against the white regime in Rhodesia was almost daily spilling across the border into Mozambique. Most ominously, the opposition movement which would eventually become known as Renamo (Resistência Nacional Moçambicana) had launched its campaign of violence in border areas. A country in such a situation would, it might be thought, grasp any hand of friendship held out to it. While it is likely that there were some in the Frelimo leadership thinking along just those lines, the personal grip of Samora Machel on the party and the government was virtually absolute at this time. Increasingly authoritarian in style and pronouncement, Machel seemed determined to assert the irrelevance of Portugal whether as friend or foe to the new revolutionary state.

There was some improvement in the relationship in the early 1980s, again as a result of Eanes's personal diplomacy. He and Machel held informal talks in Luanda at the time of Agostinho Neto's funeral in September 1979 and a formal visit to Portugal by Joaquim Chissano, then Mozambican foreign minister and number two in the Frelimo hierarchy, followed at the beginning of 1981. But this improvement in bilateral relations was to a great extent just part of a more general adjustment towards the west in Mozambican foreign policy.[31] The opening to the west was dictated by a number of factors. There was a realization that the totemic denunciation of the entire capitalist world as imperialism incarnate was not only politically misguided but economically counter-productive. Hand in hand with this new caution came a growing awareness of the technical and economic limitations of eastern bloc development aid.[32] But it was the menace posed by Renamo which was most instrumental in the re-orientating Mozambique's foreign policy in the 1980s.

Renamo had originally been set up by the Rhodesian Central Intelligence Organization. Its purpose was twofold: to provide local guides and interpreters for Rhodesian military operations against Zimbabwean nationalist guerrilla bases in Mozambique, and to act as a general focus of anti-Frelimo destabilization.[33] Its initial recruits were former African members of the Portuguese special forces, always intensely anti-Frelimo and now concerned for their future in the Frelimo state. DGS agents and informers fleeing to Rhodesia during the transfer of power reportedly took their files with them and were able to provide their hosts with recruitment lists. The movement's ranks were later joined by Frelimo dissidents who for various reasons had fallen foul of the regime.[34]

From the beginning Renamo was bereft of any comprehensible political position, defining itself only as anti-Frelimo (or, when seeking right-wing American patronage, 'anti-communist'). With the independence of Zimbabwe Renamo was 'bought-up' in its entirety by South African military intelligence. Thus the end of white Rhodesia, far from relieving Frelimo of its 'bandit problem', merely opened a new – and ultimately terminal – phase of destabilization. As Renamo attacks inflicted ever-greater destruction on infrastructure and development projects in the early 1980s, western military aid and diplomatic support became increasingly important. In a curious echo of Salazarist thinking from the 1960s, the government sought foreign investment not merely as an economic end in itself but as a means of tying western interests to those of Frelimo. The result, it was hoped, would be foreign leverage against South Africa's support for Renamo – just as the old dictator had sought to capture foreign support for his colonial policies by creating a similar community of economic interest.

In this process Portugal had only a minor role. Larger economic and diplomatic prizes like the United States and Britain were sought by Machel. There was, though, one area in which Portugal did have a particular national interest, and it was one with implications close to the centre of the Frelimo–Renamo–Pretoria equation. At independence Portugal had agreed to maintain its overall responsibility for the Cabora Bassa hydro-electric scheme and carried over 80 per cent of the debt burden associated with it. The project was finally completed in April 1977, just as the anti-Frelimo guerrilla campaign was getting underway, and Portugal was very conscious of the threat that the internal conflict in Mozambique posed to its chances of recouping its investment. Stability in Mozambique was therefore of particular economic importance to Portugal and Lisbon made considerable efforts to encourage it. The agreement signed in March 1984 between Pretoria and Maputo – the Nkomati Accord – surprised even close observers of the region. But it was in large part merely an acknowledgement by Machel of the seriousness of the Renamo crisis and the impossibility of overcoming it without at least South African neutrality. Significantly, it followed a number of expressions of concern by Portugal about the security of Cabora Bassa. Meetings in Lisbon preceded the Accord at which the Portuguese foreign minister, Jaime Gama, pressed for action to protect the project in the interests of all three parties.

Despite initial cautious optimism in Lisbon as well as Maputo it was soon evident that the Nkomati Accord had failed to restrain Renamo. While Mozambique complied faithfully with its commitment to end ANC activity in Mozambique and while it is likely that the South African government had negotiated in good faith, Pretoria's civilian politicians proved unable to control their own military. Covert SADF support for Renamo continued, though even without this, as one observer put it, Renamo 'had gained a momentum of its own which its former paymaster and arms supplier could not reverse'.[35]

The Renamo issue became a major source of conflict between Portugal and Mozambique in the 1980s. The difficulty was similar to but considerably more serious than that between Lisbon and Luanda over anti-MPLA activity in Portugal. Mozambican hostility centred firstly on the fact that a considerable part of the publicly identified leadership of Renamo were Portuguese citizens who had refused to compromise with the Frelimo state by taking Mozambican nationality at independence. This was not the case with UNITA, whose members were self-avowedly part of a historical tradition of Angolan nationalism. Secondly, Renamo's mysterious and diffuse support base included certain otherwise 'respectable' Portuguese commercial interests which looked to future business opportunities in a post-Frelimo Mozambique. These interests reportedly had influence at the highest level of the centre-right PSD which was in and out of government throughout the 1980s.[36] Relations were further strained by the abduction and murder of a leading figure in Renamo, Evo Fernandes, near Lisbon in 1988 which led to the expulsion of a junior diplomat at the Mozambican embassy on suspicion of involvement.[37]

It was perhaps this underlying tension which prevented Portugal playing the prominent role in attempts to resolve Mozambique's problems that it did in Angola.[38] While a remarkably similar (though much more successful) process of mediation, demobilization and UN-administered elections took place in Mozambique, Portugal had only a peripheral role. Although Cavaco Silva made an early contribution to the peace process in September 1989 when he sent a representative to speak to Frelimo and Renamo delegations in Kenya, the principal mediator was Italy. Taking over the organization of negotiations from a Catholic church group, the Italian government showed little enthusiasm for Portuguese involvement.[39] After a series of difficult negotiations an agreement was signed in Rome in October 1992 by Joaquim Chissano, who had become Mozambican president after the death of Machel in 1986, and the Renamo leader Afonso Dhlakama. At the end of the year, with the lessons of the Angolan failure of a few months previously ringing in its institutional ears, the UN Security Council approved the formation of a sufficiently large peace-keeping force to oversee the demobilization of Renamo and Frelimo forces and to supervise elections. The United Nations Operation in Mozambique (UNOMOZ) was 7500-strong – seven times larger than UNAVEM in Angola. Portugal was not entirely marginalized from the peace process. Although not in a central position – it was an Italian who became head of the United Nations mission – Portugal served on the Supervision and Control Commission which oversaw the demobilization and the election preparations, and UNOMOZ included a Portuguese army contingent.[40]

In the elections of October 1994 Renamo did better than expected but was still easily defeated by Frelimo which took an absolute majority in the national assembly and had Chissano returned as president.[41] Despite an early threat to withdraw from the poll as the likelihood of his defeat became apparent, Dhlakama, unlike Savimbi, was prevailed upon to accept the role of leader of the opposition. In contrast to Angola with its oil and diamonds, there were few spoils left to fight over in Mozambique.

The Islands: The Diplomacy of Hyperdependency

Portugal's respective relationships with the two micro-states created by decolonization, Cabo Verde and São Tomé & Príncipe, differed markedly. Although each was confronted by similarly dire economic conditions, they responded in different ways to post-colonial relationships. Cabo Verde, for reasons of geographical location and cultural tradition, took a highly pragmatic approach to links with the former metropole from the beginning. São Tomé & Príncipe, in contrast, had a more difficult relationship with Lisbon. Enjoying less internal stability than Cabo Verde, the MLSTP regime of São Tomé & Príncipe found itself in conflict with Portugal on the familiar issue of the latter's toleration of opposition activity.

When it became independent in 1975 Cabo Verde was in the midst of a protracted period of drought. The water problem, although a historic one for islands which are located in an Atlantic rain shadow, had been particularly severe since the 1960s. Drought was the national preoccupation in the first years of independence. By 1980 Cabo Verde had to look abroad for 90 per cent of its food requirements, and imports were costing twenty times the value of exports. The economic calculations of survival denied Cabo Verde the luxury of an ideologically confected foreign policy and its non-alignment was, in contrast to that of much of the rest of lusophone Africa, rigorously adhered to. Concerns in the west about the sensitivity of its strategic position which had been raised in the early days of the decolonization process diminished as it became obvious that no military advantage was to be gained by either cold war camp.

By the late 1980s Cabo Verde's astute management of its external relations had helped it become one of the most generously aided countries in Africa. In 1987 foreign aid accounted for half its GNP. Beyond its political inoffensiveness, Cabo Verde's appeal to foreign donors was enhanced by the energy and inventiveness of its own sustainable development programmes. Throughout the 1980s the country was mobilized in a massive tree planting campaign aimed at improving water conservation and soil retention. In 1987, in an intriguing piece of lateral thinking, the state bought 27,000 acres of arable land in Paraguay for 'distance' food production. Pragmatism in pursuit of revenue extended even to South Africa, as landing and refuelling services for South African Airlines flights continued after independence. To have done otherwise in support of the liberation struggle in southern Africa would, in President Aristides Pereira's words, have amounted to a 'suicidal solidarity'.[42] An element of self-reliance was also provided by the extensive migrant remittances from the large diaspora of Cabo Verdeans in North America, Holland, France and Portugal.

The problems of economies of scale which confronted Cabo Verde in common with all micro-states, dictated the continuation of close relations with Portugal. Realistically only Portugal could serve Cabo Verde's higher education requirements, local provision being unviable and the medium of Portuguese essential. The 1980 coup in Guiné which ended any prospect of the unification promised at independence further strengthened the Portuguese connection as the west African regional axis broke down. Presidential and prime ministerial visits between Portugal and Cabo Verde throughout the 1980s served to intensify a web of functional relationships.

Despite its evident success in managing post-independence development in Cabo Verde, the regime did not survive the wave of democratization which overtook the continent in the early 1990s. Authoritarianism and low-level corruption had been the down-side to the government's performance and, after sixteen years, there was a mood that the 'old men' of the independence campaign had had their day. In January 1991, in the first free elections held in lusophone Africa, Aristides Pereira was displaced from the presidency and the PAICV (renamed from PAIGC in 1981 after the coup in Guiné) was decisively defeated in the contest for the national assembly. The new president was a former supreme court judge, António Mascarenhas Monteiro, who led the Movement for Democracy (MPD: Movimento para Democracia), an aggressively free-market orientated party which resonated with the tone of the time in Africa.[43] Portugal's relations with the Monteiro administration were not as cordial as with that of Pereira. The MPD quickly fell victim to factionalism and Cabo Verde lost some of its enviable internal stability. In search of external agents of this instability the Monteiro regime sought to blame Lisbon for an abortive coup in 1992. Despite such upsets, though, the Cabo Verdean–Portuguese relationship will inevitably continue, bound about as it is by networks of essential functional arrangements. The 'low politics' of necessary cooperation, in this case at least, will condition the high politics of inter-state petulance.

In São Tomé & Príncipe tensions within the regime emerged soon after independence. There were various points of conflict but the most significant was that between the president Manuel Pinto da Costa and the prime minister Miguel Trovoada. Internal difficulties soon became confused with external threats, real or imagined. At the beginning of 1978 something of a panic overtook the islands as reports spread of an impending South African-inspired mercenary invasion. The immediate consequence of this was the stationing of 1000 Angolan troops in the territory, an early and unique example of lusophone cooperation.[44] Meanwhile, relations with Gabon, which in view of its pre-independence nurturing of the MLSTP would have been expected to be cordial, were complicated by suspicions over the exploitation of marine resources and Libreville's provision of facilities for São Tomense opposition factions.[45] All these political difficulties were aggravated by a deteriorating economic background as revenue from the island's cash crop, cocoa, slumped.[46]

More ideologically slanted in its non-alignment than Cabo Verde, São Tomé & Príncipe, at least up until the mid-1990s, cultivated a close relationship with the Soviet Union and was given to the frequent transmission of revolutionary rhetoric. Portugal, as the former metropole and architect of the country's declining plantation economy, was frequently the object of this rhetoric. In November 1980 another apparent coup attempt led to the arrest and then expulsion of two Portuguese citizens. Long prison sentences handed out to those implicated in this and other 'conspiracies' brought protests from Lisbon which caused further problems in relations. For its part Portugal saw no need to indulge its former colony and reacted robustly to attacks from the MLSTP regime. In 1983 Portuguese aid was suspended after the São Tomé & Príncipe minister for education criticized its quality and quantity and threatened reprisals if dissident activity in Lisbon continued to be tolerated.

In the mid-1980s relations improved a little as Pinto da Costa began to seek western aid and investment to compensate for the decline in cocoa revenues. Beyond economic concerns, he was also increasingly aware of the threat he faced from internal dissension and began to court better political relations with the west in general and Portugal in particular. Both Jaime Gama and Ramalho Eanes had successful visits to the territory in 1984 and in the following two years Pinto da Costa undertook a series of trips to western capitals, including Lisbon. The result was a number of functional arrangements similar to those already in place with Cabo Verde, including the introduction of a scheduled monthly flight to Lisbon by the Portuguese airline which provided São Tomé & Príncipe's only direct connection with Europe. The diplomatic re-orientation of the territory seemed to be confirmed in 1988 when yet another coup attempt, this time sea-borne from Equatorial Guinea, resulted in the gift of naval patrol boats from the United States.

In common with the other lusophones, São Tomé & Príncipe began on the road of political pluralism in the early 1990s. In legislative elections held in January a new opposition grouping, the Democratic Convergence Party (PCD: Partido de Convergência Democrática) took thirty of the fifty-five seats. In face of this MLSTP defeat Pinto da Costa declined to stand for the presidency and left the way open for his old rival, the former prime minister Miguel Trovoada. Now returned from exile after having been deposed and jailed in 1979, Trovoada was elected president with PCD backing in March 1991. As in Cabo Verde, factionalism and in-fighting became characteristic of the new party and Trovoada found himself in the same battles between president and prime minister that he had fought in the late 1970s, though from the opposite side. The change in regime has not, however, had any significant impact on the relationship with Lisbon.

As the divergent trajectories of Portugal and the new African states widened in the 1980s and 1990s, the intensity of the conflicts which had surrounded decolonization within Portuguese political life began to fade.[47] The public view in Portugal seemed to acknowledge the imperfections of the process without having any significant doubts about its desirability. An opinion poll published in the weekly *O Jornal* in 1984 showed that 69 per cent of those questioned regarded decolonization as 'a good thing' though only 14 per cent thought it had been 'well done'.[48] The ten years after 1974 in Portugal probably saw more profound and far-reaching change in the national world-view than there had been in the previous fifty. The mildness of the imperial hangover has been startling when the length and depth of the indulgence itself is considered. For Portugal the human consequences of empire have been remarkably light, whether in terms of its war casualties, the absorption of its settler *retornados* or the integration of its non-European refugees. A European consciousness appears to have supplanted the African one within the political culture with remarkable ease.

The experience of lusophone Africa in the aftermath of empire has been utterly different. Perhaps a million people died directly or indirectly in Renamo's war against the Frelimo regime in Mozambique and hundreds of thousands have perished in the MPLA–UNITA conflict in Angola. The physical resources of both countries have been drastically depleted, and even a stable peace will provide no more than the narrowest foothold for the beginnings of reconstruction. The prospects of sufficient external aid to achieve such reconstruction in the current world order of the 1990s are far from certain.

Amidst the human and material holocaust suffered by Mozambique and Angola and the violent factionalism of Guiné, the destruction of an idea was completed. The Afro-Marxism of Frelimo, the MPLA and the PAIGC withered and died in the 1980s. External destabilization and cold war manipulation do not provide a sufficient alibi for the failure of centralist Marxism in lusophone Africa, whatever the well-intentioned claims of its foreign enthusiasts. The revolutionary experiment would assuredly have unravelled anyway among the cultural contradictions it provoked. But it is one thing for a political idea to be tested and to fail (and perhaps leave a residue of genuine improvement in its passing); it is quite another for it to disintegrate amidst the externally contrived destruction of people and state. However inapplicable to African realities the schemes of Portugal's guerrilla enemies might eventually prove, they did offer a clear alternative to the cynical manipulation of ethnicity and the neo-colonial complaisance of the kleptocratic elites which increasingly defined African governance in 1970s and 1980s. Whatever their fate, the projects of the post-independence regimes of lusophone Africa were probably the most principled and decent ever proposed for the continent. They have not been superseded in this regard, and seem unlikely to be.

Notes

1 The terms 'corrective' and 'programmatic' are those of Eric A. Nordlinger's widely cited classification system from *Soldiers and Politics: Military Coups and Governments* (Englewood Cliffs NY: Prentice Hall 1977).

2 Ten years after the coup Melo Antunes warned against revisionist recollections of the setting in which the decolonization negotiations took place: 'I think people in Portugal, some years on, tend to forget that in the months following 25 April there was a period of revolution with all that implies – institutional disorder, disorganization of structures and, ultimately, the fragility of institutions beginning with the military itself. Everyone should remember that in the days following 25 April in the colonies the watchword among the soldiers was withdrawal. And here in the metropole the watchword among many of the groups which claimed the most advanced revolutionary tendencies was also withdrawal of the troops.' Fernando Pires, *Palavras no Tempo* (Lisbon: *Diário de Notícias* 1990), p.275.

3 The British prime minister Harold Wilson recalled that his government had been 'greatly encouraged by the first news of the revolution and decolonization in Mozambique and Angola . . . '. But he was less impressed by Costa Gomes and the MFA leadership when he had talks with them in Helsinki in mid-1975. They were, he opined, 'as choice a bunch of thugs as I have ever met'. Harold Wilson, *Final Term: The Labour Government 1974–1976* (London: Weidenfeld and Nicholson/Michael Joseph 1979), pp.168–9.

4 Spínola himself voiced the view of the right in an interview in 1994: 'If the old regime is to blame for what happened in the aftermath of April, decolonization is responsible for the fratricidal wars in Angola and Mozambique and for the unstable situation in Guiné. Democracy in Cabo Verde and São Tomé is not the achievement of the Portuguese decolonizers, they had no part in this.' *Expresso Revista*, 30 April 1994.

5 For an exploration of the factional divisions within the military leading up to

the events of 25 November see Lawrence S. Graham, *The Portuguese Military and the State: Rethinking Transitions in Europe and Latin America* (Boulder CO: Westview 1993), pp.25–30.

6 Gervaise Clarence-Smith, *The Third Portuguese Empire 1825–1975: A Study in Economic Imperialism* (Manchester: Manchester University Press 1985), p.220.

7 José Friere Antunes, *O Factor Africano* (Lisbon: Bertrand 1990), p.113.

8 Rosemary Galli and Jocelyn Jones, *Guinea-Bissau: Politics, Economics and Society* (London: Pinter 1987), p.124.

9 On the dynamics of Portuguese foreign policy in this period see José Medeiros Fereira, 'International ramifications of the Portuguese revolution', L.S. Graham and D.L. Wheeler, eds, *In Search of Modern Portugal: The Revolution and its Consequences* (Madison: University of Wisconsin Press 1983), pp.287–95.

10 The nature of the 1976 constitution is explored by Ben Pimlott, 'Portugal – two battles in the war of the constitution', *West European Politics* 4(3) 1981, pp.286–7.

11 On the PCP's relations with the MPLA and Frelimo see Alex MacLeod, 'Portrait of a model ally: the Portuguese Communist Party and the international Communist movement, 1968–1983', *Studies in Comparative Communism* 17(1) 1984, pp.49–52.

12 When he took office, Sá Carneiro of the PSD (and formerly of the *ala liberal* of the old regime's Assembly) emphatically rejected the 'Africanism' of the president and his advisers. His government's foreign policy would be 'clearly pro-European and pro-western ... there will be no trace of "Third Worldism" '. Quoted in Shirley Washington, 'Towards a new relationship', *Africa Report* March–April 1980, p.21.

13 See Norman MacQueen, 'Portugal and Africa: the politics of re-engagement', *Journal of Modern African Studies* 23(1) 1985, pp.35–51.

14 On the factionalism and power struggles within Guinean politics since independence see Joshua B. Forrest, *Guinea-Bissau: Power, Conflict and Renewal in a West African Nation* (Boulder CO: Westview, 1992), pp.55–62.

15 *Ibid.*, p.71. Enthusiasm faltered after the 1980 coup and the ensuing deterioration in relations with Cabo Verde.

16 Friere Antunes, *O Factor Africano*, p.114.

17 Basil Davidson, 'Portuguese Speaking Africa' Michael Crowder, ed., *The Cambridge History of Africa*, vol.8: *From c. 1940 to c.1975* (Cambridge: CUP 1984), p.797.

18 The relationship with Dakar has been affected by accusations of Guiné-Bissau support for separatist movements in Senegal. Difficulties between Bissau and Conakry have for the most part related to unresolved disputes over territorial waters, always important for the fishing industry but in the 1980s considerably more so as off-shore oil exploration got underway.

19 Galli and Jones, *Guinea-Bissau*, p.124.

20 The PAIGC took 64 of the 100 seats in the assembly. In the final round of the presidential poll Vieira took 52 per cent of the vote against his Balanta opponent's 48 per cent.

21 As late as 1990, the former prime minister Vítor Saúde Maria, jailed by Vieira in the 1980s and then rehabilitated as mayor of Bissau, was granted political asylum in Portugal during an official visit there.

22 J.R. Lewis and A.M. Williams, 'Social cleavages and electoral performance: the social bases of Portuguese political parties', *West European Politics* 7(2) 1984, p.133.

23 For an analysis of the coup see David Birmingham, 'The twenty-seventh of May: an historical note on the abortive 1977 coup in Angola', *African Affairs* 77(309) 1978, pp.554–64.

24 Moises Venancio, 'Portuguese mediation of the Angolan conflict in 1990–1', Stephen Chan and Vivienne Jabri, eds, *Mediation in Southern Africa* (London: Macmillan 1993), p.102.

25 According to Eanes, Soares wanted to follow the American lead in imposing

a general isolation on the MPLA regime and therefore opposed any gesture of support: *O Factor Africano*, p.112. It is worth noting that the Eanes–Soares feud was as epic in its day as the one between Spínola and Costa Gomes.

26 American policy at this time is explored by Wayne S. Smith, 'A trap in Angola', *Foreign Policy* 62 Spring 1986, pp.61–74.

27 On the superpower diplomacy surrounding the agreement see G.R. Berridge, 'Diplomacy and the Angola/Namibia accords', *International Affairs* 65(3) 1989, pp.463–79.

28 For an analysis of the 1990–91 peace process see James Hamill, 'Angola's road from under the rubble', *The World Today* 50(1) January 1994, pp.6–11.

29 Almost five million voters were registered for the elections on 29–30 September 1992 and there was a turn-out of 91 per cent. In the presidential contest dos Santos took 49.57 per cent of the vote against Savimbi's 40.07 per cent. In the election for the 220-seat national assembly the MPLA won 129 and UNITA 70.

30 'UNAVEM I' was the UN mission charged with overseeing the Cuban withdrawal from January 1989 to June 1991.

31 See Norman MacQueen, 'Mozambique's widening foreign policy', *The World Today* 40(1) January 1984, pp.24–5.

32 Allen Isaacman and Barbara Isaacman, *Mozambique: From Colonialism to revolution, 1900–1982* (Boulder CO: Westview 1983), p.186.

33 Steven Metz, 'The Mozambique National Resistance and South African foreign policy', *African Affairs* 85(341) 1986, p.493.

34 Glenda Morgan, 'Violence in Mozambique: towards an understanding of Renamo', *Journal of Modern African Studies* 28(4) 1990, p.605.

35 David Birmingham, *Frontline Nationalism in Angola and Mozambique* (London: James Currey 1992), p.87.

36 One name which has been raised in this respect is that of Carlos Mota Pinto, PSD leader in the early 1980s and deputy prime minister in Soares's PS–PSD coalition at the time of Nkomati. It was subsequently claimed that he obstructed the conclusion of a Frelimo–Renamo agreement about to be signed in Pretoria six months after the Nkomati Accord in October 1984. On this and alleged Portuguese involvement with Renamo in general see Alex Vines, *Renamo: Terrorism in Mozambique* (London: James Currey 1991), pp.32–9.

37 It was never clear whether the murder of Fernandes was solicited by Maputo or the result of one of the byzantine internal divisions characteristic of such organizations. The position of Renamo in Portugal was made even murkier by persistent suggestions of a relationship with the Portuguese secret services. Birmingham, *Frontline Nationalism*, p.113.

38 It has also been suggested that Frelimo found Italy more generous in the economic input it was willing to make to the mediation and conciliation process. Moises Venancio, 'Mediation by the Roman Catholic Church in Mozambique, 1988–91', *Mediation in Southern Africa*, p.155.

39 Scott B. MacDonald, *European Destiny – Atlantic Transformations: Portuguese Foreign Policy under the Second Republic* (New Brunswick NJ: Transaction 1992), p.115.

40 On the UN operation in Mozambique see Chris Alden, 'The UN and the resolution of conflict in Mozambique', *Journal of Modern African Studies* 33(1) 1995, pp.103–28.

41 Renamo took 112 (37.8 per cent of the vote) and Frelimo 149 (44.3 per cent) of the 250 seats in the national assembly. Only one other party, the Democratic Union, won representation with 9 seats. In the presidential election Chissano took 53 per cent and Dhlakama 33 per cent of the 4.9 million votes cast (ten other candidates shared the remainder).

42 Colm Foy, *Cape Verde: Politics, Economics and Society* (London: Pinter 1988), p.180. Ironically, it was the United States which finally shut off this source of revenue when it began to enforce sanctions against Pretoria in 1988. In the absence of South African flights to America Cabo Verde's income from SAA fell from $10m

a year to $3m. Flights did, of course, resume after the end of apartheid.

43 Monteiro won 75 per cent of votes in the presidential poll. The MPD took 56 of the 79 seats in the assembly.

44 Luanda was not motivated purely by altruism. The lodgement of forces hostile to the MPLA in São Tomé & Príncipe could have had serious consequences for Angola, given the islands strategic position in relation to the West African mainland. See Tony Hodges and Malyn Newitt, *São Tomé and Príncipe: From Plantation Colony to Microstate* (Boulder CO: Westview 1988), p.116.

45 L.M. Denny and D.I. Ray, *São Tomé e Príncipe* (London: Pinter 1989), p.120.

46 In the first ten years of independence production fell from 10,000 tons a year to 4500. Like Cabo Verde, but with less economic excuse, the territory was importing nine-tenths of its food requirements by 1985.

47 By 1994 even Spínola and the radical Rosa Coutinho appear to have been on reasonable terms. Only the 'two Marshals', Spínola and Costa Gomes, persisted in their mutual loathing. *Público Magazine*, 20 February 1994.

48

	Yes	*No*	*Don't know*
Was decolonization a good thing?	69%	22%	11%
Was it carried out well?	14%	73%	13%

O Jornal, 19–26 April 1984

Bibliography

Published Sources

ABSHIRE, DAVID M., 'From the scramble for Africa to the "New State"', David M. Abshire and Michael A. Samuels, eds, *Portuguese Africa: A Handbook* (London: Pall Mall 1969), pp.60–90.

ADELMAN, KENNETH L., 'Report from Angola', *Foreign Affairs*, 53(3) 1975, pp.558–74.

Africa Contemporary Record 1974–75 (London: Rex Collings 1975).

AGUIAR, LUÍS, *Livro Negro da Descolonização* (Lisbon: Editorial Intervenção 1977).

AGUIAR, LUÍS, *A Chamada 'Descolonização': Julgamento dos Responsáveis* (Lisboa: Intervenção 1978).

ALDEN, CHRIS, 'The UN and the resolution of conflict in Mozambique', *Journal of Modern African Studies* 33(1) 1995, pp.103–28.

ALEGRE, MANUEL, 'Convergência histórica da luta pela libertação em Portugal e da luta de libertação nacional em Angola', *Seminário: 25 de Abril 10 Anos Depois* (Lisbon: Associação 25 de Abril 1984), pp.281–5.

ALMEIDIA, DINIS DE, *A Origem e Evolução de Movimento dos Capitães* (Lisbon: Edições Sociais 1977).

ALMEIDA SANTOS, ANTÓNIO DE, *15 Meses no Governo ao Serviço da Descolonização* (Lisbon: Representações Literária ASA 1975).

ALVES, VÍTOR, 'Colonialismo e descolonização', *Revista Crítica dos Ciências Sociais* Nos.15/16/17 May 1985, pp.557–67.

ANDERSSON, HILLARY, *Mozambique: A War against the People* (London: Macmillan 1992).

ANDRADE, MÁRIO DE and OLLIVER, MARC, *A Guerra em Angola* (Lisbon: Seara Nova 1974).

ANSPRENGER, FRANZ, *The Dissolution of the Colonial Empires* (London: Routledge 1989).

ARRIAGA, KAÚLZA DE, *Guerra e Política* (Lisbon: Referendo 1987).

ARRIAGA, KAÚLZA DE, (*et al.*), *África: A Vitória Traida* (Lisbon: Intervenção 1977).

AVILLEZ MARIA JOÃO, *Do Fundo da Revolução* (Lisbon: Público 1994).

AZEVEDO, MÁRIO, "'A sober commitment to liberation"? Mozambique and South Africa 1974–79', *African Affairs* 79(317) October 1980, pp.567–84.

BAKLANOFF, ERIC N., *The Economic Transformation of Spain and Portugal* (New York: Praeger 1978).

BAKLANOFF, ERIC N., 'The political economy of Portugal's old regime: growth and change preceding the 1974 revolution', *World Development* vol.7 (1979), pp.799–811.

BENDER, GERALD, *Angola under the Portuguese: The Myth and the Reality* (London: Heinemann 1978).

BENDER, GERALD, 'Angola, the Cubans and American anxieties', *Foreign Policy* 31, Summer 1978, pp.3–30.

BENDER, GERALD, 'Angola, left, right and wrong', *Foreign Policy* 43, Summer 1981, pp.53–69.

BENDER, GERALD, 'Peacemaking in southern Africa: The Luanda–Pertoria Tug of War', *Third World Quarterly* 11(2) 1989, pp.15–30.

BERRIDGE, G.R., 'Diplomacy and the Angola/Namibia Accords', *International Affairs* 65(3) 1989, pp.463–79.

BIRMINGHAM, DAVID, 'The twenty-seventh of May: an historical note on the abortive 1977 coup in Angola', *African Affairs* 77(309) 1978, pp.554–64.

BIRMINGHAM, DAVID, 'Angola revisited', *Journal of Southern African Studies* 15(1) 1988, pp.1–14.

BIRMINGHAM, DAVID, *Frontline Nationalism in Angola and Mozambique* (London: James Currey 1992).

BLUME, NORMAN, 'Portugal under Caetano', *Iberian Studies* 4(2) 1975, pp.46–52.

BRAGANÇA, AQUINO DE, 'Independence without decolonization: Mozambique 1974–1975', Prosser Gifford and William Roger Louis, eds, *Decolonization and African Independence: The Transfers of Power 1960–1980* (New Haven CT: Yale University Press 1987), pp.427–43.

BRANDÃO ALVES, MANUEL, 'Alguns aspectos da situação económica em Moçambique durante os anos de 1974–1975', *Seminário: 25 de Abril 10 Anos Depois* (Lisbon: Associação 25 de Abril 1984), pp.345–52.

BRIDGLAND, FRED, *Jonas Savimbi: A Key to Africa* (Edinburgh: Mainstream 1986).

BRUCE, NEIL, *Portugal: The Last Empire* (Newton Abbot: David & Charles 1975).

BRUNEAU, THOMAS C., 'Out of Africa into Europe: an analysis of Portuguese foreign policy', *International Journal* 32(2) 1977, pp.288–314.

BRUNEAU, THOMAS C., 'Continuity and change in Portuguese politics: ten years after the revolution of 25 April 1974', *West European Politics* 7(2) 1984, pp.72–83.

CABRAL, AMÍLCAR, *Revolution in Guinea: An African People's Struggle* (London: Stage One 1969).

CAETANO, MARCELLO, *Depoimento* (Rio de Janeiro: Record 1974).

CAMILO, CARLOS, 'Moçambique: os acontecimentos de 7 de Setembro e 21 de Outubro de 1974', *Seminário: 25 de Abril 10 Anos Depois* (Lisbon: Associação 25 de Abril 1984), pp.341–3.

CHABAL, PATRICK, 'The social and political thought of Amílcar Cabral: a reassessment', *Journal of Modern African Studies* 19(1) 1981, pp.31–56.

CHABAL, PATRICK, *Amílcar Cabral as Revolutionary Leader* (Cambridge: CUP 1983).

CHABAL, PATRICK, 'People's war, state formation and revolution in Africa: a comparative analysis of Mozambique, Guiné-Bissau and Angola', *Journal of Commonwealth and Comparative Politics* 21(3) 1983, pp.104–25.

CLARENCE-SMITH, GERVAISE, *The Third Portuguese Empire 1825–1975: A Study in Economic Imperialism* (Manchester: Manchester University Press 1985).

COSTA GOMES, FRANCISCO DA, *Discursos Políticos* (Lisbon: ENP 1976).

COSTA GOMES, FRANCISCO DA, *Sobre Portugal: Diálogos com Alexandre Manuel* (Lisbon: A Regra do Jogo 1979).

CRESPO, VÍTOR, 'Descolonização de Moçambique', *Seminário: 25 de Abril 10 Anos Depois* (Lisbon: Associação 25 de Abril 1984), pp.319–37.

CRUZ, POMPÍLIO DA, *Angola: os Vivos e os Mortos* (Lisbon: Intervenção 1976).

CUNHAL, ÁLVARO, *A Revolução Portuguesa* (Lisbon: Dom Quixote 1975).

DACOSTA, FERNANDO, *Os Retornados estão a Mudar Portugal* (Lisbon: Relógio d'Água 1984).

DAVIDSON, BASIL, *For the Liberation of Guiné* (Harmondsworth Middlesex: Penguin 1968).

DAVIDSON, BASIL, *In the Eye of the Storm: Angola's People* (Harmondsworth Middlesex: Penguin 1972).

DAVIDSON, BASIL, *No Fist is Big Enough to Hide the Sun: The Liberation of Guiné and Cabo Verde – Aspects of an African Revolution* (London: Zed 1981).

DAVIDSON, BASIL, 'Portuguese speaking Africa', Michael Crowder, ed., *The Cambridge History of Africa*, vol.8: *From c.1940 to c.1975* (Cambridge: CUP 1984), pp.775–806.

DAVIDSON, BASIL, *The Fortunate Isles: A Study in African Transformation* (London: Hutchinson 1989).

DAVIS, NATHANIEL, 'The Angola decision of 1975: a personal memoir', *Foreign Affairs* 57(1) 1978, pp.109–24.

DIMAS, VICTOR ed., *O Programa do MFA e dos Partidos Políticos* (Lisbon: Edições Acrópole 1975).

DUFFY, JAMES, *Portuguese Africa* (Cambridge MA: Harvard University Press 1959).

DUFFY, JAMES, 'Portuguese Africa 1930 to 1960', L.H. Gann and Peter Duignan, eds, *Colonialism in Africa 1870–1960*, vol.2: *The History and Politics of Colonialism 1914–1960* (Cambridge: CUP 1970), pp.171–93.

EBINGER, CHARLES K., 'External intervention in internal war: the politics and diplomacy of the Angolan civil war', *Orbis* 20(3) 1976, pp.669–99.

EGERO, BERTIL, *Mozambique: A Dream Undone – The Political Economy of Democracy 1975–84* (Uppsala: Scandinavian Institute of African Studies 1987).

FABIÃO, CARLOS, 'A descolonização da Guiné-Bissau. Spínola: a figura marcante da guerra na Guiné', *Seminário: 25 de Abril 10 Anos Depois* (Lisbon: Associação 25 de Abril 1984), pp.305–11.

FIELDHOUSE, D.K., *The Colonial Empires: A Comparative Study from the Eighteenth Century* (London: Macmillan 2nd edn. 1982).

FIELDS, RONA M., *The Portuguese Revolution and the Armed Forces Movement* (New York: Praeger 1975).

FIGUEREDO, ANTÓNIO DE, *Portugal: Fifty Years of Dictatorship* (Harmondsworth Middlesex: Penguin 1975).

FIRST, RUTH, *Black Gold: The Mozambican Miner, Proletarian and Peasant* (Brighton: Harvester Wheatsheaf 1983).

FORD, GERALD, *A Time to Heal* (London: W.H. Allen 1979).

FORREST, JOSHUA B., 'Guinea-Bissau since independence: a decade of domestic power struggles', *Journal of Modern African Studies* 25(1) 1987, pp.95–116.

FORREST, JOSHUA B., *Guinea-Bissau: Power, Conflict and Renewal in a West African Nation* (Boulder CO: Westview 1992).

FOY, COLM, *Cape Verde: Politics, Economics and Society* (London: Pinter 1988).

FRIERE ANTUNES, JOSÉ, *O Factor Africano* (Lisbon: Bertrand 1990).

FRIERE ANTUNES, JOSÉ, *Kennedy e Salazar: a Leão e a Raposa* (Lisbon: Difusão Cultural 1991).

FRIERE ANTUNES, JOSÉ, *Nixon e Caetano: Promesas e Abandono* (Lisbon: Difusão Cultural 1992).

FRIERE ANTUNES, JOSÉ, *Salazar e Caetano: Cartas Secretas 1932–68* (Lisbon: Difusão Cultural 1994).

GALLAGHER, TOM, 'Controlled repression in Salazar's Portugal', *Journal of Contemporary History* 14(3) 1979, pp.385–402.

GALLAGHER, TOM, *Portugal: A Twentieth Century Interpretation* (Manchester: Manchester University Press 1983).

GALLAGHER, TOM, 'From hegemony to opposition: the ultra right before and after 1974', L.S. Graham and D.L. Wheeler, eds, *In Search of Modern Portugal: The Revolution and its Consequences* (Madison: University of Wisconsin Press 1983), pp.81–103.

GALLI, R.E., 'The political economy of Guinea–Bissau: second thoughts', *Africa* 59(3) 1989, pp.371–80.

GALLI, ROSEMARY and JONES, JOCELYN, *Guinea–Bissau: Politics, Economics and Society* (London: Pinter 1987).

GARCÍA MÁRQUEZ, GABRIEL, 'The Cuban mission to Angola', *New Left Review* Nos.101–102 February–April 1977, pp.123–37.

GIL FEREIRA, HUGO and MARSHALL, MICHAEL W., *Portugal's Revolution Ten Years On*, (Cambridge: CUP 1986).

GRAHAM, LAWRENCE S., *Portugal: The Decline and Collapse of an Authoritarian Order* (London: Sage 1975).

GRAHAM, LAWRENCE S., 'The military in politics: the politicization of the Portuguese armed forces', L.S. Graham and H.M. Makler, eds, *Contemporary Portugal: The Revolution and its Antecedents* (Austin: University of Texas Press 1979), pp.221–56.

GRAHAM, LAWRENCE S., *The Portuguese Military and the State: Rethinking Transitions in Europe and Latin America* (Boulder CO: Westview 1993).

GRAYSON, GEORGE W., 'Portugal and the Armed Forces Movement', *Orbis* 19(2) 1975, pp.335–78.

GREEN, G., *Portugal's Revolution* (New York: International Publishers 1976).

GREY, ROBERT D., 'The Soviet presence in Africa: an analysis of goals', *Journal of Modern African Studies* 22(3) 1984, pp.511–27.

GRUPO DE PESQUISA SOBRE A DESCOLONIZAÇÃO PORTUGUESA, *A Descolonização Portuguesa: Aproximação a um Estudo*, vol.1 (Lisbon:

Instituto Democracia e Liberdade 1979).

GRUPO DE PESQUISA SOBRE A DESCOLONIZAÇÃO PORTUGUESA, *A Descolonização Portuguesa: Aproximação a um Estudo*, vol.2 (Lisbon: Instituto Amaro da Costa 1982).

GUERRA, JOÃO PAULO, *Memória das Guerras Coloniais* (Porto: Afrontamento 1994).

HALL, MARGARET, 'The Mozambique National Resistance Movement: a study in the destruction of an African country', *Africa* 60(1) 1990, pp.39–68.

HALLET, ROBIN, 'The South African intervention in Angola 1975–76', *African Affairs* 77(308) 1978, pp.347–86.

HAMILL, JAMES, 'Angola's road from under the rubble', *The World Today* 50(1) January 1994, pp.6–11.

HAMMOND, RICHARD J., *Portugal and Africa 1815–1910: A Study in Uneconomic Imperialism* (Stanford CT: Stanford University Press 1966).

HAMMOND, RICHARD J., 'Uneconomic imperialism: Portugal in Africa before 1910', L.H. Gann and Peter Duignan, eds, *Colonialism in Africa 1870–1960*, vol.1: *The History and Politics of Colonialism 1870–1914* (Cambridge: CUP 1969), pp.352–82.

HAMMOND, RICHARD J., 'Some economic aspects of Portuguese Africa in the nineteenth and twentieth centuries', Peter Duignan and L.H. Gann, eds, *Colonialism in Africa 1870–1960*, vol.4: *The Economics of Imperialism* (Cambridge: CUP 1975), pp.256–79.

HANLON, JOSEPH, *Mozambique: The Revolution under Fire* (London: Zed 1984).

HANLON, JOSEPH, *Mozambique: Who Calls the Shots?* (London: James Currey 1991).

HARGREAVES, JOHN D., *Decolonization in Africa* (London: Longman 1988).

HARSGOR, MICHAEL, *Portugal in Revolution* (London: Sage 1976).

HARSGOR, MICHAEL, 'Aftereffects of an "exemplary decolonisation"', *Journal of Contemporary History* 15(1) 1980, pp.143–67.

HARVEY, ROBERT, *Portugal: Birth of a Democracy* (London: Macmillan 1978).

HASTINGS, ADRIAN, *Wiriyamu* (London: Search Press 1974).

HASTINGS, ADRIAN, 'Some reflections upon the war in Mozambique', *African Affairs* 73(292) 1974, pp.263–76.

HEIMER, FRANZ-WILHELM, *The Decolonization Conflict in Angola: An Essay in Political Sociology* (Geneva: Institut Universitaire de Hautes Etudes Internationales 1979).

HENDERSON, L.W., *Angola: Five Centuries of Conflict* (Ithaca NY: Cornell University Press 1979).

HENDERSON, ROBERT D'A., 'Relations of neighbourliness: Malawi and Portugal, 1964–74', *Journal of Modern African Studies* 15(3) 1977, pp.425–55.

HENRIKSEN, THOMAS H., 'People's war in Angola, Mozambique and Guinea-Bissau', *Journal of Modern African Studies* 14(3) 1976, pp.377–99.

HENRIKSEN, THOMAS H., 'Portugal in Africa: comparative notes on counterinsurgency', *Orbis* 29(2) 1977, pp.395–412.

HENRIKSEN, THOMAS H., 'Marxism and Mozambique', *African Affairs* 77(309) 1978, pp.441–62.

HENRIKSEN, THOMAS H., *Mozambique: A History* (London: Rex Collings 1978).

HEYWOOD, LINDA M., 'UNITA and ethnic nationalism in Angola', *Journal of Modern African Studies* 27(1) 1989, pp.47–66.

HODGES, TONY, 'How the MPLA won in Angola', Colin Legum and Tony Hodges, *The War over Southern Africa* (London: Rex Collings 1976), pp.47–64.

HODGES, TONY and NEWITT, MALYN, *São Tomé and Príncipe: From Plantation Colony to Microstate* (Boulder CO: Westview 1988).

HOLLAND, R.F., *European Decolonisation 1918–81* (London: Macmillan 1985).

HUMBARACI, ARSLAM and MUCHNIK, NICOLE, *Portugal's African Wars* (London: Macmillan 1974).

ISAACMAN, ALLEN and ISAACMAN, BARBARA, *Mozambique: From Colonialism to Revolution, 1900–1982* (Boulder CO: Westview 1983).

ISAACMAN, ALLEN, 'Regional security in southern Africa: Mozambique', *Survival* 30(1) 1988, pp.14–38.

ISAACSON, WALTER, *Kissinger: A Biography* (London: Faber & Faber 1992).

JAMES, W. MARTIN III, *A Political History of the Civil War in Angola 1974–1990* (New Brunswick NJ: Transaction 1992).

KAY, HUGH, *Salazar and Modern Portugal* (London: Eyre and Spottiswoode 1970).

KLINGHOFFER, A., *The Angolan War: A Study in Soviet Policy in the Third World* (Boulder CO: Westview 1980).

LAIDI, Z., *The Superpowers and Africa: The Constraints of a Rivalry 1960–1990* (Chicago: University of Chicago Press 1990).

LARRABEE, STEPHEN, 'Moscow, Angola and the dialectics of detente', *The World Today* 32(5) May 1976, pp.173–82.

LEGUM, COLIN, 'Foreign intervention in Angola', Colin Legum and

Tony Hodges, *The War over Southern Africa* (London: Rex Collings 1976), pp.9–43.

LEWIS, J.R. and WILLIAMS A.M., 'Social cleavages and electoral performance: the social bases of Portuguese political parties', *West European Politics* 7(2) 1984, pp.119–37.

LOPES, CARLOS, *Guiné–Bissau: From Liberation Struggle to Independent Statehood* (Boulder CO: Westview 1987).

LOPES, DOMINGOS, 'A derrota político-militar, base da vocação descolonizadora do MFA. A situação em Moçambique', *Seminário: 25 de Abril 10 Anos Depois* (Lisbon: Associação 25 de Abril 1984), pp.291–3.

MACDONALD, SCOTT B., *European Destiny – Atlantic Transformations: Portuguese Foreign Policy under the Second Republic* (New Brunswick, NJ: Transaction 1992).

MACLEOD, ALEX, 'Portrait of a model ally: the Portuguese Communist Party and the international Communist movement, 1968–1983', *Studies in Comparative Communism* 17(1) 1984, pp.31–52.

MACQUEEN, NORMAN, 'Mozambique's widening foreign policy', *The World Today* 40(1) January 1984, pp.22–8.

MACQUEEN, NORMAN 'Portugal and Africa: The politics of re-engagement', *Journal of Modern African Studies* 23(1) 1985, pp.31–51.

MAILER, PHIL, *Portugal: The Impossible Revolution* (London: Solidarity 1977).

MARCUM, JOHN, *The Angolan Revolution*, vol.1: *The Anatomy of an Explosion, 1950–62* (Cambridge MA: MIT Press 1969).

MARCUM, JOHN, A., 'Lessons of Angola', *Foreign Affairs* 54(3) 1976, pp.408–25.

MARCUM, JOHN, *The Angolan Revolution*, vol.2: *Exile Politics and Guerrilla Warfare, 1962–76*, (Cambridge MA: MIT Press 1978).

MARCUM, JOHN A., 'Regional security in southern Africa: Angola', *Survival* 30(1) 1988, pp.3–14.

MAXWELL, KENNETH, 'The thorns of the Portuguese revolution', *Foreign Affairs* January 1976, pp.250–70.

MAXWELL, KENNETH, 'Portugal and Africa: the last empire' in P. Gifford and W.R. Louis, eds, *The Transfer of Power in Africa: Decolonization 1940–1960* (New Haven CT: Yale University Press 1982), pp.337–85.

MAXWELL, KENNETH, 'As colónias portuguesas e a sua descolonização', *Revista Crítica dos Ciências Sociais* Nos.15/16/17 May 1985, pp.529–47.

MEDEIROS FERREIRA, JOSÉ, 'International ramifications of the Portuguese revolution', L.S. Graham and D.L. Wheeler, eds, *In Search of Modern Portugal: The Revolution and its Consequences* (Madison: University of Wisconsin Press 1983), pp.287–95.

MEDEIROS FERREIRA, JOSÉ, 'Descolonização e a política externa portuguesa', *Seminário: 25 de Abril 10 Anos Depois* (Lisbon: Associação 25 de Abril 1984), pp.391–5.

MEDEIROS FERREIRA, JOSÉ, *O Comportamento Político dos Militares: Forças Armadas e Regimes Políticos em Portugal no Século XX* (Lisbon: Estampa 1992).

MELO, JOÃO DE, ed., *Os Anos da Guerra 1961–75: Os Portugueses em África* (Lisbon: Dom Quixote 1988) [2 vols].

METZ, STEVEN, 'The Mozambique National Resistance and South African foreign policy', *African Affairs* 85 (341) 1986, pp.491–507.

MIDDLEMASS, KEITH, *Cabora Bassa: Engineering and Politics in Southern Africa* (London: Weidenfeld and Nicholson 1975).

MILLER, JOSEPH C., 'The politics of decolonization in Portuguese Africa', *African Affairs* 74 (295) April 1975, pp.135–47.

MINTER, WILLIAM, *Portuguese Africa and the West* (Harmondsworth Middlesex: Penguin 1972).

MOITA, LUÍS, 'Não ha uma mas várias descolonizacões', *Seminário: 25 de Abril 10 Anos Depois* (Lisbon: Associação 25 de Abril 1984), pp.287–90.

MOITA, LUÍS, 'Elementos para um balanço da descolonização portuguesa', *Revista Crítica dos Ciências Sociais* Nos.15/16/17, May 1985, pp.501–5.

MONDLANE, EDUARDO, *The Struggle for Mozambique* (Harmondsworth: Penguin 1969).

MORGAN, GLENDA, 'Violence in Mozambique: towards an understanding of Renamo', *Journal of Modern African Studies*, 28 (4) 1990, pp.603–19.

MORRISON, RODNEY J., *Portugal: Revolutionary Change in an Open Economy* (Boston: Auburn 1981).

MUNSLOW, BARRY, *Mozambique: The Revolution and its Origins* (London: Longman 1983).

MUNSLOW, BARRY, 'Mozambique and the death of Machel', *Third World Quarterly* 10 (1) 1988, pp.23–36.

NETO, MANUEL L., 'Descolonização e democratização', *Seminário: 25 de Abril 10 Anos Depois* (Lisbon: Associação 25 de Abril 1984), pp.301–3.

NEWITT, MALYN, *Portugal in Africa: The Last Hundred Years* (London: Hurst 1981).

NEWITT, MALYN, *A History of Mozambique* (London: Hurst 1995).

NORDLINGER, ERIC A., *Soldiers and Politics: Military Coups and Governments* (Englewood Cliffs NY: Prentice Hall 1977).

OGUNBADEJO, OYE, 'Angola: ideology and pragmatism in foreign policy', *International Affairs* 57(2) 1981, pp.254–69.

OLDBERG, INGMAR, 'The Portuguese revolution in US foreign policy', *Cooperation and Conflict* XVIII (1982), pp.179–89.

OLIVEIRA MARQUES, A.H. DE, *History of Portugal*, vol.2: *From Empire to Corporate State* (New York: Columbia University Press 1972).

OPELLO, WILLIAM, *Portugal: From Monarchy to Pluralist Democracy* (Boulder CO: Westview 1991).

PAIGC, *História da Guiné e Ilhas do Cabo Verde* (Porto: Afrontamento 1974).

PEZARAT CORREIA, PEDRO, 'O processo de descolonização em Angola. Do 25 de Abril ao Alvor', *Seminário: 25 de Abril 10 Anos Depois* (Lisbon: Associação 25 de Abril 1984), pp.353–8.

PEZARAT CORREIA, PEDRO, 'Uma perspectiva sobre a descolonização', *Revista Crítica dos Ciências Sociais* Nos.15/16/17, May 1985, pp.549–59.

PEZARAT CORREIA, PEDRO, *Descolonização de Angola: A Jóia da Corona do Império Português* (Lisbon: Inquérito 1991).

PEZARAT CORREIA, PEDRO, 'Portugal na hora de descolonização', António Reis, ed., *Portugal Contemporâneo*, vol.VI (1974–1992), (Lisbon: Alfa 1992), pp.117–69.

PEZARAT CORREIA, PEDRO, *Questionar Abril* (Lisbon: Círculo de Leitores 1994).

PIMLOTT, BEN, 'Socialism in Portugal: was it a revolution?', *Government and Opposition* 12(3) 1977, pp.332–50.

PIMLOTT, BEN, 'Were the soldiers revolutionary? The Armed Forces Movement in Portugal 1973–1976', *Iberian Studies* 7(1) 1978, pp.13–21.

PIMLOTT, BEN, 'Portugal – two battles in the war of the constitution', *West European Politics* 4(3) 1981, pp.286–96.

PIRES, FERNANDO, *Palavras no Tempo* (Lisbon: *Diário de Notícias* 1990).

PORCH, DOUGLAS, *The Portuguese Armed Forces and the Revolution* (London: Croom Helm 1977).

PORTO, MANUEL, 'Portugal: twenty years of change', A.M. Williams, ed., *Southern Europe Transformed: Political and Economic Change in Greece, Italy, Portugal and Spain* (London: Harper and Row 1984), pp.84–112.

POULANTZAS, NICOS, *The Crisis of the Dictatorships: Portugal, Spain and Greece* (London: New Left Books 1976).

RAMA, MANUELA DE S. and PLANIER, CARLOS, *Melo Antunes: Tempo de ser Firme* (Lisbon: Liber 1976).

Revolução das Flores: do 25 de Abril ao Governo Provisório (Lisbon: Aster 1975?).

ROBINSON, R.A.H., *Contemporary Portugal: A History* (London: George Allen and Unwin 1979).

ROSA COUTINHOIA, 'Notas sobre a descolonização de Angola', *Seminário: 25 de Abril 10 Anos Depois* (Lisbon: Associação 25 de Abril 1984), pp.359–66.

SALES GOLIAS, JORGE, 'O MFA na Guiné', *Seminário: 25 de Abril 10 Anos Depois* (Lisbon: Associação 25 de Abril 1984), pp.313–17.

SAMUELS, MICHAEL A., 'The Nationalist Parties' in David M. Abshire and Michael A. Samuels, eds, *Portuguese Africa: A Handbook* (London: Pall Mall 1969) pp. 389–405.

SAMUELS, MICHAEL A. and HAYKIN, STEPHEN M., 'The Anderson plan: an American attempt to seduce Portugal out of Africa', *Orbis* 23 (3) 1979, pp.649–69.

SARAIVA DE CARVALHO, OTELO, *Alvorada em Abril* (Lisbon: Ulmeiro 1977).

SAUL, JOHN S., 'Nkomati and after', John S. Saul, ed., *A Difficult Road: The Transition to Socialism in Mozambique* (New York: Monthly Review Press 1985), pp.391–418.

SAUL, JOHN S., 'Rethinking the Frelimo state', Ralph Miliband and David Panitch, eds, *Real Problems False Solutions – Socialist Register 1993* (London: Merlin 1993), pp.139–65.

SCOTT, C.V., 'Socialism and the "soft state" in Africa: an analysis of Angola and Mozambique', *Journal of Modern African Studies* 26(1) 1988, pp.23–36.

SERAPIÃO, LUÍS B. and EL-KHAWAS, MOHAMED A., *Mozambique in the Twentieth Century* (Washington DC: University Press of America 1979).

SILVA CUNHA, JOAQUIM DA, *O Ultramar, A Nação e o "25 de Abril"* (Coimbra: Atlântida 1977).

SILVEIRA, JOEL DA, 'As guerras coloniais e a queda do império', António Reis, ed., *Portugal Contemporâneo*, vol.V (1958–1974), (Lisbon: Alfa 1990), pp.71–106.

SILVÉRIO MARQUES, SILVINO, *Portugal: e Agora* (Lisbon: Tempo 1978).

SMITH, WAYNE S., 'A trap in Angola', *Foreign Policy* 62, Spring 1986, pp.61–74.

SOARES, MÁRIO, *Democratização e Descolonização: Dez Meses no Governo Provisório* (Lisbon: Dom Quixote 1975).

SOARES, MÁRIO, *Portugal's Struggle for Liberty* (London: George Allen and Unwin 1975).

SOBEL, LESTER, *The Portuguese Revolution* (New York: Facts on File 1976).

SOMERVILLE, KEITH, 'Angola: Soviet client state or state of socialist orientation?', *Millenium* 13(3) 1984, pp.292–310.

SOMERVILLE, KEITH, *Angola: Politics Economics and Society* (London: Pinter 1986).

SOMERVILLE, KEITH, 'Angola: reaping a deadly harvest', *The World Today* 51(8–9) August–September 1995, pp.156–9.

SOUSA FERREIRA, EDUARDO DE, *Aspectos do Colonialismo Português* (Lisbon: Seara Nova 1974).

SPÍNOLA, ANTÓNIO DE, *Portugal e o Futuro: Análise da Conjuntura Nacional* (Lisbon: Arcádia 1974).

SPÍNOLA, ANTÓNIO DE, *Portugal and the Future* (Johannesburg Perskor 1974).

SPÍNOLA, ANTÓNIO DE, *Ao Serviço de Portugal* (Lisbon: Ática 1976).

SPÍNOLA, ANTÓNIO DE, *País sem Rumo: Contributo para a História de uma Revolução* (Lisbon: Scire 1978).

STEVENS, CHRISTOPHER, 'The Soviet Union and Angola', *African Affairs* 75(299) April 1976, pp.137–51.

STOCKWELL, JOHN, *In Search of Enemies: The CIA in Angola* (New York: Norton 1978).

STORY, JONATHAN, 'Portugal's revolution of carnations', *International Affairs* 52(3) 1976, pp.417–33.

SUNDAY TIMES INSIGHT TEAM, *Portugal: The Year of the Captains* (London: Deutsch 1975).

SYKES, JOHN, *Portugal and Africa* (London: Hutchinson 1971).

SZULC, TAD, 'Lisbon and Washington: behind the Portuguese revolution', *Foreign Policy* Winter 1975–76, pp.3–63.

TORP J.E., *Mozambique* and Denny, L.M. and Ray, D.I., *São Tomé e Príncipe* [combined volume] (London: Pinter 1989).

TVEDTEN, INGE, 'US policy towards Angola since 1975', *Journal of Modern African Studies* 30(1) 1992, pp.31–52.

VAIL, L. and WHITE, L., *Capitalism and Colonialism in Mozambique* (London: Heinemann 1980).

VASCO GONÇALVES, *Discursos, Conferências de Imprensa e Entrevistas* (Lisbon: no publisher cited 1976).

VENANCIO, MOISES, 'Portuguese mediation of the Angolan conflict in 1990–1', Stephen Chan and Vivienne Jabri, eds, *Mediation in Southern Africa* (London: Macmillan 1993), pp.100–16.

VENANCIO, MOISES, 'Mediation by the Roman Catholic church in Mozambique, 1988–91', Stephen Chan and Vivienne Jabri, eds, *Mediation in Southern Africa* (London: Macmillan 1993), pp.142–58.

VINES, ALEX, *Renamo: Terrorism in Mozambique* (London: James Currey 1991).

WASHINGTON, SHIRLEY, 'Towards a new relationship', *Africa Report* March–April 1980, pp.17–22.

WHEELER, DOUGLAS L., 'The military and the Portuguese dictatorship 1926–1974: "The Honour of the Army" ', L.S. Graham and H.M. Makler, eds, *Contemporary Portugal: The Revolution and its Antecedents* (Austin: University of Texas Press 1979), pp.191–219.

WIARDA, HOWARD J., *Corporatism and Development: the Portuguese Experience* (Boston: University of Massachusetts Press 1977).

WILSON, H.S., *African Decolonization* (London: Edward Arnold 1994).

WILSON, HAROLD, *Final Term: The Labour Government 1974–1976* (London: Weidenfeld and Nicholson/Michael Joseph 1979).

WOLFERS, MICHAEL and BERGEROL, JANE, *Angola in the Frontline* (London: Zed 1983).

YOUNG, TOM, 'The politics of development in Angola and Mozambique', *African Affairs* 87(347) 1988, pp.165–84.

Press and Documentary Sources

A Capital
A República
Diário de Notícias
Diário do Governo
Diário Popular
Expresso
O Jornal
O País
O Século
Público
The Guardian
The Times
United Nations General Assembly Documents 1974–76

Maps

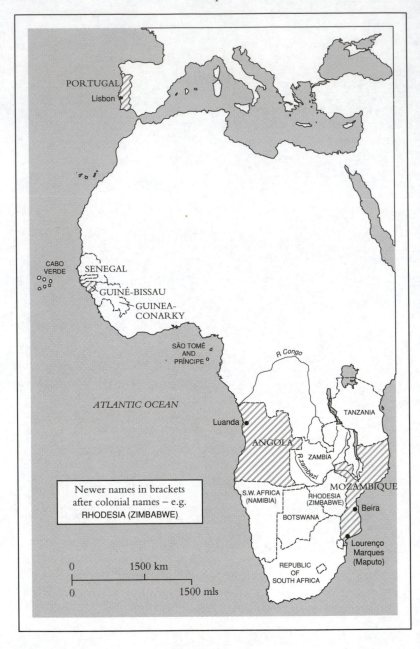

Map 1   The Portuguese Empire in Africa

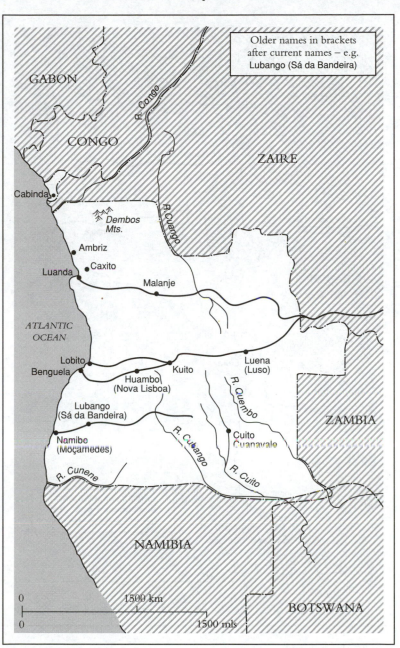

Map 2 Angola

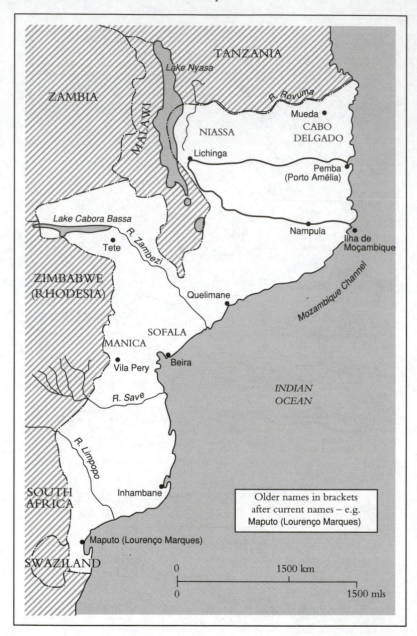

Map 3 Mozambique

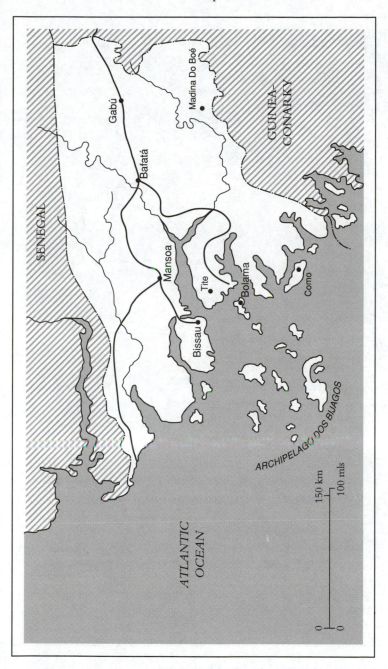

Map 4 Guiné-Bissau

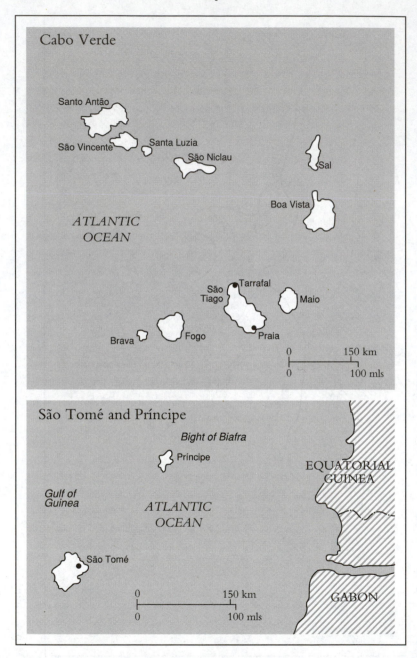

Map 5   Cabo Verde and São Tomé & Príncipe

Index

259